REMAKING ISRAELI JUDAISM

To Dani, Olga, Eli and Ita
and to
Benji, Jessica and Raphi

DAVID LEHMANN
BATIA SIEBZEHNER

Remaking Israeli Judaism

The Challenge of Shas

OXFORD
UNIVERSITY PRESS

2006

OXFORD
UNIVERSITY PRESS

Oxford University Press, Inc., publishes works that further
Oxford University's objective of excellence
in research, scholarship, and education.

Oxford   New York
Auckland Cape Town Dar es Salaam Hong Kong Karachi
Kuala Lumpur Madrid Melbourne Mexico City Nairobi
New Delhi Shanghai Taipei Toronto

With offices in
Argentina Austria Brazil Chile Czech Republic France Greece
Guatemala Hungary Italy Japan Poland Portugal Singapore
South Korea Switzerland Thailand Turkey Ukraine Vietnam

Published by Oxford University Press, Inc.
198 Madison Avenue, New York, New York 10016
www.oup.com

Library of Congress cataloging-in-publication data is available

ISBN 13: 978-0-19-530693-4

ISBN 0-19-530693-7

1 3 5 7 9 8 6 4 2

Printed in India on acid-free paper

ACKNOWLEDGEMENTS

The idea which eventually led to the writing of this book was born in 1998 in Rio de Janeiro from a suggestion by Bila Sorj. For that and for her help in the early days of the project we remain extremely grateful. During fieldwork and as we developed our ideas we accumulated an unusually large debt of gratitude to a lively and caring group of supporters in Israel, notably Nurit Stadler and Kobi Shahar, Mario and Laura Sznajder, Gadi Sznajder and Oren Golan, who have been like a family to us over a period of six years, as have Menachem and Tamar Friedman. Nurit and Mario have read extensive drafts and we are extremely appreciative of their advice in correcting factual errors and analytical misapprehensions, as we are to Shmuel Eisenstadt, whose comparative and theoretical frames of reference are an ever-present source of wisdom. We thank Menachem Friedman for his inexhaustible fund of knowledge and stories. Zeev Emmerich and Gal Levy have been faithful friends to our project from a very early stage and have also commented on drafts. Guillermo O'Donnell and Gabriela Hippolito O'Donnell gave us the confidence that our work would also be of interest to people whose primary concern was neither Israel nor Judaism. Shlomo Fischer generously made unpublished writings available and has commented on draft chapters, and Ari Engelberg provided excellent support and unusual commitment as a research assistant, while Einat Wilf made a crucial contribution to the coverage of our interview material. At a very early stage Tali Loewenthal gave invaluable help and a very friendly welcome in London, and in the latter stages Risa Domb gave generously of her time to avoid mistakes in the glossary.

We are especially grateful to the Leverhulme Foundation for the award of a fellowship and to the Nuffield Foundation and Cambridge University for grants and travel expenses. We are also grateful for institutional support to Beit Berl College and to the Harry

S. Truman Institute for the Advancement of Peace at the Hebrew University.

Although the convention is that informants remain anonymous, some of them made such important contributions that they deserve to be mentioned in person, and that is why, with his agreement, we wish to mention Rachamim Harbel, a man of enormous generosity of spirit, who helped us with no afterthought as to what we might write about him and his movement.

We are also very grateful indeed to students at Beit Berl for their interest in our project and for providing us with contacts for interviews.

Support for this venture from quite an early stage from our publisher Michael Dwyer and from Maria Petalidou, has been a source of indispensable confidence to us as authors.

Parts of Chapter 6 have appeared in Birgit Meyer (ed.), *Religion, Media and the Public Sphere*, Indiana University Press (2006). We thank Birgit for inviting us to present our work at the seminar in Amsterdam in 2001 where that book originated.

We are extremely grateful to Alex Levac for his help in selecting photographs taken by him and to Rohen Keden for permission to use his photograph.

None of those mentioned, of course, bears any responsibility for errors and omissions in the final outcome.

The support—much more than purely administrative—of Clare Hariri and Julie Coimbra at the Centre for Latin American Studies; of Odette Rogers, Deborah Clark and Norma Wolfe at the Social and Political Sciences Faculty in Cambridge, England; and of Hagit Ronay-Tal at Beit Berl has facilitated our arrangements in innumerable ways. We are very grateful for their professionalism and, personally, for their innumerable human qualities.

Jerusalem   D.L.
May 2005   B.S.

CONTENTS

vii

GLOSSARY

Agudat Yisrael
: (*Agudas Yisroel* in its followers' Yiddish pronunciation) Historically the political organ of European Orthodox Judaism founded in 1912; today an Israeli political party, but under other names since 1988.

Ashkenazi(m)
: Jews of European descent and culture and, by extension, the music, rituals and culture of European Judaism.

avrech/avrechim (pl.)
: Devout persons; full-time *yeshiva* students.

ayin ha-ra
: The evil eye.

ba'al t'shuva/ba'alei t'shuva (pl.)
: A 'returnee', a secularised Jew who has turned to religious observance.

bachur
: 'Young man' Often used to refer to yeshiva students.

chozer/chozrei bet'shuva (pl.)
: Same as *ba'al t'shuva* and *hozer bet'shuva*.

Chassidim
: Ultra-Orthodox Jews who follow in the more mystical tradition of a movement which arose in Eastern Europe in the late eighteenth century and whose religiosity lays more emphasis on bodily religious expressions than the 'Lithuanians'. Chassidim usually recognise the authority of a single, dynastic Rebbe, and Chassidic sects are in principle endogamous, though not dogmatically so.

chug/chugim (pl.)
: Discussion group(s) (lit. circle).

dati/dati'im (pl.)
: Religious, or devout person.

Degel Hatorah
: Israeli political party representing the ultra-Orthodox community, which emer-

	ged in 1988 from a split within Agudat Yisrael, with which it later came to work jointly.
emouna	Trust in God, or faith.
gemach	A charitable body, sometimes a purchasing co-operative, a rotating credit fund or simply a very low cost local, voluntary supplier of goods and services. An acronym of the Hebrew *Gemilut Hasadim* (acts of kindness).
Gemara	see Mishnah.
goy/goyim (pl.)	Literally nation, by extension non-Jews or gentiles.
Halakha	The legal corpus of Rabbinic writings relating to daily life, viz. running of the home, marriage etc.
haredi/haredim (pl.)	Literally those who tremble (before God); generic term referring to ultra-Orthodox Jews, including Chassidim, 'Lithuanians' and others, to be distinguished from Orthodox, or what are now called 'modern Orthodox'.
Haskalah	The Jewish Enlightenment, an intellectual movement which propounded engagement with modernity and the Enlightenment of late eighteenth-century and nineteenth-century Europe, provoking much Rabbinic hostility but also giving rise to Reform Judaism, which is less stringent than the Orthodox version. Its most prominent early representative was Moses Mendelssohn.
hillula	Pilgrimage (see also *mimouna*).
hiloni/hilonim (pl.)	Secularised person(s).
hozer beshe'ela	A term used in the secular world to describe those who return with a question, i.e. who abandon religious observance.
hozer bet'shuva/hozrim bet'shuva (pl.)	Literally to return with an answer; a 're-turnee', One who is returning or has

	returned to religious observance. Synonymous with *ba'al t'shuva*.
Kabbala	Literally 'tradition'. Corpus of mystical writing originating in twelfth-century Provence, which later found followers in Spain, leading to the compilation of the *Zohar*.* For the purposes of this book the Kabbala's extremely esoteric character should be stressed as well as the protection of that character, the exclusion of all but a select élite from detailed contact with the Kabbalistic tradition and the attribution of special powers to those well versed in the Kabbala.
kibbutz	A collective unit of (usually agricultural) production, managed collectively but not owned by the members (i.e. not alienable). For the purposes of this study the kibbutz symbolises the vision and achievement of the pioneering generations of mainly European Zionists, who ran kibbutzim on the basis of secularist and egalitarian collectivism (Dieckhoff, 2003).
Knesset	The Israeli Parliament
kollel/kollelim (pl.)	Centres of Torah learning attended by married men, often on a daily and (in Israel) even full time basis.
kosher (abstract noun: *kashrut*)	Food which conforms to laws of ritual cleanliness as interpreted and certified by Rabbinic authorities. This applies not only to meat and is extended in different ways by different Rabbinic authorities depending on the breadth of their interpretation of the concept of contamination. Thus in Israel, although there is a state-supported kashrut certification authority under the Chief

rabbinate, some sects or communities prefer to follow certification by their own authorities.

lashon hara   Gossip, lit. the evil tongue (cf. *ra*—evil)

Likud   The right-wing political party which first came to power under Menachem Begin in 1977 and in 2005 was headed by Ariel Sharon.

Lithuanians   A name reserved in principle for people trained in yeshivas who follow the Lithuanian method of study as developed by the Gaon of Vilna (1720–97). In practice the word refers to non-Chassidic ultra-Orthodox Jews. Lithuanians are also developing certain sect-like features, notably endogamy.

MAPAI   The Israeli Labour Party led by David Ben-Gurion, formed in 1930. Led all governments, as MAPAI and later as Labour, till 1977 and remains the emblematic representation of Zionist social democracy.

MAPAM   The more left-wing party of Israeli Social Democracy, which governed together with MAPAI as junior partner, but eventually divided and merged into other parties.

masorati   'Traditional'. Used in Israel to refer to people, especially Sephardim, who are not strictly observant but are respectful of the customs of their parents and grandparents. In the United States, in contrast, *masorati* or *masorti* refers to 'Conservative' synagogues, equivalent to what in the UK is called 'Reform'.

mezuzah   A small case fastened to a doorpost containing a tiny scroll on which the prayer 'Hear O Israel, the Lord our

God, the Lord is One' (the *Shema*, Deuteronomy, 6:4) is inscribed. Found in many Jewish houses and institutions, not only those belonging to the ultra-Orthodox, and ubiquitous in Israel.

mikveh Ritual bath used by observant Jewish women to purify themselves after menstruation.

Mimouna A festivity, celebrated in Israel by North African Jews, that takes place at the end of the Passover.

minhag/minhagim (pl.) Customs, as distinct from laws.

Mishnah The corpus of Rabbinic teaching compiled at the end of the second and beginning of the third century BCE. The Babylonian Talmud and the Palestinian Talmud are commentaries on the Mishnah, the whole forming the Gemara.*

mitchazek/ mitchazekim (pl.) Those who are 'strengthening' in their religious observance.

mitnaged/mitnagdim (pl.) Literally 'opponents': those who 'opposed' the Chassidic movement when it developed in Eastern Europe in the late eighteenth century.

mitzvah/mitzvot (pl.) A commandment, or pious deed.

Mizrachim Eastern or Oriental Jews, from *mizrach*—the East. In Israel the word is used more or less interchangeably with Sephardim, though the persons to whom it refers seem to prefer the latter. Another formula is *edot hamizrach* or 'peoples of the East'.

mohel Man qualified by religious authorities to perform circumcision.

moshav Agricultural co-operative and settlement whose members own their land and cultivate it individually. For the purposes of this study the *moshav* is asso-

	ciated more with immigrants from North Africa, in contrast to the kibbutz.
musar	Literally 'instruction' or 'reproof'. The *musar movement*, which developed in the yeshivas of nineteenth-century Lithuania, represents an approach to study in which the development of the inner self through introspection is a necessary complement to textual study.★
Rabbanit	Wife of a Rabbi (Yiddish *Rebbitzen*).
Rebbe	Yiddish version of 'Rabbi', used specifically to refer to the leaders of Chassidic sects.
sabra	Literally a prickly pear; used to describe Israeli-born Jews, the phrase was widely used in the early days of the state when most of the population were foreign born, but it is now heard less often.
Sephardi(m)	Literally 'Spanish', in reference to the Jews expelled from Spain in and after 1492. Their descendants settled mostly on the northern shores of the Mediterranean and in what is now Northern Morocco, but today the term is used to refer to Jews of the Mediterranean basin as a whole and also to those from the Middle East (but not from Yemen or Ethiopia).
shadchan	Marriage broker, from *shiddouch*, an arranged commitment to be married.
Shasnik	Follower or adept of Shas, cf. 'beatnik', 'peacenik' etc.
shtetl	Yiddish word denoting Jewish villages or communities in pre-Holocaust Eastern Europe.
Shulchan Aruch	Literally 'the table laid'. Title of the systematisation of the laws of daily life

compiled by Joseph Karo (1488–1575) in Tsfat (Safed).★

smolanim   Leftists (from *smol*—left).

Talmud   see Mishnah.

tefilin   Leather binding laid over the right arm and round the forehead during week-day morning services. (cf. Deuteronomy 6:8). *Tefilin* are conventionally rendered in English as 'phylacteries', as in Matthew 23:5, from the Greek 'phylacterion' meaning 'to protect'. This implicit allusion to *tefilin* as devices to ward off evil spirits is not found in Deuteronomy.

tinokot shenishbu Imprisoned babies (Jewish children born into a secular, non-observant family).

Torah   Strictly, the Five Books of Moses or Pentateuch; in daily parlance among *haredim*, the corpus of Jewish law and Rabbinic works, and even more generally the study of Jewish law and wisdom, or simply, the law.

t'shuva   Repentance, or return, or an answer.

tzaddik   A pious or righteous person, a saint in the eyes of popular tradition; a Chassidic Rabbinic leader.

tzedaka   Charity (from the adjective *tzaddik*).

tzitzit   Fringes. White tassels on the edge of the prayer shawl (*tallit*) (Numbers 15:38). Observant men permanently wear a vest with *tzitzit*, and ultra-Orthodox Jews often wear it so the fringes show outside their clothes, as do many on the more uncompromising wing of Israeli nationalism, notably West Bank settlers.

yeshiva/yeshivot (pl.) Centre of Torah learning, attended by young unmarried men. The word is also used to refer generally to the 'world of Torah learning'.

yetzer ha-ra   The 'drive to evil' or 'instinct for evil'.
Yiddish   The version of German spoken by East
                     European (but not German) Jews and
                     written in Hebrew characters. Yiddish
                     has been revived as the language of
                     everyday life by Chassidic sects and also
                     in Lithuanian circles. The structure and
                     core vocabulary of Yiddish is German,
                     but it contains innumerable Hebrew
                     words, while Yiddish words permeate
                     Israeli Hebrew.
Yishuv   Literally settlement. The period and
                     institutions of Jewish settlement in Pal-
                     estine before the founding of the state
                     of Israel.

* See, Jacobs, Louis, 1995, *The Jewish Religion: a Companion*, Oxford University Press.

1

INTRODUCTION

This book is about Israel, about Judaism and about contemporary religion. Its purpose is both descriptive and analytic. As a case study, it shows there is much in common between certain trends in Judaism and broader trends in world religion, but it also aims to elucidate Israeli Jewish society, especially its many cross-cutting ethnic and religious frontiers, the very distinctive patterns of political mobilisation which proliferate around them, and the changes which are coming about in contemporary Judaism as a consequence of the *t'shuva* movement of 'return' to strict observance.

The focus for these themes is Shas, a political party and social movement which has by common consent been a highly unsettling intruder in Israel's cultural firmament and in the Israeli political system since it entered the Knesset in 1984, sharpening the tense interaction between ethnic and religious forces in Israeli society. The party carries a banner for Israel's Sephardi Jews, who constitute almost half of the Jewish population, and whose underprivileged position is widely recognised. But our interest is in the many ironies embedded in the relationship between Shas and the rest of Israeli society. First, this is not a routine party of social protest: rather than demanding expanded welfare programmes, civil rights, and social democratic reforms, its leaders, who come from the yeshiva world, have harnessed their grievances to the cause of religious renewal, principally for Sephardim but also for Israel as a whole. Furthermore, although the renewal they proclaim is described as a return to the past glories of Sephardi Judaism, the content of the observance and religious study they promote is overwhelmingly Ashkenazi. This is

highly counterintuitive when set against the background of centuries of disconnection between the Jewish worlds of Europe, North
Africa and the Middle East, and also of the sometimes furious
rhetoric of Shas leaders against both the Ashkenazi Rabbinic élite
and the equally Ashkenazi Israeli secular élite. While they denounce
the patronising treatment they have suffered at the hands of the
former, they symmetrically accuse the latter of having subjected
North African immigrants to a ruthless process of acculturation in
the early decades of the Jewish state.

The case is also of interest in contemporary social science because
it allows us to trace in unusual detail the interweavings of religious
and ethnic frontiers and their oscillation between thickness and
porousness: ethnic and religious markers can be very thick, very
visible, yet they can be shifted to either include or exclude people
with remarkable agility. Israel presents a paradox, for while ethnic
and ethno-religious categories abound in daily speech, as if they
were ready-made and self-evident, there are also numerous instances
of the redrawing of those categories—as for example in the construction of the idea of the Sephardi itself, which strictly speaking
refers to the Judaism of Spanish Jews and their Northern Mediterranean descendants, and yet has now come to be used in reference to
Jews from the whole of North Africa and the Middle East, as well as
from Greece, Turkey and so on, though not from Yemen.

Aside from ethnicity and religion there is of course politics. The
mode of Shas's intrusion into Israeli politics is of interest also because
it raises questions about corporatism and liberal democracy. Conventional wisdom nowadays teaches that the inclusion of the excluded proceeds by a combination of mobilisation of pressure groups
from below and reform from above: the reform from above is meant
to be universalistic and impartial, whether it veers towards the
bureaucratic allocations of the social democratic welfare state or the
market-driven incentives of neo-liberal approaches to welfare. Israel,
however, which we would describe as a democracy, though not a
liberal democracy, follows different rules: Shas has shown that an
outside force can break into the system by establishing bridgeheads
in the state system and exploiting them in ways that are anything but
universalistic. The results may be hard to detect in social indicators,

but in terms of political influence and visibility they have been impressive. This observation has in turn led us to a reflection on Israel's 'society of enclaves' and its corporatist politics which is essential if we are to understand how the Shas phenomenon developed.

The Shas phenomenon also links in to certain trends in Judaism worldwide, notably the *t'shuva* movement of return to religion. Pioneered in the early postwar period by the Lubavitch Chassidim, also known as Chabad, *t'shuva* is now an established feature of Jewish life which is reshaping the culture and institutions of Judaism. The organisation and propagation of *t'shuva* takes many forms and both the message and the experience of the returnees themselves vary widely, but, as we shall explain, variety makes a movement strong. *T'shuva* is also to some extent related to the growth of messianic nationalism in Israel, though that subject is not dealt with directly here.

The questions raised by this subject are by no means peculiar to Israel or to Judaism. Indeed one of the purposes of this book is to take a cosmopolitan view of its subject and place it in the framework of worldwide religious change within which *t'shuva* is just one example of the conversion-based movements that are reshaping religion everywhere, including evangelical Christianity, Pentecostalism and Islamic renewal. That this research comes after previous work on Latin American Catholicism and Pentecostalism is no accident.

Religious change arises from religious movements, so we have approached our subject matter as a multi-levelled and multi-faceted social movement, which we analyse in what we call an 'epidemiological' framework. In a country with such a short history using structural explanations without begging questions about agency is not easy, and we have been repeatedly impressed by the state of permanent mobilisation which seems to characterise so much of Israeli life: this mobilisation takes advantage of the most diverse opportunities, so that a theory of social movements which relies on hierarchy and organisational models is much less helpful than one which allows for an openness to initiative from below. Again, this is not peculiar to Israel or to Judaism: indeed, it has been seen and studied in the mobilisation of evangelicals in Latin America and elsewhere. Once again, the comparative dimension of this study and the similarities between the reshaping of Judaism and the reshaping of religion worldwide come to the fore.

ISRAEL AS A SOCIETY OF ENCLAVES

The author of one of the classic texts of political science (Sartori, 1976), after failing to fit Israel into his elaborate typology of party systems, begins his few pages on the country as follows: 'Israel is a most baffling case—and this quite apart from the fact that it is a microcosm of all the conceivable complexities' (*ibid*.: 151), and concludes despairingly by describing the country as 'definitely a case by itself to be understood as such' (*ibid*.: 155). Sartori's problem is that Israel's politics cannot be categorised either as a polarised two-party system or as a centripetal multi-party system. However, this is only the beginning, for the difficulty of fitting Israel into a standard category of political institutions goes beyond the party system: the political culture and political practices range from the sectarian and corporatist to the ultra-liberal and impersonal; its welfare benefits system, for example, has features of a classic social democratic arrangement and others which are highly particularistic; it has a single judicial system for public law, but for private law has separate systems for three religions, so that lawful marriage, for example, can on occasion be a very complicated business. Above all, Israel remains a society in which fundamental disagreements simmer, notably but by no means exclusively, over the relationship between religion and the secular state, and implicitly over the extent to which modern impersonal institutions can prevail over the very different concepts of authority and legitimacy prevalent in the ultra-Orthodox and ultra-Nationalist communities (which to some extent of course overlap, though only to some extent). When the Israeli Arabs (one sixth of the population and growing fast) are brought into the picture the polarisation becomes further accentuated and complicated. Although we do not deal with the Arab population at all, our analysis is enough to illustrate how the tension between modern democratic practices and the ethno-religious definition of the state itself continues to haunt the land, to the point where some authors describe the country as an ethnic democracy, while others speak, perhaps tendentiously, of an 'ethnocracy' (Yiftachel, 1998).

A text such as this one, which focuses on religion and on social movements in Israel, will inevitably emphasise the less liberal and more corporatist aspects of the Israeli state, whereas one which focused on, say, monetary policy or higher education, or on the judicial system, would show a more impersonal and liberal face. The word corporatist is used to refer to groups, often corporate bodies, so entrenched within the state that they manage institutions of interest to themselves, either directly—as when, say, the pineapple growers manage the pineapple subsidy regime—or indirectly—as when they are in close and maybe unseemly touch with the officials allocating the scarce and also subsidised credit for pineapple growers. We derive our use of the term from the literature on Latin America where until, and even since, neo-liberal economic policies began to take hold, business interests have taken a formal and often controlling part in the management of state agencies (Schmitter, 1974; O'Donnell, 1977). The term was used with reference to European politics for a certain period to describe the involvement of economic interest groups in policy-making and government-sponsored ('concerted') collective bargaining (Molina and Rhodes, 2002), but the Latin American example is more appropriate for Israel because of the connotation that to some degree corporatism allows fiefdoms to exist within the state but largely beyond the control of central government, and also because of the shared history of protectionist economic policies known as 'import substitution'. The word fiefdoms also denotes the effects of class structure, whereby representation of corporate interests is monopolised by particular groups, and is not a product of an impersonal, let alone transparent, procedure. (Thus in our notional example, the pineapple growers' representatives would tend to be the owners of the biggest pineapple plantations.)

So just as Sartori had trouble with the party system, we have trouble reconciling a system which combines both modern bureaucratic institutions, and an often (but not always) fiercely independent judiciary, with the capture of certain institutions by civil society interest groups. The political science literature on Israel has used the term consociationalism to describe 'arrangements which conferred partial autonomy on political movement "enclaves"' (Horowitz and Lissak, 1987: 152): 'In this model, social enclaves tend to form around movements which act as secondary centers that mobilize and allocate resources and commitments, receiving continuity through socialization and indoctrination' (*ibid*.: 28). These arrangements had developed during the mandate under the Yishuv, the inter-war period when Jewish self-government was effective and operative but not institutionalised as a state: as used by Horowitz and Lissak, consociationalism refers to the existence of a 'political-communal centre' (*ibid.*: 151) and to the prominent role of political parties with strong ideological commitments in running education, housing, culture, even sports. Horowitz and Lissak speak of a 'far-reaching politicization of all spheres of life' during that period (*ibid.*), and it is easy to forget the dominance at that time of socialist ideology and highly centralised party organisation. Subsequently, after 1947, the trade union movement (Histadrut) became a vast apparatus which both owned many industries (today mostly privatised) and at the same time represented the workers in a fairly classic European-style corporatist system, while the welfare state became a more conventional social-democratic operation, and secular education, previously controlled by different political forces, was unified under the Ministry of Education.

In the classic account of consociational democracy the state may support and accept communally specific educational systems or marriage arrangements, for example, and at the extreme may reserve parliamentary seats for one or another community or even—as in Lebanon before the country fell into civil war—reserve certain posts for members of one or another community (Lijphardt, 1969). In Israel some of this communal pattern exists, as in the *haredi* educational system and in the separate religious courts with jurisdiction over personal status laws. But Israel has also exhibited party or movement monopolies over certain institutions, in the kibbutzim, and today in Shas's separate school system, and there is room for opening up quite wide-ranging de facto prerogatives, as in the West Bank settlements since 1977.

Beyond corporatism or consociationalism, the notion of enclaves encompasses all these practices, and others, very conveniently, because of the connotation of frontier and boundary maintenance which is a pervasive feature of Israeli life. For example, the Israeli concept of a Cabinet seat is unique: to our knowledge, in no other country are Cabinet votes announced publicly, nor do Ministers campaign against Prime Ministerial policies they disagree with. Ministers, in certain respects, seem to treat their Ministries as quasi-fiefdoms protected by the Knesset members of their party in an eventual vote of confidence. During Ehud Barak's government the Shas party, for example, held several high-spending Ministries, but despite their open disagreement with Barak's foreign policy, only resigned briefly in a sort of muscle-flexing gesture: later they returned because of the need to retain access to the government budget for their educational and promotional activities. Ministers also habitually use their Ministries for partisan purposes—as in the admittedly extreme case of the Minister of Tourism Effi Eitam, sacked for his aggressive campaigning against the Sharon government's foreign policy in 2004, or Sharon himself, who as Minister of Agriculture in previous governments devoted himself little to agriculture, but much to encouraging and funding West Bank settlement. Other ministers who opposed Sharon's foreign policy in 2004, but who had stronger bases in Parliament, were not sacked. Apart from Ministerial fiefdoms (which may change hands or be redistributed) there are corporatist fiefdoms, of which the best known, or most widely denounced, examples are the now-defunct Ministry of Religious Affairs which has served the interests of the *haredi* communities almost exclusively, and the Ministry of Agriculture, within which a quasi-autonomous Department was created to fund settlements in such a way that it bypassed provisions that would have prevented the funding being directed so specifically at one set of communities (*Ha'aretz*, 25 June 1999).

The Israeli enclave arrangements, though, are not always as exclusionary as, for example, Latin America's corporatist systems have been. The case of Shas illustrates this point well, raising the question of how a political force 'breaks in' to a political system. From the early 1980s Shas proclaimed itself as the voice of the economically and culturally dispossessed Sephardi population, children and grandchildren of immigrants from North Africa and the Middle East, with the added and unaccustomed element of a call to return to strict orthodox observance. The party's success in breaking into a system which, according to its own rhetoric, had previously managed to exclude or suffocate the Sephardi voice is particularly interesting because it was achieved thanks to those very corporatist features which one usually assumes to be exclusionary and to favour incumbents against newcomers. Although by 2004 Shas was out of power and its leadership were behaving somewhat like 'lost souls', it nevertheless was an established force with eleven out of 120 Knesset members (down from the peak of seventeen in the 1999 elections) and a school network all its own, and remained the political face of a vast movement of religious renewal reaching far beyond the Sephardim. Shas turned the corporatist system in its favour by hard bargaining with coalition partners, and in particular by making sure that the party obtained its own 'fiefdoms' in the form of the school system and numerous mechanisms to subsidise Shas-affiliated activities and organisations. The question for political theory is whether the party and the people for whom it stood could have fought their way into the political system with such success if instead of playing the game of corporatism and enclaves, it had continued to support Labour as the Sephardim had done until 1977, with meagre and, in the view of many, humiliating results. To avoid any hint of triumphalism, however, it must also be noted that their successes are in visibility and occupancy of the political stage: the material gains, in terms of income and life-chances and access to the socio-economic élite, of the children and grandchildren of the Sephardi immigrants, remain uncertain and unquantified. Furthermore, even if there has been advance among this population, the extent to which it is the result of Shas's passage through government would be yet another question. The Israeli political system favours those who would adopt Shas's approach, that is, using the control of Ministries to consolidate their political support through patronage rather than adopting universalistic welfare state type policies. Of course Israel's elaborate welfare state is run on a universalistic basis, even though, as in other countries, it seems to have done little to prevent the increasing social inequality—even within the Jewish population—associated in this case with the period of rapid growth post-1967 and the growing neo-liberal emphasis of economic policies since 1985.

Legal expressions of the enclave system

The division of the territory which is now Israel, and of Jerusalem in particular, into enclaves can be traced back to the Ottoman Empire's 'millet' system of tax collection: the point was noted in passing by Ernest Gellner in his *Muslim Society*: 'in Modern Israel, the legal institutions of the Ottoman autonomous community, the "millet" system, are kept alive by political stalemate' (Gellner, 1981:2). Under this system the territory was divided among tax-farming overlords, and Jerusalem was divided into 'quarters'. Already at the time of the

Crusades the territory was divided among various kingdoms and fiefdoms, so the history of parcellised government, of division into autonomous and quasi-autonomous units governed according to different rules and customs, is very ancient, and also very enduring. In that respect, it is perhaps not fundamentally different from other former Ottoman possessions in the Middle East and the Balkans.

The British Mandate itself perpetuated the pattern of communal separation and legal distinctiveness by allowing indigenous Arabs, immigrant Jews and Europeans, or Muslims, Christians and Jews, to run their own affairs in the spheres of family, civil law and education. The corporatist arrangements described above, which existed during the Yishuv, with funding from the international Jewish community (Swirski, 1999), fitted into this scheme. Among the legacies of those successive periods of more or less indirect imperial and colonial rule the practice is observed in Israel of allowing a degree of juridical autonomy to different religions, especially in the fields of family and civil law. This is not unique to Israel, it is also found in India, where Muslim and Christian courts operate family law side by side with the secular judiciary (Nussbaum, 2000). On the eve of Independence in 1947, and then during the 1948 war, Ben Gurion and the leaders of the religious community negotiated an agreement, under which the religious community was allowed certain exemptions, such as military service for women and for Torah students, and certain autonomies, notably for their education system. It became known as the 'status quo' because initially the religious representatives sought a preservation of the arrangements that had prevailed under the Mandate and the Yishuv, which allowed them much autonomy (Friedman, 1995). As a result there is an intricate involvement of the state in appointments to both religious bodies and to the judiciaries that follow the various religious denominations; for example, the Ministry of Justice appoints judges and officials of religious councils (a function transferred on abolition of the Ministry of Religious Affairs in 2003), but allows different degrees of autonomy to different religious communities, so that inevitably Muslims are much more dependent than the Christians (Eisenman, 1978; Louër, 2003). Eisenman explains the powers of Muslim courts but notes that they have difficulty in getting the authorities to enforce their decisions. Louër has some ironic points, noting that on occasion a mullah may be glad to have the protection of a state salary against the intrigues of his Mosque committee. The ultra-Orthodox parties in Israel are able more or less to dictate the membership of local Religious Councils, which administer marriage, funerals, *kashrut* and the like, and employ large numbers of officials for the purpose, although certain municipalities, amid much controversy, recently began to flex their muscles by appointing women and non-ultra-Orthodox Rabbis (as a result the Jerusalem Religious Council did not meet for two years, see *Jerusalem Post*, 19 March 2004).

Education and enclaves

Education is at the heart of Israel's enclave pattern: the state funds not only different streams with different curricula, but also different sets of institutions which operate under different inspection regimes, different accountability regimes, and different resource allocation mechanisms. Thus, in addition to the State Secular system, which takes the majority of pupils, there are separate educational institutions for the State Religious, for the Arab and Druze populations, for the ultra-Orthodox in general, and since 1988 a separate ultra-Orthodox network under the aegis of Shas. Those for the ultra-Orthodox and Shas are not directly managed by the state. Hence the delicate formula 'Non-official recognised education', reflecting the fact that they are funded by the state but the state has limited control over the education they offer. For example, the ultra-Orthodox and Shas networks appoint their own inspectors. Until 2003, towards the end of the first Sharon government, when the Attorney General put an end to the practice, the yeshivas for under-18 year old pupils run by Agudat Yisrael and Shas were receiving additional funds ('double funding' in the Attorney General's words) from the Ministry of Religious Affairs, which was held by a Shas Minister.

The State Secular system is directly funded and managed by the Ministry of Education which also pays the teachers. The 'State Religious' (*Hinuch mamlachti dati*) system, however, was developed under the close eye of the National Religious Party and continues to be influenced by it. It is managed by a separate department within the Ministry but its teachers are also directly paid by the state and are subject to a similar but separate inspection regime. Religion has a far greater place in their schools' curriculum, but they teach all standard secular subjects and prepare their secondary students for the *bagrut* examination which is the stepping stone to university. However, the distinction between State Secular and State Religious Schools, and the lower likelihood that students from the latter will proceed to university, seems to be social and socio-cultural as much as curriculum-related: the latter's intake comes from lower income strata, who also happen to include proportionately more pupils of North African and Middles Eastern origin. Nevertheless, the State Religious System also has some prestigious high-achieving schools. There are also a small number of non-religious, non-official recognised schools devoted, for example, to progressive models of education.

Crudely stated, the State Secular system remains dominant, with 66 per cent of primary and 70 per cent of secondary pupils in 1998/99. However, the ultra-Orthodox increased their share of pupils from 6 per cent to 14 per cent of primary pupils and from 6 per cent to 11 per cent of secondary pupils in the 1978/79 to 1998/99 period (*Statistical Abstract of Israel, 1999,* Table 22.16), and according to *Ha'aretz* (26 August 2004), quoting Central Bureau of Statistics figures, the proportion of Jewish elementary school children in ultra-Orthodox schools reached 23.6 per cent in 2002. This reflects the general expansion of *haredi* numbers and influence, and not only the emergence of the Shas network.

Within these institutions there are of course innumerable further non-legislated differences related to location, social class and so on, but the institutional differentiation itself sets pupils on radically different life-courses, especially when the ultra-Orthodox and Shas school systems are compared to the other two systems aimed at the Jewish population. Since the *haredi* ethos rejects the social life of the university and also the academic criteria of scholarship that prevail in university education, these institutions do not offer secular studies of the kind that would enable pupils to go on to university. The characteristic education of *haredi* children offers a minimum of secular subjects, and only until the age of fourteen, with very little science or foreign languages. Some teaching of religious subjects is in a combination of Hebrew and Yiddish (save in Shas schools). After they have left school these students will be confined to making their living within the ultra-Orthodox society/enclave. Indeed, there have been efforts to retrain *haredim* for non-religious occupations, but reports in 2004 were that it was very difficult to achieve results since the trainees had never been exposed to learning with the purpose of acquiring skills: the yeshiva life is a life of study as an end in itself.

This issue of a state-funded education system that does not provide its pupils with what are widely regarded as the basic skills needed for life in a modern society has been the subject of legislation and court cases. There is a core curriculum which is in principle obligatory for all schools: since 2001 these 'non-recognised' but funded schools have been obliged to teach 55 per cent of that curriculum. By 2004 the implementation of this provision had still not begun and, in response to a petition from the Association of Secondary School Teachers, the Supreme Court gave the government three years to negotiate a transition with the schools. Whether this will actually take place is another matter, but the prestigious Rabbi Shalom Elyashiv declared that no part of the programme should be allowed into the schools (*Jerusalem Post*, 16 December 2004). The Ministry, it seems, was not relishing the confrontation, even if it talked of negotiation, while even a seasoned 'broker' who often acts as an intermediary in these sorts of situations, said that the state was looking for a conflict, and could have achieved all these aims so long as it had not mentioned the provocative words 'core curriculum'.

This unusual differentiation, under which the state funds schools with different philosophies, different funding regimes and different conceptions of the purposes of education, dates back to the early days of the Zionist movement in Europe and its implantation in Palestine, when Agudat Yisrael was, as it still is, a powerful voice of religious Judaism and strongly opposed to the secularist and modernising ethos of the Zionist movement (Swirski, 1999). The details, which can be found in Swirski and in Horowitz and Lissak, are of less concern here than the pattern, whereby the education of children is entrusted not only to a state education system with standard modern academic objectives catering to the majority of the Jewish population, but also to an ideological religious movement—Agudat Yisroel—a particular political party—the National Religious Party—and now to another political party, namely Shas. However, the Shas education network is much more political than the State Religious system, since the latter is fully incorporated within the state and subject to civil service procedures and Ministry inspection, so its ideological thrust is less exposed to view. A further element is the Yeshivot Hesder, which have developed into élite yeshiva institutions catering for the 14–23 age group, offering both academic and Talmudic study for young religious men intending to do military service (Eisenstadt, 1985: 259). Shas, as we shall see, has focused on religious content, but even here there is some variation.

The enclave pattern of construction and settlement

Israeli land and housing markets bear no resemblance to a free market, nor to the variously regulated, subsidised and controlled land markets which operate in Western Europe and North America, nor even to the unregulated (or ill-regulated) but imperfect markets of Latin America. This distinctiveness is grounded legally in the fact that the land is owned by the state, and it is reinforced by the political nature of construction, which in the early years of the state was driven by the imperative of occupying the territory, and which even now is very often a highly political matter, independently of the issue of the West Bank settlements. For urban territory and neighbourhoods to acquire a degree of ethnic, class or communal homogeneity—encapsulated in expressions such as 'ghetto' and 'gated community'—is by no means unusual in any country, but in Israel the process of occupation and control of the territory is distinguished by explicit and purposive political mobilisation and by arguments adducing the desirability on religious grounds both of certain groups living together, and of other groups living elsewhere (because their way of life is offensive to the religious, for example). To this is added the mobilisation of support within the state apparatus, which controls subsidies, permits and even design. The most visible examples are those areas in and around Jerusalem and elsewhere (most notably the de facto *haredi* town of Bnei Brak, but also in Ashkelon, Ashdod, in some West Bank settlements and in newly built dedicated *haredi* towns dotted around the country) which are more or less 100 per cent occupied by people leading a highly observant lifestyle. These have increased as the ultra-Orthodox population has expanded in numbers and political leverage. In Jerusalem, where the area of strictly observant communities was once known as Me'a Shearim, after one single street, the areas dominated by the wearing of distinctive dress and meticulous observance of the

Sabbath extended first into adjacent neighbourhoods and then into
the post-1967 areas of the city. These consist of rapidly built and to
some extent uniform housing complexes made up of three and four
storey blocks all faced in standard rugged carved blocks of yellow-
white Jerusalem stone (in compliance with a famous regulation
enacted under the Mandate). The post-1967 expansion has divided
the city broadly between 'black'—or ultra-Orthodox—areas to the
north and the more secular to the south, added to previous territorial differentiation between Sephardim and Ashkenazim, and
between income groups (Sasson, 1993). The central area of strict
observance which spread out from Me'a Shearim is barred—following much political mobilisation—to all traffic during the Sabbath, contains innumerable synagogues and yeshivas, large and small,
majestic and dingy, and is characterised by small shops and artesanal
outlets that sell devotional and Rabbinic literature and religious paraphernalia, kosher food and kosher clothing (made with unmixed
cloth), and also provide in-demand services, including the provision
of food, tailoring, cleaning and the repair of push-chairs. It is
'another world', near to another 'other world' in the Old City,[1] and
at the centre of a bustling modern city (not least because a multitude
of bus services connecting far-flung suburbs pass through its narrow
streets). It is unthinkable for a non-observant person to live here
openly, though one hears of secretly non-observant *haredim*. Even
the public services regard it as something of a no-go area: the streets
are dirtier than elsewhere, and on one occasion we observed how a
fire in a video shop was not cleaned up for days, apparently left to
smoulder by the fire service. (The shop, it should be added, had been
torched on suspicion of selling pornographic material, and a Rabbi
had died in the mêlée.)

In neighbourhoods built since 1967 the combination of business,
politics and communal pressure has been very effectively managed
by various groups, including the ultra-Orthodox: the state allocates
land for construction, a developer sees an opportunity, and community representatives enter into the arrangement with their stipulations for size of houses, numbers of rooms, design of kitchens,
public religious buildings (synagogues, ritual baths and the like) and

---

[1] Itself divided into enclaves as a result of the establishment of nationalist and ultra-
Orthodox strongholds within the Arab Quarter.

a ready-made list of purchasers for the entire project. Mortgage and other finance may also come directly or indirectly from the government. In addition, where religious observance is at issue, subsequent sale and purchase is governed by a committee, operating under the legislation governing NGOs, which ensures that apartments are only bought by suitable people. The Council of Torah Sages—the Rabbinical authority which governs the *haredi* world—plans housing projects in *haredi* areas which, whatever the private or public agents and authorities may say, cannot proceed without their permission, including design approval, to the extent that they held up the *haredi* area for eight years in Bet Shemesh, an expanding town near Jerusalem to which we shall return. In mid-2000 rumours had been circulating according to which ultra-Orthodox people would move into particular neighbourhoods, as a result of which prices went down and certain types of potential inhabitants were discouraged from moving there. Bet Shemesh itself is a striking illustration of the enclave system, and not only because of the presence of *haredim*: the town is built on a large hill, the prosperity of the inhabitants rising towards the top: around the small central shopping area live Ethiopians and Sephardim; the Russians live in newly constructed housing a little below. Not far from them is the large, also newly constructed, *haredi* neighbourhood, and at the top of the hill the 'Anglos'—mostly 'modern Orthodox' immigrants from the English-speaking diaspora.

An instance of the financing of these schemes can be found in a case which reached the High Court in 2000. A suit had been brought by the Am Chofshi (A Free People) NGO, a secularist pressure group represented by Yossi Paritzki, subsequently a short-lived Minister for the militantly secularist Shinui party in the 2003 Sharon government. The suit claimed it was illegal for the State, through the Department of Building and Residence, to provide more advantageous mortgages to the 'ultra-Orthodox town of Elad' than to purchasers of houses in neighbouring communities. The complaint was upheld with respect to the preferential mortgages, but significantly the Court said 'there was no legal problem with establishing a *Haredi* settlement' (*Ha'aretz*, 31 May 2000). The case shows it has been standard practice for the state not only to establish settlements or neighbourhoods for designated religious groups, but also to provide subsidised housing for them. This reflects, doubtless, the political influence of the religious parties and organisations, and recognition by the Court and the government of a de facto reality, that in the final analysis, ultra-Orthodox residents, when they have reached a critical mass, exercise discreet, or sometimes not so discreet, pressure on other residents to leave (Friedland and Hecht, 1996). The Supreme Court, reviled by ultra-Orthodox spokesmen, who see it at best as secularist and at worst as a force for the destruction of Judaism, has frequently had to find difficult compromises on cases such as this one and on others involving, for example, the de facto exclusion of Israeli Arabs from purchase of land or access to mortgages (Shafir and Peled, 2002), as on numerous other sensitive subjects on the religious/ secular, majority/minority or nationalist/liberal borderlines.

The segregation of ultra-Orthodox communities is further accentuated by their economic isolation. With the exception of the Ge'ulah (next to Me'a Shearim) in the centre of Jerusalem and the main street in Bnei Brak, their communities have very few shops and more or less no public eating places, the latter because those frequenting them would 'inevitably' risk illicit sexual relations, giving rise to the birth of children of uncertain parentage and the like. Having low incomes, or perhaps simply because they prefer it, the ultra-Orthodox make extensive use of co-operative shopping schemes and elaborate mutual aid arrangements which keep their reliance on public retail outlets to a minimum and create a certain degree of autarchy. The separateness of these areas, notably Ge'ulah, is accentuated also by their manifest aesthetic indifference to the quality of public, secular space: commercial premises are unkempt and dingy, and streets are laden with more rubbish than elsewhere.

One might say that this is a 'system' in which those in competition for land make headway by creating facts on the ground. This of course was how the State was created. As a result, the Arab population within the 1967 borders are almost invisible, even though they number about 1 million, constitute 14 per cent of the country's population (*Statistical Abstract of Israel*, 1999) and are far more numerous than the *haredim*. They have been de facto confined to their own enclaves, in Haifa, in Galilee and in the east in the 'Triangle', in separate villages with separate occupations and schools and truncated citizenship rights—most notably their exclusion from military service, and their de facto exclusion from most of the civil service. Also, Arab municipalities receive funds according to less advantageous rules than those applying to all others. They can be thought of as an enclave of exclusion, while the more powerful or self-empowered have used enclaves to gain inclusion—access to resources, leverage and land—sometimes by legal means and often by creating 'facts on the ground'. This is how Gush Emmunim, the settlers' movement, acquired the settlements on the West Bank under way in the early 1970s[2] (Sprinzak, 1991), and we shall see how Shas activists also implant themselves in urban settings. The pattern is even to some extent repeated among the Arab population: Jerusalem planners are said to be in despair at their inability—despite one or two high-profile evictions—to control the building of illegal or unauthorised extensions and houses in East Jerusalem.

However, the appearance of enclaves is not only the work of ethnic or religious or messianic nationalist groups: it is a pattern which has caught on and, of its very nature, tends to reproduce itself, so there are also neighbourhoods in the cities and sectors in the newly-built towns in which one finds only secularised Israelis, or 'yuppies' as some of them are often described. This is well evoked by an analysis of electoral results in 1996 which shows the territorial distribution of voting between the globalised, more prosperous, English-speaking middle classes, who mostly live on the coastal plane and support the 'left'—at that time in the person of Ehud Barak—and the popular classes who live in the interior (Elazar, 1998). Barak won overwhelmingly in Tel Aviv (two to one), through most of the coastal plane and especially in 'classic upper-middle-class suburban cities', one of which registered a nine to one proportion in favour of Barak, and in selected purpose-built suburbs in the interior, including one which Elazar describes as for 'Israeli WASPS' (White Ashkenazi *sabras*[3] with *protectsia* or influence). In Jerusalem the secularist parties won 11 per cent, (the ultra-Orthodox Shas 17 per cent), but beyond that the secularist parties won over 10 per cent in only three interior cities.

Thus the enclaves separate not only the religious from the secular, but also what Yiftachel describes as 'Jewish ethno-classes', and the

---

[2] A pattern that goes back to the days of the Yishuv when the territory and the boundaries of the future state were far from being established.

[3] See glossary.

pattern has been intensified by the establishment of 'more than 150 small ex-urban developments' in which a 'whole range of mechanisms' were 'devised and implemented … to erect fairly rigid lines of separation between various Jewish ethno-classes', involving 'the provision of separate and unequal government services (especially in education and housing), the development of largely separate economies, the organization of different types of localities in different statewide "settlement movements" and the uneven allocation of land on a sectoral basis' (Yiftachel, 1998). Illustrating how the practice of selection and exclusion described here is not peculiar to ultra-Orthodox communities, Yiftachel states, 'movement across boundaries has been restricted by allowing most new Jewish settlements to "screen" their residents', leading 'predictably' to 'domination by middle class Ashkenazis' (*ibid.*: 11). However, the denomination 'ethnocracy' seems too tendentious, especially when placed in opposition to democracy, while the notion of ethno-classes does not sufficiently reflect the fact that the enclave frontiers can be religious, ethnic, or simply related to income or lifestyle, and may also cut across one another. These are practices that have arisen in the context of a modern state with legal institutions and a political system which may not satisfy the conditions of a liberal democracy, but which is democratic nonetheless, and can be interpreted as products more of a hyper-mobilised society than of a coherent politico-legal design.

Social enclaves

The enclave system can also be thought of as one aspect of the ostentatious exhibition and mobilisation of social frontiers which is so characteristic of Israeli Jewish society. In this book readers' attention will be drawn to the many boundary-defining devices maintained and produced by *haredi* Jews to distinguish themselves from each other and from the rest of the world. But the concern for defining and maintaining boundaries and their signs is by no means restricted to them, and is possibly unusually prevalent in Israel. Whether or not this is the case, it is important to be aware of the ways in which Israelis mark themselves off from one another. Dress is the most obvious example amounting almost to a uniform in some groups: secular women are careful to calibrate the length of their skirt, because if it only reaches the calf then they might look like a *dossi*—ironic Yiddish slang for a *haredi* woman. A whole array of skullcap (*kippa*) styles has developed to denote different political loyalties: the standard difference between the black velvet kippa, which denotes a *haredi*, and the knitted, coloured, varieties worn by the National Religious, who are observant and Zionist unlike the *haredim*, has been amplified and finely graded. The modern Orthodox do not adopt the 'black' dress style, but do wear non-velvet black skullcaps, while the settler movement, now dominant in the National Religious Party, has developed its own version of what might be called '*haredi* fatigues': dress which is utterly informal and not colour-coordinated (unlike the *haredi* men), but which exhibits protruding fringes (*tzitzit*) and large skulls-caps, while the women on the settlements, though dressed in an entirely functional way, have adopted the *haredi* practise of covering their arms, their heads and their legs—using headscarves instead of the hats or wigs of their urban counterparts. Found at what might be called 'the other end of the spectrum' is the aggressive secularism of male fashion, with shaved heads, large sunglasses and something like an exhibition of the male body.

Although a preference for intra-ethnic socialising is noticeable among many groups, it must dilute in the second and third generations; nevertheless the Russian community has been less assimilative than others and is well known for building up all sorts of enclave characteristics: a thriving press; availability of Russian TV; after-school classes to teach Russian and to compensate for what is regarded as the inferior science teaching in Israeli schools; shops selling imported food from Russia; predominantly Russian neighbourhoods.

These features of everyday practices contribute, together with the enclave system and the corporatist features of the political system, to a picture of a society in which social boundaries are extremely important, even though without systematic international comparison it is obviously not possible to state whether they are more important, or thicker, than in other countries. At the same time, they are not set in stone. Thus already in 1985 Eisenstadt remarked on the high rate of intermarriage between Ashkenazim and Sephardim, reaching 20.4 per cent of all marriages among Jews in 1980 (Eisenstadt, 1985: 310), and today estimated at almost 30 per cent. The enclaves are multi-faceted: they are social, religious and even political, so that the erosion of one does not imply a weakening of the enclave system as such. The system should be thought of as the superimposed mobilisation of a variety of markers and ties—economic, political, ethnic, cultural, symbolic, phenotypical, even linguistic—in any one case, but not the same in all cases. Religion adds to the list not just because of coincidences between religious affiliation and these other ties, but also because it is in the nature of religion to create boundaries, a subject to which we turn in the next section.

Although we have alluded to ethnic frontiers (Sephardi, Ashkenazi, Russian), we have not mentioned ethnic enclaves. The reason, of course, is that although ethnic belonging and origin, expressed in terms of geographical origin, pervades Israeli daily speech, it is not institutionalised. Furthermore, ethnic terminology in Israel—and probably elsewhere and perhaps everywhere—is usually a shorthand for a combination of frontiers and markers. The analyst's task is to deconstruct these markers, asking why they become frozen in social categories or even institutionalised by a combination of legal, bureaucratic or political mechanisms. Colour or race, as descriptions of ethnic belonging, are metaphors or at least shorthand. There is in principle no analytical difference between markers and frontiers expressed in terms of physiognomy or geographical origin, on the one hand, and those expressed in terms of religion, language, income or profession on the other. The analytical concerns of social scientists focus especially on, first, the interaction of ascription differences (gender, geographical origin, phenotype) with those of wealth, status and power; and, second, on the idea of cultural markers as representing packaged 'identities'. Although we evidently recognise the existence of a politics of identity and of ethnicity, we ourselves have great difficulty in using the words as categories of analysis. Ethnic affiliations are combinations of markers calling for deconstruction; while identity is a word borrowed from psychoanalysis, impossible to apply coherently to social processes save in the political sense of the rhetoric of identity used to promote particular causes or groups (Bayart, 2005). This is illustrated by our difficulty in deciding whether to use the term 'Sephardi' or 'Mizrachi' in our analysis.

Strictly 'Sephardi' is a religious category which, although it now covers a wide array of geographically-rooted liturgical and ritual practices (dress, music, Hebrew pronunciation and much besides), is opposed to, but on equal terms with, 'Ashkenazi'. (Ashkenazi itself ranges widely, in terms of ritual, liturgy and geography, across Western and Eastern Europe.) The word Mizrachi (Eastern) is more broadly social in its connotation, but connotes lower social status when set against the principally Ashkenazi élites. But people also speak of *edot hamizrach*—peoples or communities of the East— reflecting their diversity but not necessarily a lower status. As we shall see, people from Iran, Iraq and Egypt have generally fared better economically than those from North Africa. Also, the word Ashkenazi has clearly different meanings in different contexts. In a secular context it refers to European origin, both East and West. Nonetheless it excludes post-1980 immigration from Russia (known simply as 'Russian', though doubtless having its own internal differentiation). We have decided to use the word 'Sephardi', partly because this is what Shas invokes as its religious heritage, and partly for the sake of simplicity in a text concerned so centrally with religion. Our usage is a pragmatic choice: we do not claim that it is better than or preferable to alternatives used by other authors (cf. Shafir and Peled, 2002).

RELIGION AS ETHNICITY

Religious affiliation is constructed out of boundaries and is sustained by boundary-maintenance mechanisms which vary in intensity, but should not be thought of as conceptually different from ethnic boundaries. It is not by accident that most religious affiliation is—still—inherited, or that the minimum religious observance consists of the rituals accompanying birth, marriage and death, nor is it by accident that stringency in observance in all the world religions focuses on the control of sexuality, especially women's sexuality. These are all mechanisms of intervention in social reproduction, and the more closely the religious organisation can control them, the more it can ensure its own reproduction and eventually expansion.

At the 'soft' extreme of boundary maintenance we may note the availability of the Church of England to conduct rites of passage for people who may otherwise never set foot in a church. It is, as Grace Davie has noted, a vicarious sort of religious institution, a kind of moral or ceremonial guarantor desired by a passive, non-participating and non-contributing support population, whose attitude can be described as 'believing without belonging' (Davie, 2002). These 'unchurched populations' manifest their 'latent sense of belonging' mostly by their attitudes, but it is not without significance that, insofar as they do manifest their belonging in their actions, it is by participation in rites of passage, not, for example, in Good Friday or even in Christmas services. Among Jews we find a similar pattern with barmitzvahs and weddings. Pascal Boyer describes rituals as, among other things, a way of enabling individuals to realise that their intuitions about sometimes unfathomable changes—like the loss of life in a dead body, or the removal of a woman from sexual availability by marriage—are shared by others: 'attending a wedding may well give you the intuition that your relations to the newly-weds will now be different, and that this may be the case for other participants too... a ritual may give you a simple representation of why these changes are so clearly co-ordinated in all participants since the event is itself a salient and mutually manifest reference point' (Boyer, 2001: 292). But in addition 'not performing a ceremony, when others do, very often amounts to defecting from social co-operation' (*ibid.*). It is therefore not surprising that conversion-based movements multiply rituals, because this is a way of ensuring co-operation and preventing defection.

The proliferation of rituals is also a way of creating boundaries between the group and the outside, so it is equally unsurprising that in so many contexts religion is hard to disentangle conceptually from ethnicity. This is not to suggest that religion necessarily follows boundaries of colour, language or territory (though there are of course many instances where these boundaries are superimposed) but rather that the two operate in similar ways—to keep people in, and to keep people out. In fact, one very striking finding of our own and others' research in Latin America has been how in that continent religious change seems to have cut across other ethnic boundaries. The surprising success of Protestant sects—fundamentalist and Pentecostal—among indigenous groups has been widely noted (Gros, 1999; Muratorio, 1980; Rostas, 1999; Vilaça, 2002), often changing the content of their cultural practices quite profoundly without necessarily weakening the boundaries which keep them separate: 'We face a disjuncture when interpreting the relationship between religious transformation and cultural boundaries. Although we take it for granted that large-scale religious changes are intertwined with encounters between cultures ... we find it increasingly difficult to conceptualize the word "culture" in this somewhat concretized sense of superimposed multiple boundaries of language, religion, race, politics and so on. So unless we disentangle our notion of cultural boundary or cultural interchange we are caught between the crudity of assuming that cultural boundaries are superimposed on innumerable others (social, economic etc.) and the absurdity of denying their existence altogether.' (Lehmann, 2001:53) In other words, we need not be surprised that Protestant preachers, who do nothing to hide their contempt for the belief systems of the indigenous peoples to whom they are bringing their message, attract and retain more active adepts among indigenous peoples than the much more cautious Catholic activists who make valiant attempts to see the world through indigenous eyes and emphasise social issues such as land rights and multiculturalism. The assumption that indigenous people think of their rituals, their magic and their ethnicity as a single and undifferentiated whole seems to be mistaken, and we find a similar unbundling, a similar bricolage, in the outcomes of campaigning by Shas and its many affiliates and associates. Conversion campaigns depend too much for their success on local initiatives for central control over every detail to be feasible: their unity derives from affinity rather than hierarchy.

In the process, the evangelical churches, like Shas, draw new boundaries and create a 'quasi-ethnicity', thus strengthening the ties of dependence of their members and followers. Some of course are more dependent and more deeply involved than others, but the link between creating dependence and constructing boundaries is clear: people are encouraged to attend services very frequently, and some do so daily; they are obliged by various techniques to make regular subscriptions as well as supplementary donations to their churches. They adopt distinctive modes of dress and their lives acquire a distinctive rhythm which sets them apart. Having cut many, even all, of their previous social ties, their incentive to comply is strong. Thus it can be seen why the original title of this research was 'Crossing Frontiers in Israel'. Dynamic religious movements seem to rearrange allegiances, recomposing symbolic clusters which we too readily assume to be definitively 'packaged'. If this bricolage worked in Brazil or Africa, why should it not 'work' elsewhere?

THE GROWING PROMINENCE OF
CONVERSION-BASED RELIGION

Changing what it means to be religious

In innumerable contexts across the world, religion itself has changed. These contexts straddle wealth and poverty, cut across the standard divisions between religious traditions, and cut across political and ethnic divides. The transformation goes beyond the routine sense in which religion is forever changing, because it is bringing about a change at the heart of religious institutions and traditions. The change in question is conversion, by which we mean campaigns both to bring people in and—equally important—to bring people *back*. Of course, mass conversion itself is a far from new phenomenon: the Spanish empire was defined from its very inception as an evangelising undertaking—as was, to a not inconsiderable extent, the British Empire in sub-Saharan Africa—and the Pentecostal churches whose followers are now a majority of Protestants throughout the world have conversion and evangelisation as their defining feature. What is new today is the extent to which, following the example of, and also competing with, Pentecostalism, the initiative has passed to the periphery and to the grass roots, for example in Africa with the 'Ethiopian' churches (Campbell, 1995) and Zionist messianic movements (Sundkler, 1948; Comaroff, 1985) and in Latin America with the founding of the Assemblies of God in Brazil in 1918 (Martin, 1990). The conversion movements of today are anti-establishment, transnational and transcultural (Lehmann, 1998), and they draw their dynamism from poor and disenfranchised sectors of the population and indeed from poor countries. Even in developed countries the dynamic comes from diaspora populations (Haar, 1998; Hunt and Lightly, 2001), both Muslim and Christian. For Christians, including Catholics, and even for Jews, Pentecostalism has provided the prime model for many movements outside Protestantism which centre their organisation on growth through proselytising activity, making every member a missionary, and have also borrowed doctrinal or quasi-doctrinal elements such as belief in the gift of the

Spirit and in divine healing (Martin, 1990; Csordas, 1997; Freston, 2001a; Martin, 2001; Chesnut, 2003).

Even among Hindus, who might not be thought to have a very strong tradition of even worrying about who is 'inside' and who is 'outside', this trend can be observed (Rajagopal, 2000), and this book shows that, even in its ultra-Orthodox manifestations, Judaism, usually thought of as a conversion-resistant religious culture, is itself being reshaped by conversion movements. The targets of these movements may be almost exclusively 'returnees', but the process and its effects bear much similarity to those observed in Christianity and Islam.

Saying that religion is being reshaped by conversion movements is obviously not a claim that the majority of adherents of Christianity, Judaism or Islam are converts, or 'reverts' or 'returnees', or even that a majority are involved in conversion campaigns. In religion the majority of adherents are apathetic and participate only passively and intermittently. The claim rather is that the converts and returnees are liable to be disproportionately represented among the most enthusiastic and committed adherents and among the missionaries, and the activity of conversion, campaigning and 'outreach' becomes increasingly central to the leading religious institutions.

The qualitative importance of the conversion phenomenon can be observed in the extent to which religion's public face is that of the revivalist preacher, of the campaigner, speaking not only or even principally to the faithful following, but to potential new followers and to those who have abandoned the religion of their ancestors. This face can be seen in the mass media and on the street. It can be observed in the proliferation of courses, classes, seminars, specialised institutions and specialised roles devoted to the attraction of converts and providing for their religious and non-religious needs: the words missionary or evangelist, for example, are attached to particular sorts of position in Pentecostal Churches; the Jewish Chabad sect has a worldwide apparatus of missionaries (*shlichim*) and other sects not usually known for their 'outreach' activities, run courses for returnees; the powerful Lithuanian community in Israel has established whole yeshivas specially for returnees, where they can study for many years; the Catholic Charismatic Renewal, which consists of prayer groups largely run by unordained people who are specialised in managing communities of the born again, is becoming very prominent in some countries, especially in Latin America, as the public face of Catholicism, in mass meetings and mediatic occasions (Csordas, 1997; Chesnut, 2003; Lehmann, 2003). The once-Brazilian, now global, Universal Church of the Kingdom of God, is organised as a vast marketing apparatus, aimed at bringing outsiders into Church, including TV and radio stations and 'nuclei' of members who work the streets and houses of a neighbourhood to convince people to join (Birman and Lehmann, 1999; Birman, 2001). The Islamic movement Tablighi Jama'at, which also has a presence across the globe, though it takes pains to keep out of the headlines, is devoted entirely to religious revival and renewal (Kepel, 1987; Metcalf, 2002) and is quantitatively much more important than the hyper-politicised fundamentalist groups that command so much attention.

Shas is not the only conversion-led force that has influenced Israeli Judaism and Israeli politics. The messianic nationalism that drives the settlement movement, and is a very strong influence in the Likud party, is another variant on the same theme, for many of its militants are people who have given up another way of life to become settlers and to drive the cause. So when the two are taken together, the importance of conversion or 'reversion' in Israel's politics is clearly not to be minimised. In addition, the presence of converts and reverts or returnees generates a particular dynamic within a movement, which is discussed in Chapter 6, and which is common to movements across religious boundaries.

Conversion as life crisis

For millions of Pentecostals across the globe conversion is a defining element of the existence and mission of their churches and of their own life and identity as church followers, and even people born into Pentecostal families are often not regarded as full members of the community until they have been through a conversion-like experience in which they profess to have seen 'the world', to have been tempted and to have recovered or retrieved themselves from that experience. When researchers ask Pentecostals to recount their lives the response has a standardised, almost formulaic quality and changes little from one person to the next. In these accounts their conversion, which is the central event in their lives, is usually described as a fulminating experience linked to healing and often also to family and psychological problems, during which an individual is disoriented or experiences some sort of trance, interpreted as receiving the gift of the Holy Spirit. In Judaism returnees may not mention healing, but like Pentecostals they describe their return as much more than just the adoption of a new religious label, or the paying of membership fees to a different synagogue. For them, as for Pentecostals, and also for members of the Tablighi Jama'at, and doubtless other Islamic movements of regeneration, the process brings moral change, as described by the converts and the *ba'alei t'shuva* (returnees) themselves. In all cases we observe radical material changes: in a person's social milieu; in the mode of dress; in the carrying of the body; in personal financial arrangements; in taboos surrounding sexual relations; in rituals of eating. The list can be very long. The non-material, ethical, transformation is of course harder to document than more tangible changes, but it is proclaimed in a standard language which includes for example, a 'change of life', renunciation of this-worldly aspirations for the 'world to come' and of short-term illusory pleasures for more enduring happiness, living by the rules laid down in a sacred text (as interpreted by religious professionals), and living in a stable family in which couples live in peace and children obey their parents. Among Pentecostals the account describes more of a fulminating experience than among the *ba'alei t'shuva*, but in all the cases perhaps the most encompassing common thread is joining a new community and then becoming dependent upon it. Among Jews it can take time, but the outcome is the same, and the chapters that follow show how the dependence unfolds. The dependence is deeper, probably, than in the generality of Pentecostal communities, but this is only a matter of degree. Jews who 'return' also differ in their social background and personal trajectory: in France, and quite possibly in other Western countries, it is linked, for a particular generation, to rejection of a youth dedicated to alternative lifestyles and left-wing causes (Podselver, 2002), rather than to the social marginality which is widely credited with Pentecostal conversion and Islamic 'return'. Even though all three examples come with a history of migration (Pentecostals in Europe coming predominantly from Africa and the Caribbean, and Muslims from

North Africa and South Asia) the particular histories are too different to allow for a common explanation in terms of discontinuous
family histories. Yet despite radically different trajectories, the similarities of outcome are too strong to be ignored.

The conversion phenomenon has also made its presence felt inside
establishment institutions, so that it is no longer accurate to think of
it as belonging only in dissenting institutions or communities. We
have already mentioned the Charismatic Renewal movement within
the Catholic Church, which has only existed since the late 1960s but
already counts its followers in millions (Chesnut, 2003), but we
should go further and mention the 'Pentecostalisation' which Chesnut describes as affecting congregations in historic Protestant churches in Latin America, and which can also be observed in the
'evangelical' wing of the Church of England for example. Within
Judaism, practices associated with the *t'shuva* movement are becoming standard in communities where not so long ago they would have
been regarded as unthinkable, such as among Chassidim, some of
whose leaders now support the provision of courses for returnees.
We can see *t'shuva* in all sorts of manifestations: the adoption of
increasingly orthodox practices among Reform synagogues, such as
gradual increases in the use of Hebrew, or adoption or revival of
tunes identified with the orthodox tradition; the ever more widespread use of skullcaps by Jews all over the world (in tune with the
growing use of ethnic or religious markers by others); the increasing
adoption by 'modern Orthodox' Jewish women, who are regarded
as strict but not ultra-Orthodox or *haredi*, of styles of modest dress
which resemble, though they never exactly replicate, that of their
haredi counterparts—long sleeves, calf-length skirts, close-fitting
bonnets etc.

The mechanisms whereby ultra-Orthodoxy is gaining influence
are not always what they seem. Although the main tendency among
Jews is still probably a shift away from observance, among people
who continue to identify themselves as Jews, *t'shuva* is a growing
trend, and one which is increasingly influential. In addition, the
intermarriage rate among Jews may well be strengthening the *t'shuva*
movement and compensating for attrition, because Jewish communities have become increasingly open to the spouses of those who
marry out. They and their children need religious education and

induction, which means more outreach work for the *t'shuva* movement: these newcomers and converts may not shift across to ultra-Orthodox observance, but they and their children may well be taught by ultra-Orthodox Rabbis, because often they are the only teachers available, and because of the massive over-production of qualified Rabbis due to the culture of intensive Torah study which has taken hold of ultra-Orthodox communities worldwide.[4] Furthermore, prayer books and religious texts produced by the ultra-Orthodox publishing house Artscroll are becoming standard in synagogues of many different persuasions (Stolow, 2004). These are not the only reasons why ultra-Orthodox Rabbis have established themselves as guarantors of tradition, and their practices as a yardstick against which others measure themselves. One has to take into account other factors which will emerge in the course of this book, such as the power they wield inside their own communities and the extent to which they are able to mobilise their followers to act politically and in unison, which enables them for example to achieve almost 100 per cent turnout in Israeli elections, and to present an extremely strong front in Jewish politics.

SOCIAL MOVEMENTS

The epidemiological pattern of spread

Although evangelicalism, Pentecostalism, charismatic churches and fundamentalism are routinely described as 'movements', analysts of these phenomena do not usually link their interpretations with the literature on social movements. Likewise those who write theories of social movements only rarely pay attention to religious movements. In contrast, we treat religious movements similarly to other social movements, because the pattern of their development can be analysed with the same tools. Possibly, the case of Shas is particularly suited to this approach because of its explicit invocation of social and

---

[4] It is increasingly common, in our experience, to find missionaries from the best known evangelical Jewish sect, the Lubavitcher, also known as Chabad, in highly secularised communities such as Madrid, Santiago de Chile, São Paulo and Rio de Janeiro. Chabad is an acronym made of the first letters of the Hebrew words for Wisdom, Judgment and Discernment, while Lubavitch is the town where the sect was founded.

especially ethnic conflict and injustice, and also because of the explicit political dimension present from its birth. The social and the religious are in any case closely intertwined in the historical narratives and language associated with, and propounded by, Shas and its most faithful followers, as well as in more symbolic spheres such as architecture and music. Furthermore, one is entitled to ask whether this supernatural dimension in religious movements is fundamentally different from the quasi-magical element which is present in much social and political mobilisation: the insiders' jargon, the emblems, sometimes the flags and uniforms, the rituals associated with certain sorts of gathering, the almost unlimited trust sometimes placed in charismatic leaders.

In our conception social movements do not have clear boundaries or defined objectives in the way that formal organisations do: they are multi-stranded, multi-layered and indeed multi-directional, and cannot be pinned down to lists of objectives or to certain named organisations. We think of a movement as having a culture, but at the same time as being borne not by ideas or identities, but by large, even vast, numbers of individuals, and although movements are evidently a context or shelter for formal organisations with defined structure and objectives, these can never be enumerated as if they amounted to a specific number. A movement exists as the object of allegiance on the part of innumerable individuals, but not as a structure or even a defined set of ideas. Of course it has a name, or names, and identities which evoke ideas and ideals, but outside the specialised institutions of research these are effective as banners and sources of solidarity rather than concepts or theories. Social movements necessarily encompass institutions, and networks of institutions, which organise to defend certain interests, develop doctrine and ideology, provide services, and mobilise opinion. However, these institutionalised attributes are not quite enough: emblems and slogans and codewords provide signs under which individuals congregate, mobilise, agitate, or sometimes just relax. Movement boundaries are shifting, varied and locally defined, and the content of the boundaries may relate to lifestyle, age, social class, ethnicity, in fact almost anything in their self-conception that individuals might have in common with others. In some parts of a movement there may be organisations with very tight membership or participation requirements, while in others they may be loose or only vaguely connected to the movement's ideological emblems and positions. Even if individual followers are members of an organisation which adheres to some movement ideas, that will only account for a small part of their lives and does not exclude adherence to many other causes and organisations.

Since individuals express allegiance for many different reasons and certainly do not all have the same idea of the movement, their connection to each other should be thought of as epidemiological rather than organised or hierarchical. In saying this we draw an analogy with epidemiology in the image of Sperber's notion of an epidemiology of representations: just as he points out that for a group to share a cultural representation its members do not have to replicate or duplicate it exactly, but simply to transform it so as to produce a 'degree of resemblance between the communicator's and the audience's thoughts' (Sperber, 1996: 83). So we would claim that movements bring together people whose aims and ideals are not all the same, and certainly not hierarchically regimented by their membership in an organisation. Rather they come together because each one shares something with an other, and also because they come to the movement through their connection with others, not, as a general matter, through their adherence to a leadership or an ideal. The reasons for a movement, a slogan, even a category of feeling becoming a force for change or a collective phenomenon are to be found in individual, sometimes even random, contacts, like the spread of a flu epidemic (Gladwell, 2001). One might add that this applies even (perhaps in particular) where individuals express slavish and absolute obedience to certain stated ideals and to the leadership, since our studies show that slavish obedience to a text or idea means in fact authoritarian imposition of one particular reading and thus obedience to the person imposing that interpretation, independently of any close examination of ideas or of a text. It is intensity of connection to a particular individual leader, and not only a high-profile leader, which explains the hyper-commitment to an idea, rather than the other way round.

The epidemiological concept implies that people join because of their connections to others in their immediate vicinity, so it is a local matter (though not necessarily local in an exclusively geographical sense). Ours, therefore, is a very broad and generous conception, and clearly differs from other current conceptions which emphasise identity—associated with Manuel Castells among others (Melucci, 1989; Castells, 1998)—or leadership, as in Lenin or in 'resource mobilisation' approaches (McAdam, McCarthy *et al.*, 1996). The epidemiological metaphor highlights the importance of movements' ability to penetrate the interstices of society, a conception which stands in contrast to one which emphasises hierarchy and efficiency in marshalling resources and laying siege to institutions. We say this not because such skills and resources are unnecessary, but because they are only partial aspects of a movement, and may even exist successfully with no basis in any movement at all.

The argument can be illustrated by reference to European social democracy, which could lay claim to being a prime model of a social movement: social democracy, at the height of its power and legitimacy, was an entire culture, enjoying intellectual representation in academia and the press, pervasive influence throughout the welfare state, sponsoring and managing an infinity of private and public social interventions, and providing the arena for wide-ranging debate about the meaning of social democracy itself. Contemporary examples would include the international NGO-development movement, and possibly the anti-globalisation movement. Developmental NGOs taken together constitute a vast network of networks with a common culture, a common vocabulary, but also with fierce disagreements and debates on all sorts of issues (Hulme and Edwards, 1997; Crewe and Harrison, 1998). In Israel itself the Zionist movement in the pre-state period evidently fitted this multi-layered, multi-directional model, containing within itself, again, violent ideological disputes (Dieckhoff, 2003), a wide array of educational institutions and religious styles, and also divergent economic interests. Yet these contradictions do not necessarily prevent institution-building: some NGOs, notably Amnesty International and Oxfam, have 'come from nowhere' to international status and influence, and Zionism, through its many networks, set up a proto-state. The strategy of building pressure and institutions from below—giving rise to the enclaves already mentioned—has retained effectiveness and legitimacy in contemporary Israel: the West Bank settlers could be seen as the irredentist spearhead of a wide-ranging movement which, like Shas, has succeeded in shifting one of the fulcrums of Israeli politics

(Sprinzak, 1991): they have their own parties and have penetrated the mainstream right-wing Likud and the National Religious Party, and they have established their own institutions—notably the Yeshah Settlers' Council—in effect to manage the settlements as their own local government, not in place of the state but as an enclave within it, enjoying numerous complicities and subsidies, open and hidden (see, for example, *Ha'aretz*, 25 June 1999). All these movements are multi-levelled mobilisations, impinging on many different instances of power and in many different spaces, unified less by ideas than by core symbols and emotional attachments.

To merit the name, a social movement must be a vehicle for social change on a grand scale. That implies, among other things, that it should engage with conflicts at the heart of a society's system of accumulation and reproduction. The classic example of a core mechanism of reproduction is the wage-labour nexus: obviously this relationship is at the heart of the capitalist system and by challenging the level of wages and the mechanisms of fixing them, European social democracy changed the capitalist system. The women's movement also exemplifies the point: it has contributed to fundamental changes in women's labour force participation, in sexual behaviour and much else besides, all of which have contributed in some measure to changing core mechanisms of demographic and economic reproduction. Also, the international NGO movement has successfully pressed the international development system to open its decision-making processes to civil society and NGOs and, as a result in no small measure of their efforts, the themes of environment, gender, and human rights, are unavoidable and prominent in all international development programmes. In addition, though, we should remember that involvement with major international institutions also influences the NGOs, whose style has over time shifted to a more accommodating stance *vis-à-vis* international institutions (Fox and Brown, 1998)

Nevertheless, a very high profile event or set of events does not of itself make a social movement. To bring about social change on a significant scale, social movements need to make themselves felt and heard in a multiplicity of institutional contexts and niches of society. An epidemic of demonstrations, even large ones across many countries, is not a guarantee that enduring social change can be achieved.

Demonstrations, after all, are ephemeral events. Even if occasionally they achieve the status of historic turning points, it will not be the demonstration itself, but the follow-up which explains that outcome. To become a social movement, collective fervour has to be translated into purposive action, sustained presence and engagement with other social forces, lobbies and interest groups in institutional contexts capable of generating tangible outcomes, and this has to be done in people's daily life, not just in formal institutions. The anti-globalisation movement offers a good example of a media event or protest phenomenon still waiting to be transformed into a social movement. Until about 2001 it gained much media coverage, but unless it can develop an institutional presence in decision-making forums and a project or set of projects of its own, it will be remembered only as a series of street spectacles, and the underground global spread of an attitude of distaste, rejection or simply fatigue with respect, for example, to global brand names and other more political emblems. The Israeli peace movement ('Peace Now') offers an interesting contrast in the light of its relative failure (especially compared to the settlers). The peace movement's supporters may be more numerous than the politically active settler vanguard, and their international support is substantial. They also have no shortage of intellectual spokespersons with access at least to the printed media in Israel and outside. Yet they have failed to gain the penetration that the settlers now possess in institutional niches especially in the state, and in their campaigning in civil society they may suffer from an elitist style and a cosmopolitanism which does not have much grassroots appeal. There may also be a difference in the degree of commitment among followers:[5] settler militants probably devote a much higher percentage of their time to their cause, first because they have decided, somewhat in the manner of converts, to devote their entire lives to it, and second, because they benefit from government subsidies which enable them to divert their energies from earning a living to political campaigning.

To say that social movements need to engage institutionally does not imply that they can only succeed if they work 'within the

---

[5] For a graphic account of the most active settlers' campaign to turn the Likud ballot against Sharon's Gaza withdrawal plan in May 2004, see: 'Sharon feels wrath of settlers he long supported', *Wall Street Journal*, 15 June 2004.

system', that is, if they adopt moderate, gradualist strategies. But it does mean to say that appearances, both of radicalism and of gradualism, can be deceptive, just as the changes which follow from high profile media exposure or from collective or institutionalised violence are not always profound or intended. Likewise in religious movements: the most strident, even the most violent, those commanding most media attention, may not, in the end, produce the most revolutionary social changes. Although Shas has without doubt produced changes in Israel's political system, it is still unknown how much change in social indicators, if any, has resulted from its rise, or from the evangelical movements we previously studied in Latin America, despite their undoubted symbolic and mediatic presence.

In modern societies a core element of the reproduction of society is the boundary between the religious and the secular, and radical religious movements are heavily involved in trying to shift that boundary, thus changing explicit or implicit 'rules of the game'. This is evident in public and political debate on issues such as abortion and sex education, as well as the spread of AIDS, in rich and poor countries. Religious movements intervene beyond the locally defined, conventional boundaries of the religious in secular spaces such as politics, education and the media, to introduce, sometimes to impose, changes in the mechanisms of reproduction of the religious sphere itself, and its relationship with the state and the institutions of secularism. We can see this in Latin America where evangelical Protestant churches have claimed parity with the Catholic Church in the formal apparatus of the state, for example by acquiring the right to conduct marriage ceremonies, by taking their place alongside Catholic-sponsored and secular charities receiving state support and by broadcasting on innumerable radio stations and increasingly on television, sometimes even to the point of owning their own television networks or cable broadcasting stations. We see it wherever Islamist movements are putting pressure on states to apply their version of Islamic law; and we shall of course see it in Israel where the frontier is a source of permanent conflict in law, housing, schooling, public finance, even in disputes over who can hire a municipal theatre. By redrawing the boundaries dividing the religious from the secular in social circumstances where secularism has become a central institution of modernity religious movements engage with core mechanisms of reproduction.

Apart from shifting legal and institutional boundaries, and others drawn by inherited convention, religious movements also try to bring about changes in the symbolic presence of the religious in the popular imaginary by, for example, constructing grandiose church buildings in Brazil on a scale previously associated with the Catholic Church (Birman, 2001) or organising mass gatherings of the faithful in Israeli basketball or football stadiums, normally regarded as strongholds of secularism. At the other extreme, missionaries violate the anonymity of the street and accost passers-by with the message of Jesus or the importunate question 'Are you Jewish?'

The core of social reproduction must be biological, and it is not by accident that all religious movements—indeed more or less all religious institutions—concern themselves intimately with marriage, birth control, sexual behaviour and education. Jewish ultra-Orthodoxy exemplifies this feature with particular salience, in the explicitness of its rules and exhortations regulating sexual behaviour and the extraordinary success of the different branches of Jewish ultra-Orthodoxy in dictating the conduct of family life, through fertility strategies and education. Similarly, fundamentalists and, to a slightly lesser extent, charismatics and evangelicals, push back the frontiers between the secular and the religious by political agitation, but also by making sexual behaviour itself a frontier or marker of religious belonging, as in the obsession with the 'SBM' ('sex before marriage' in their jargon) among young British evangelicals. The drawing and redrawing of frontiers goes hand in hand with the penetration of new social niches, because once a niche is marked out the barriers must be thrown up, and sexual frontiers are particularly suitable for this purpose: they are cheap to erect financially (but not socially) and they create a competitive and gossipy atmosphere which raises the costs of non-conformity, as in Atran's central question about religion: what leads people to adopt costly and hard-to-fake patterns of behaviour? (Atran, 2003b).

A project of cultural transformation

To think that the strength of a movement lies in the clarity and coherence of an idea, a slogan, or even a doctrine is tempting. But although ideas are obviously extremely important, to know how they are represented by those who proclaim their belief or faith in them is not always easy. They may be expressing an underlying trust in those who would propagate the ideas. Their belief may be of an aesthetic, or romantic kind, or alternatively it may derive from their conception of their own economic self-interest. In any of these cases, ideas reach individuals in packaged and simplified form, so that an analysis based on the original, erudite form may not explain their popularity. Religious movements are a very good example of this, because the counterintuitive character of claims about the supernatural—which is what religious claims are—makes it hard to speak of their clarity or coherence. But political ideas also have a quasi-magical flavour, at least when stated in the sound bites and catch-phrases that form the staple of political discourse: are people of average, or even low, intelligence ever really any more convinced that a new government will, for example, 'abolish poverty, reduce taxes and increase public expenditure' all at the same time—or even that it could achieve one of these in a short period—than they are likely to believe in virgin birth or reincarnation? Of course one can cavil about the precise meaning of the word 'believe' in this context, but the point we are making is that a movement's success cannot be explained by the leadership's capacity to convince people of such claims. Instead, somehow such claims and doctrines must be translated into rules for the conduct of daily life, and this means debate and sometimes quite technical discussion among professionals, intellectuals and experts: how else can the doctrine of the Trinity, or of transubstantiation be made meaningful for individuals' concrete existence, or translated into real-life ritual? This is why the Catholic Church has staged such elaborate events as the Second Vatican Council, or proclaimed documents such as the Syllabus of Errors, to take two politically contrasting examples. It is also why the great institutionalised religions have given rise to theology as a profession, debating the supernatural in a framework of rational debate in which reign the impersonal practices and procedures of intellectual exchange. The absence of such intellectual ferment limits the influence and durability of a movement: for all their massive quantitative success, evangelical churches have far less influence in society as a whole than Catholic and Anglican élites do in Africa, or than the Catholic Church does in Latin America. In the case of ultra-Orthodox Judaism, the influence may appear greater than it really is because of their unusually high fertility and, in Israel, because of their efficacious use of the political system: their success in marshalling society behind their agenda, however, has been small. This is especially striking when we compare the relative success of the settlers in drawing to their side large segments of public opinion, and even segments of intellectual opinion which might have been thought to veer towards more liberal positions.

Contemporary religious movements will remain as sects—even large sects—with a limited impact on society as a whole if they continue to allow those who hold positions of political and managerial power to exercise, in addition, a monopoly on doctrinal or theological authority, and therefore also to prevent intellectual reflection. To achieve influence in modern society religion must allow the development of spaces of argument about religion's own concerns in which trust, reason and honest exchange prevail. Of course, religious movements can, and sometimes unfortunately do, try violence, but that leads where it leads. Although violence is still rare, verbal violence is common, as is the movements' rabid hostility to intellectuals and academic culture. For the Universal Church of the Kingdom of God theology is 'both useless and diabolic, a sort of possession which confuses people and distracts from the true task of religion, namely to cure and deliver them from the devil, to put an end to their suffering. Jesus, its leader reminds us, did not waste time on theology—he devoted himself to healing the sick and casting out evil spirits' (Lehmann 2002, summarising Campos, 1997). This argument also applies to ultra-Orthodox Judaism, for which learning is esoteric and legalistic, where, if our fieldwork is to be believed, creationism is widely accepted and advocated, and where the tools of modern science—archaeology, linguistics and so on—are excluded from the study of Rabbinic texts.

Of course in the short and medium term, charismatic and fundamentalist movements can sometimes exert powerful pressure in the political system and often in the local community, *inter alia* because of their numbers and because their followers obey their leaders and therefore vote as a solid bloc. In some situations and countries religious movements exercise an influence out of all proportion to their numbers, sometimes even by using violence, but, as Gilles Kepel has insisted in the case of political Islam (Kepel, 2002), this is a reflection of weakness rather than strength, and will not help the achievement of the religious reformation to which some of them claim to aspire.

If a movement is to endure and to bring about a change in the culture in which it moves—if, in Alain Touraine's phrase, it is to bring about a change in the control of '*historicité*' or of a '*champ d'action historique*' (Touraine, 1973)[6]—then it has to allow the intelligentsia to develop their own sodalities and symbolic ties. If this does not happen the project will suffer the fate of official marxism in state socialism, or of Jewish thought in the ultra-Orthodox world, where it has been subordinated to limits imposed by authoritative bodies, especially in Israel.

The intelligentsia in their turn develop as a movement within the movement, with their networks, their power plays and their public disputes. Visions and projects will be discussed researched and analysed in universities, and in the media, publishing houses will host some ideas and not others, and so the movement can take its place in the public sphere. We shall see in our study how Shas has largely failed in this department, despite one or two isolated efforts to carve out a niche for itself. This is explained partly by political contingencies, and by the incompatibility of the anti-intellectualism of ultra-Orthodoxy with the culture of the secular intelligentsia.

THE RESEARCH

The research presented in this book was first suggested by Bila Sorj in a conversation in Rio de Janeiro in 1998. Shas seemed to offer an extreme case of 'crossing boundaries' while thickening new ones: it invoked the Sephardi identity and the resentments and nostalgias of the second generation North African and Middle Eastern immigrants, but at the same time proclaimed a return to religion in the style of the Eastern European Ashkenazi *haredim*.

The research began in the summer of 1999, with the collaboration of Bila Sorj at first and then of Batia Siebzehner, and continued until 2004. In this period Israel went from Barak to Sharon,

[6] Our analysis of social movements—apart from the epidemiological approach—owes much to Touraine, whose model is well expressed in Chapter VI of the book quoted.

and Jews and Arabs went from an uneasy peace to the nightmare of a
war and a sense that they might be compelled to live forever in unre-
solved tension. Our book deals with hardly any of this. We are not
experts on the subject and have little new to say about it, and our
analytical focus is on issues in the comparative study of religion.
Comparisons apart, the phenomenon under study is fascinating in
itself, and our account and our interpretation of Shas and the *t'shuva*
movement provides a window on aspects of Israeli Jewish society
which are either little known outside Israel or are understood only
in a highly schematic way. Thus this is a case study in a comparative
context, offering thick description with the intention of grasping
the multi-layered and multi-faceted character of the movement.
Comparative studies in the social sciences always run the risk of sac-
rificing richness of description in the pursuit of a general theory,
based on neatly pigeonholed data, finely tuned variables and refined
indicators. This is very profitable in certain spheres, where abundant
high quality data are available, but in subjects where subjective dispositions are a prime focus, such as religious movements, the results
of controlled comparisons are unlikely to be very profitable. The
risk with case studies, of course, is that by immersion in detail they
come to be too self-absorbed, provincial and monographic. However, in addition to Geertz's thick description, we have the soaring
example of Max Weber to demonstrate that the comparative interest
of a case study arises from the choice of the case, and the fertility of
analysis undertaken in awareness of a set of defined themes derived
from a comparative background. The thick description notion is
particularly applicable in this study because it involves so many situations in which words and symbols have been wrenched out of an
accustomed context and are used in ways which evoke several different meanings for different listeners: this applies as much, for example, to habits of religious observance as to methods of teaching and
study or even gestures of political loyalty.

As has been stated in various ways, to grasp a movement means
understanding many facets and levels, which means the process of
research has to be a very open one. Since one is trying to discover
connections, and since the object of the research is not a structured,
bounded institution, one has to adopt the view of the explorer:
the movement has innumerable points of contact and the contacts

themselves have many other contacts. There is no list of institutions from which one can select. Thus one has to follow leads, and in this way we were able to appreciate Shas's penetration in the interstices of Israeli society. Over three years we visited schools, yeshivas, synagogues and radio stations, and attended study groups, consciousness-raising sessions, public meetings and political discussions. We made contacts at meetings with people who sometimes were open to further meetings and interviews, and sustained relationships with some of them over a period of time. In short, the research was conducted by networking. The focus is much more sociological or anthropological than political, and this has been our intention. We did not, on the whole, become involved in the factional politics of Shas, or in the relations between Shas and other parties, or in the mechanics of electoral campaigning, because this would have been for another type of study. Our focus was more on Shas's dimension as a movement than as a party, even though the subject is obviously deeply political.

There has been excellent research on Shas, though only a small amount has so far been published in English. This research has, with some exceptions (Leon, 1999; Fischer, 2004a; Lupo, 2004), been from a political science viewpoint. The view of Shas in Israel is two-fold: many people see it as a largely political phenomenon designed to gather votes and to wield political influence in the interests of its leadership, yet often the same people also remark that it is a very important phenomenon and express their sense that it reflects underlying and troubling features of their society. We address this second set of concerns and in doing so are aware of the somewhat preliminary nature of an inquiry which, based on two people's fieldwork, nevertheless attempts to grasp a large and complex phenomenon in its entirety.

2

T'SHUVA MEETS ETHNICITY: THE SHAS RELIGIOUS PROJECT

This chapter provides the background needed to understand the confluence of ethnic resurgence and religious renewal in the political party and movement Shas. If the two themes are intertwined this is not only because they are related in the narrative, but also because, as explained in the previous chapter, they are extremely difficult to separate analytically. What the chapter describes is nevertheless unusual in the context of the Jewish experience: the movement of return is by now an established feature of Jewish life, but the strategy followed by Shas of linking it explicitly to ethnic and social resentment is unprecedented, though it makes excellent sense for its protagonists in the Israeli context.

The word *t'shuva*, which has become a standard element in Jewish parlance worldwide, has two meanings, 'penitence' and 'answer', and is linked with the idea of 'return' as in *hozer bet'shuva* which means a person who returns (*hozer*) in (*be-*) penitence (*t'shuva*), often rendered in English as 'returnee'. In addition, Mazlish points out the derivation from the Biblical word *shuv* (again), which evokes the sense of a new beginning, or even being 'born again' (Mazlish, 1984). On Yom Kippur, the Day of Atonement, and during the Ten Days of Penitence preceding it, the service includes a frequently repeated prayer, using these self-same words, asking God to 'bring us back in penitence to you'. The extent to which *t'shuva* in everyday usage has a connotation of penitence, rather than return, is unclear. Another less usual allusion is to *t'shuva* as an answer, sometimes contrasted with *beshe'ela*, a question, as in the contrast between a person who questions religion and one who finds the answer in return. The term *ba'al t'shuva* (*ba'alat t'shuva* for women) is used interchangeably with *hozer bet'shuva. T'shuva* has become a far-reaching and multi-faceted project in Judaism worldwide, and in Israel, but this book focuses on an Israeli social movement and political party, which, uniquely in Judaism, has combined the religious renewal of *t'shuva* with an anti-discriminatory campaign and also a practical renewal or recovery of a particular ethnic tradition.

CHABAD AND SHAS: CONTRASTS AND SIMILARITIES IN *T'SHUVA*

By now it is commonplace that the growth of the *haredi* or ultra-Orthodox community worldwide has been one of the most note-worthy, but no longer surprising, features of post-war Judaism. Even without the Holocaust, the trend towards secularisation and the influence of the consumer society was expected to reduce the community to mere remnants, like the decline of religious observance in other religions. However, the community has in fact experienced a remarkable comeback, and although it obviously remains a quanti-tative minority among Jews worldwide, its political and religious influence has grown considerably. It is, of course, a heterogeneous phenomenon, whose component parts include the traditionally separate 'Lithuanian' and Chassidic communities. The former share a common experience in yeshiva education and adult study centres, they speak of themselves as a community and, crucially for their def-inition as such, if at all possible they marry endogamically. However, they do not have an official common leadership, which is diffused among yeshiva heads, who command more influence than com-munity Rabbis (Soloveitchik, 1994). The Chassidim are grouped into numerous communities which—as always with an exception—re-cognise single unified leadership in the person of a *tzaddik*, a su-preme Rabbi who is said to be consulted by all his followers on all matters of importance (especially marriage). The largest single Chassi-dic community is Satmar, stretching across Western Europe, the United States, Latin America and Australia, though the Satmar view the state of Israel with even greater disdain and disapproval than most Chassidim. Chassidim are regarded as more mystical but less open than the Lithuanians, although in practice it is increasingly dif-ficult to tell them apart save through the practice of endogamy and distinctive codes of dress. Neither liturgy nor methods of Torah study, dietary rules, or political positions provide clear clues to the lines of demarcation. The ultra-Orthodox non-Chassidim are also known as *mitnagdim*, the 'opponents', because of rifts that emerged at the birth of Chassidism in the late eighteenth century when it represented an ecstatic, messianic variant and was virulently opposed by the revered sage, the Gaon of Vilna (hence 'Lithuanian'). Today such ideological differences are of little importance and the fight against permissiveness and secularism holds them together. The demographic growth of the Chassidic sects, which have extremely high fertility rates, has been remarkable, as has their ability to build community institutions for education, welfare and the conservation of their way of life.

This is a well known and widely documented phenomenon (Heilman, 1992), though distinct, analytically, from the conversion movements that have fuelled the growth of Pentecostalism and Islamism worldwide, and from the *t'shuva* movement spearheaded by the Lubavitch, or Chabad Chassidim and Shas. The growth of the religion of those who return, and the movements which bring them back and in which the returnees themselves then become activists, is not the same phenomenon as the resurgence of sects and institutions that existed before the Holocaust. Those traditions provide Shas and Chabad with the religious content, the raw material, which, after small but crucial modifications, endows these movements with a distinct identity, and a distinct set of markers.

Chabad and Shas, in their different ways, represent a bold, proactive, comprehensive, multi-faceted approach to *t'shuva*, adding a powerful 'supply-side' drive to the 'demand-side' predisposition arising from structural and personal circumstances. Since the 1960s Chabad, once a relatively small Chassidic sect, has grown into a vast worldwide complex of organisations, all apparently controlled from headquarters in Crown Heights, Brooklyn (Friedman, 1994). It has had remarkable success in establishing institutions, in providing rabbis for students in universities in North America and Europe and for isolated communities worldwide, and in attracting people 'back' to what Chabad followers call '*yiddischkeit*' (Jewishness). This involves helping people to establish a kosher household, guiding them towards stricter Sabbath observance, providing lessons in Kabbalistic mysticism or Talmudic classes and discussion groups, sponsoring lectures and weekend seminars, teaching children to speak Yiddish, and much besides, all in the context of insertion in an all-encompassing communal framework which monopolises an individual's social life. Its constituency is revealing itself to be—or is becoming—increasingly diverse, including, for example, extremely comfortable families living in a newly-built exclusively *haredi* suburb of Jerusalem (Ramat Shlomo), ultra-militant settlers on the West Bank, dentists and psychoanalysts in North London, children of highly secularised middle-class families in Mexico, Brazil, Argentina and Chile, and young Sephardim in France.

Chabad offers a service to the people who are attracted to the movement, helping people who have lost touch, or never been in touch, with the Judaism of their parents or grandparents, to 'return', for example through 'how-to' pamphlets about preparations for major festivals, classes in mysticism and drop-in centres for businessmen, but extending, depending on the degree of commitment—or dependence—to much more pervasive involvement in the details of their lives. The organisation is particularly interested in influencing the education of the younger generation. If children are brought in early enough they attend Chabad schools where religious education dominates, in particular Rabbinic learning for the boys, and where secular education takes second place and is not offered at all after the age of about sixteen. At that age, in London, girls usually go to a seminary, while boys go to a boarding yeshiva. Chabad is more attentive to women's public role than other Chassidic sects. In the long run girls will become mothers and schoolteachers or maybe social workers and may well play an important role as Rabbis' wives (*rebbitzin*). The boys go to yeshivas in London, Manchester and many other places, from Israel to Argentina, after which quite a number join the growing ranks of Lubavitcher Rabbis and activists around the world.[1] The eventual employment of the young men we have spoken to in the Lubavitch yeshiva in North London, for example, whose education has been almost entirely religious, remains a mystery, for there cannot be religious stipends for them all.

Chabad is organised in concentric circles. At its core are the missionaries (*shlichim*) spread across the globe, who gather once a year in

[1] These observations are based on fieldwork in London during 1998–9, and also on conversations with Chabad Rabbis in Brazil and Chile.

November in Crown Heights. They are born into very large Chabad families and thus are, so to speak, unpolluted by association with the outside world or with recent converts. It takes a generation or two for the children or grandchildren of converts to be admitted to the core—which means being allowed to marry someone from a fully-fledged Chabad family. Coming, like all *haredim* nowadays, from large families, its core followers (best thought of as cadres[2]) have innumerable relatives who are also members of the core. Consequently, each one of them will have cousins in far-flung countries and will meet frequently in the never-ending round of weddings, circumcisions and barmitzvahs[3] (which also multiply as a result of the size of families). If they live in places where there is no available suitable education they may send their children to live with relatives or to board in another country.

Chabad's strategy of penetration leads its emissaries to establish themselves in universities, in communities which lack a Rabbi[4] and even in Reform synagogues whose members would hardly be expected to have any respect for ultra-Orthodoxy. Chabad houses have been set up on many US campuses (UCLA for example) and in Cambridge, England among many others. Missionaries are subsidised for two or three years, during which time they are expected—like Pentecostals—to build a self-sustaining local basis for their mission. They are also prepared to go to the difficult corners of society, to bring Jews back from drugs and social marginality and to welcome those who have fallen by the wayside. It provides them,

[2] It is often difficult to decide what words to use in connection with membership, affiliation and adherence to these sects and movements. There is obviously no formal membership 'card', but there are different categories of involvement: thus some people are certified graduates of institutions proclaiming their adherence to a movement; others are employed by charitable bodies clearly identified with it, but most are just followers—yet followers are also bound in to a tightly knit set of relationships which profoundly influence their daily lives, their decisions about marriage and education, and also the way they earn their living. The term 'cadres' is used to refer to office-holders—Rabbis, activists on the payroll of an association, teachers in religious institutions etc.

[3] Though the barmitzvah is less important and not always celebrated publicly in Chabad and other *haredi* circles: for them marriage, which is a teenage event, is the main moment of passage into adulthood.

[4] In Madrid for example, with its heterogeneous community of Ashkenazi and North African Sephardi Jews.

and all returnees, with a firm context and a strict set of procedures
and timetables for daily life: they know there is always someone to
listen, there is always something to do, if only to study, and that a wife
or husband will be found for them, as will a Sabbath meal. They also
know there is an answer to every question: what can I cook? what
can I wear? what is the blessing over this type of food? and so on ad
infinitum. All these questions have an answer, based in a text, a story,
an analogy, an embedded message concealed among the letters of a
text, or just 'tradition', which becomes authoritative if invoked by a
person in a position of authority. They join a 'meaning-rich' world
and one in which most of their leisure time can be devoted to
activities organised by and in support of Chabad.

In Israel, however, Chabad's presence as an organisation is less
prominent than in Europe and the United States. There are followers of Chabad and there is a township known as Kfar Chabad,
but the sect's presence is diffuse.[5] The Lubavitch Rebbe, when he
was alive, exercised some political influence in Israel, especially in his
opposition to territorial concessions on the West Bank and in his
followers' campaigning against Sabbath traffic, as a result of which an
intersection in Jerusalem's Mea Shearim neighbourhood is popularly known as Chabad Square. However, he never went to Israel and
was never fully committed to the idea of the state in its current form.
Despite their diffuse presence in Israel, they are the most prominent
organisations proclaiming t'shuva in open public spaces—enabling
hospital secular patients to celebrate Sabbath rituals and inviting
passers-by to engage in simple rituals like putting on *tefilin*.[6] The
t'shuva movement is very widespread, though, and, apart from Chabad's quantitatively and qualitatively high profile in so many countries, there are many other groups and organisations who seem to
follow a similar model, which is in turn similar to the model used by

---

[5] Lubavitch followers are known in Israel for their hospital visits with candles and
bread to encourage the sick to celebrate the Sabbath, and for planting outsize candelabra in public places at the time of the Hanukkah festival, as well as for soli-
citing money on behalf of the poor. Kfar Chabad owes it origins to personal
contacts between the Chabad Rebbe, Schneersohn, and the then Israeli representative at the United Nations—and subsequent President of Israel, 1963–73—
Zalman Shazar, who came from a Chabad family. (Information from Menachem
Friedman.)

[6] Known in English, and in the New Testament Greek, as 'phylacteries'. See Glossary.

evangelical conversion movements in other traditions. Thus the Aish Hatorah (The Fire of Torah) organisation, established in Israel but largely for the benefit of Americans in 1974, has developed '120 programmes in cities worldwide' to bring Jews back to religion. Their method of persuasion—start gently and gradually involve people more, selecting the most committed to become a full-time corps of evangelists—is very similar to that of the Arachim ('Values') organisation described in Chapter 3 (Tapper, 2002). The *t'shuva* movement appears as an ever more pervasive and institutionalised feature of Jewish life worldwide, generating its own youth culture and accompanying jargon—as in the standard abbreviations 'BT' (*ba'al t'shuva*) and 'FFB' (*'frum* from birth'—*frum* being the Yiddish for 'observant').

Among the Ashkenazim, Lithuanian institutions and Chassidic sects in Israel have opened spaces for the education and reception of *ba'alei t'shuva* to a much greater extent than in the diaspora. The Arachim Organisation for the diffusion of Jewish Consciousness, which provides support for *t'shuva* campaigning by organising courses, mass meetings and home visits, and providing speakers when requested, is apparently a Lithuanian creation originally established to attract professionals and scientists back to religion. The large Netivot Olam (Paths of the World) yeshiva was set up by the Lithuanian leader Rav Schach specially for returnees in the *haredi*-dominated town of Bnei Brak, near Tel-Aviv, in the 1970s. Our informant there told us that Rav Schach had predicted that the setback of the Yom Kippur war in 1973, with its surprise effect and the high casualties suffered, after the triumph of the 1967 war, would produce a moral crisis in secular Israel and would lead people to return to religion. We were told so often, and in different contexts, that the Yom Kippur War marked the start of the *t'shuva* movement that it came to sound like a myth of origin, but there are indications that this is a founding moment for the *t'shuva* movement in Israel. In 1967 the first yeshiva specifically for *ba'alei t'shuva* was founded in Har Tzion in Jerusalem, funded first by donations and then by the state, in the form, successively, of the Jewish Agency, which is concerned with immigration and absorption, the Ministry of Education and other Welfare agencies (Mazlish, 1984). The Ministry funded extra-curricular activities for those attending the *t'shuva*-oriented yeshivas, and welfare agencies started to fund them to take in people with a 'difficult, deviant or delinquent background'. Mazlish does not speculate on the motivations for this involvement of the state, but it can be seen as an example of how a grassroots movement finds a niche (i.e. enclave) in the state apparatus. Less institutionalised initiatives have sustained themselves over the same period, associated with mediatic figures like the singer Schlomo Carlebach, with the Bratslav Chassidim and their alternative lifestyle, and various mystical and Kabbalistic ventures.

The 'social' aspect of Chabad's work seems particularly to have influenced Reuven Elbaz, who in the 1960s founded the Or Hachayyim ('The Light of Life') network of yeshivas, schools and adult study centres (*kollelim*), whose ritual and intake are distinctly Sephardi, and which today is very closely tied in to the political and religious agenda of Shas. It was prominent among the organisations receiving state funds for taking in 'difficult' cases and by 2000 its students were receiving monthly stipends like other full-time yeshiva students. Elbaz is recognised for his courage and patience, having started out in 'the billiard halls' seeking out the most marginalised of Israeli Jewish society. The students in Or-Hachayyim are *ba'alei t'shuva* who often tell of their earlier life of dissolution, when they loved drinking, partying and worse, and who have now found a wife and a vocation in Or-Hachayyim.

Shas uses techniques of organisation that closely resemble Lubavitch, and they both share the underlying idea that *t'shuva*—as opposed for example to political-secular Zionism—is the way forward for the whole Jewish people. But Shas has been shaped by, and has also been shaping, its Israeli context and is much more prepared to take a full part in secular politics than Chabad and the other *haredi* communities. Shas's ethnic appeal and political vocation differentiate it from Chabad, as do differences on specifically religious practices and beliefs, not least Chabad's notorious messianism. The insistence with which a large faction of the Lubavitch continue to affirm that their Rebbe, who died in 1994, was and remains the Messiah, is a particularly sensitive point within Judaism[7] (Dein and Littlewood, 1995;

---

[7] On 22 June 2004, the tenth anniversary of the Rebbe's death, there were two commemorative ceremonies in Israel. One was held in the Bat Yam stadium and was attended by thousands who believe that the Rebbe still lives but is hidden, the other in the Yad Eliahu stadium, which also attracted thousands who straightforwardly commemorated his death. The former also had a distinctly political tinge with talk of the religious prohibition on returning occupied land to Palestinians.

Berger, 2001). Indeed it was one of the things which led Rav Schach, the most prominent *haredi* figure in Israel and Shas's founding patron,[8] to describe Chabad sarcastically as 'the nearest thing to Judaism'. It is hardly surprising, therefore, that when, in our experience, the comparison is mentioned to Shas activists, they point out very firmly that Shas does not share Chabad's predilection for the external expression of religious emotion—dancing, chanting, and high-profile displays such as outsize open-air candelabra. By implication, they are saying that they do not share Chabad's messianism.[9] Chabad veneration for their late 'Rebbe', which sometimes borders on hysteria, has no parallels in modern Jewish history, but it does bear some resemblance with the veneration, bordering on a cult of the personality, for Rabbi Ovadia Yosef among Shas followers, endlessly quoted and praised in person and in print, and known for example as 'the saint (*tzaddik*) of our generation'.

There is also a broader context favouring *t'shuva* movements which is neither structural nor supply-led, but political, even psychological, and could be described as the receptivity of certain Jewish communities or simply certain individuals to *t'shuva* undertakings. As a result they find all sorts of niches in the state and the community. We can observe Chabad Rabbis who have established themselves as either officially recognised community leaders or in positions of influence, especially over the education of children, in Moscow, Madrid, Santiago de Chile, Rio de Janeiro, São Paulo and notably in weak or vulnerable communities which do not grow their own religious leadership (Fishkoff, 2003). In Israel, however, there is a collective dimension to *t'shuva*, shaped by social issues (as we shall see) and by the state apparatus. One author spoke already in 1991 of a 'Judaization industry' with 230 yeshivas, 4,400 returnee students and 80 organisations of one sort or another, adding (crucially) that '40 per cent' of the budget for these activities comes from the government (Beit-Hallahmi, 1991). The account, based on data from the late 1980s, mostly predates Shas or the Sephardi renewal, but already found fifty-six branches of Chabad in Israel, and highlights

---

[8] The relationship did not survive a political dispute after the elections of 1980.

[9] This may well reflect the Lithuanian training of the Shas leadership and their application of the Lithuanian 'method' in their approach to Rabbinic study, as well as their adoption of similar modes of dress for their men, and a certain austerity of comportment which Shas shares with the Lithuanian yeshiva culture.

the way in which the *t'shuva* movement has found niches in the state: for example, the Prison Service sponsors 'prison yeshivas' and instruction directed towards 'Judaization', and judges tend to reduce sentences where the convicted person is a returnee.[10] Rav Elbaz' Or Hachayyim would now have to be added to the list of beneficiaries of state subsidies. This indulgence on the part of the state with respect both to evangelisation and the ultra-Orthodox generally, is also observable, for example, in the tolerance of 'pirate radios', dealt with in Chapter 6, and in the unwillingness of certain authorities to inquire too closely into issues of ultra-Orthodox sensitivity community, such as intra-family violence or disputes, even though Shasniks (as Shas followers are popularly known) and other ultra-Orthodox do not tire of describing the state as their persecutor and the nemesis of religious life generally. However, since the 2003 elections there has been a reduction in state support for *haredi* life: it is already harder for young men to look forward to a life of full time Torah study, and some Israelis think this trend will affect the entire *t'shuva* movement.

WHAT OBSERVANCE MEANS AND WHO CODIFIES THE RULES

The simplest and most concrete manifestation of *t'shuva* is the adoption of a more observant lifestyle. The individual starts out for example by changing eating habits, by observing the Sabbath, by changing just a few areas of daily life. Young men and women still living with their parents are encouraged to set aside a niche in the family kitchen for their own food, and to make sure they do not alienate their parents, at least in the early stages—for one also hears accounts of families which remain at odds over the change of lifestyle of a member and the resulting break in relationships. Women may begin to attend classes or discussion groups where they learn what keeping kosher involves, when to go to the ritual baths (*mikva*), and what dressing modestly involves, often in great detail: the acceptable style of hat, or length of skirt or whether Sephardi women cover their heads with hairnets or wigs. People brought up in an Orthodox milieu imbibe these habits in their own childhood and youth, but those who

---

[10] Evangelical churches in Brazil also devote considerable efforts to work in prisons, where prisoners who convert have a better chance of early release, and not infrequently then become missionaries on the churches' behalf.

embark on the *t'shuva* process have to learn them in a more public setting in adulthood.

It is often said, as if it were a self-evident truth, that Judaism confers upon practical observance of rules and rituals of everyday life an importance far greater than most Christian churches, Protestant or Catholic, which are taken to place greater emphasis on doctrine and belief. However, this is to misunderstand the ubiquitous distinction in all religious traditions between the official apparatus and the daily religious life of all followers (including the scholars, managers and functionaries themselves), sometimes also described as the distinction between official or erudite religion and popular religion. In fact, there is much similarity between the popular practice of religion at least across all Abrahamic traditions, as some call them, and possibly to religious behaviour even more generally. The differences are the product of bureaucratic and doctrinal elaboration which of course has an interest in 'product differentiation' and in the pursuit of power and the accumulation of wealth (Boyer, 2001). Pentecostal churches, which express little interest in doctrine or theology, may appear to pay less close attention to the regulation of everyday life than the Rabbis who so often refer to the '613' commandments in the Torah, in the sense of Pentateuch, and to the centuries of Rabbinical pronouncements and learned disquisitions, but the underlying reality is that the lives of both Pentecostals and ultra-Orthodox Jews are regulated by the dynamics of everyday life, and of power, in the community. The Halakha or corpus of legal codification, built up over generations and assembled most notably by Joseph Karo in the sixteenth century in Palestine, which is said to govern daily life, is not susceptible of impersonal, rational application and leaves individual Rabbis infinite latitude for interpretation. This is particularly evident in the light of technological change: how does one apply the prohibition of lighting a fire on the Sabbath—to take a notorious example—to the era of the mobile phone? In the contemporary atmosphere the standard answer is, if in doubt say 'no', but that could change, and to some extent Ovadia Yosef is himself an exception. So what then is the role of the official deliberative and adjudicatory system?

The need for interpretation of the rules in the light of changing circumstances and the immanence of debate and argument in Talmudic learning might confuse newcomers. An observer schooled in an academic or legal discipline might think that it would be hard to explain how, on the one hand, rules must be followed strictly while on the other, there is not always—maybe never—a recognised single legitimate authority to settle any differences. But that is to misunderstand the nature of authority in the *haredi* world. Authority in this context is embodied in individuals who are taken to be persons of great learning and subtle reasoning, but who are also possessed of an aura of spiritual authority, observed in the rituals of deference surrounding their movements and public appearances, and in the wide range of their pronouncements and of the subjects on which their opinions are sought, and whose authority carries weight well beyond a professional specialism. Most Rabbis earn a living as teachers or ritual practitioners, administering *kashrut*, circumcision, marriage, divorce, funerals and so on, but prestigious Rabbis, who gain their position simply by the number of their followers, can pronounce on all manner of subjects. Thus Shas's spiritual leader Ovadia Yosef has pronounced on the acceptability of the water of Lake Galilee at Passover[11] and the legitimacy of Israel's foreign policy. Self-appointed Rabbinic groups or councils have on occasion issued authoritative pronouncements and even excommunications on no authority other than their own.[12] The paradox seems to be that thousands upon thousands of yeshiva students and Rabbis subject Rabbinic texts to endless examination, yet this has scarcely any relevance to the rules governing daily life of even the most observant, many of which—for example the male practice of covering the head at all times, or of wearing black coats and suits with white shirts at all times, or the age sequence of daughter marriage—are not in the texts in any case.

[11] An issue arose in 2004 because the Minister of Infrastructure refused, for technical reasons, to block the lake's water supply to households as had been customary during Passover: apparently it is feared that the water may contain bread thrown into the lake by tourists, and bread is of course strictly forbidden on Passover. Ovadia Yosef decided it was acceptable to drink the tap water if strained through a piece of muslin.

[12] In the summer of 2004 some Knesset members called on the Attorney General to open a criminal investigation into a Rabbi who, during a lecture at a 'West Bank settlement outpost' had spoken 'in a philosophical or moral sense' of a law which would make it permissible to kill 'anyone who transfers parts of the land of Israel to non-Jews'. The usual mud-slinging ensued, but the Rabbi himself issued a statement saying that 'under no circumstances should his words be interpreted as permission to attack any Jew... since in terms of practical halakha...[the law] does not exist today'. *Ha'aretz*, 1 July 2004.

The observer might ask, if, as is evident, 99 per cent of practices are taken for granted and deeply woven into the fabric of everyday *haredi* life, and are never discussed or debated, what is the point of all this legal disquisition? The answer is that this 'learning'—an English borrowing of the Yiddish and German word 'lernen' meaning 'to study'—is not an academic activity in the usual (literal or metaphorical) sense, let alone an adjudicatory activity, but rather a ritual activity. The point is illustrated by the head of the distinguished Porat Yosef yeshiva of Jerusalem, in an address given at the French Hill synagogue, when he said that by learning, scholars save the children of Israel and defend the land just as the soldiers do by fighting; or, in a more popular context, by the words of a lady who dedicates her life to *t'shuva* work, when she conjured up the image of Rabbis 'with their hair nailed to the ceiling' to save the Jewish people.[13] In 2002 Ovadia Yosef recalled the yeshiva students from their Passover holidays when the Army called up reservists, perhaps on the grounds that the Torah students contribute as much to the security of the country through their study as the soldiers do with their arms, though the motivation may have been more pragmatically political. This is evidently a standard sort of analogy: already in September 2000 in the weekly Shas-supported devotional publication *Ma'ayan Hasheva* (published by the Education Fund for Sephardi Heritage) Ovadia Yosef wrote, 'every page of the Gemara is a gun, every chapter of the Psalms is a missile.'

The learning is undertaken in pairs, and is sometimes punctuated by ritualised dispute, in which individuals shout at one another as if their lives depended on it. After completion of yeshiva, which is broadly that part of their education which can be said to move ahead in steps, and after getting married, graduates become full-time attendants at a *kollel* where they follow an annual cycle of texts. Their vocation is to be present at the study venue. The act of learning is even physically ritualised, as those studying rock back and forth in the same motion as when they are at prayer.

So undertaking *t'shuva* involves accepting a certain type of authority over one's life and also, for men, incorporating the ritual of study

---

[13] It is a very arresting image, though not one we have come across elsewhere: but the underlying idea that the masses of people studying Torah contribute to the salvation of the world is a very common one.

into it. The inter-generational transmission by non-formal, deeply embedded, mechanisms of family and socialisation works well for communities which have maintained a degree of historical continuity and are not looking to introduce newcomers. But for the Sephardim who are adopting Orthodoxy, the fabric of everyday life into which orthodoxy is woven must be learned. Sephardi renewal in Israel has required, or perhaps has been created by, a framework for the construction anew of observance, and thus also for the construction of authority, producing a novel, quasi-hierarchical Rabbinate for the first time since the destruction of the Temple by the Romans.

NORTH AFRICA AND MOROCCO: JEWISH LIFE BEFORE EMIGRATION

Whatever the intrinsic interest of the *t'shuva* movement, the focus here is on its connection to ethnicity and ethnic revival. Hence, the following pages provide background on the religious life of Israel's Sephardi population, so that the singularity of this particular, and highly successful, version of *t'shuva* can be grasped.

Even the name of this population is a matter of divergence, if not of dispute. In the early days of the Israeli state, and perhaps until Shas came into the limelight, the non-European immigrants, who were mostly from the Middle East, were known as Mizrachim, Easterners, or *edot hamizrach* (peoples of the East). Although not geographically accurate for those from North Africa, who differed from the Middle Easterners in the way they spoke Hebrew, their music and, in small but—as always—crucial ways, ritually, the term was extended to include them and stuck even as they became the majority of non-European Jews. For Shenhav (Shenhav, 2000; 2004) the Mizrachi name, which was for a long time more current than Sephardi, and is still preferred by some writers (for example Shafir and Peled), was an essentialist imposition by the Zionist institutions on a heterogeneous set of groups whose individual identity was thereby denied. This notion does have some merit, but principally in the sphere of religious ritual, and cannot be said to have a transcendent importance for the people involved. It would seem that if they themselves did express any dissatisfaction with that usage, it was by adopting the word 'Sephardim', but not by resuscitating their local identities

(Moroccan, Libyan etc.). Eventually the term '*mizrachi*', as distinct from 'Sephardi', may have come to reflect a more secular outlook on the part of the speaker, but that is not clear. We shall use Sephardi because that is how our interlocutors described themselves.

Pointing to the innovations and the 'constructions of tradition' in contemporary *haredi* life is easy, as is enumerating the ways in which, despite appearances to the contrary, it is very different from life in Lithuania and Eastern Europe generally before the Holocaust. These differences include (especially in Israel where it enjoys state subsidy) the commitment of men to full time Torah study and the fierce pressure to have very large families. But this image of innovation, attractively counter-intuitive as it is, can be exaggerated. Compared to the Sephardim the systems and structures of Ashkenazi *haredi* life, and their rhythms and habits of observance, have been less fundamentally disrupted by the creation of the Israeli state: the trauma and demographic collapse in the Holocaust were followed by demographic recovery on a grand scale in Israel and in the diaspora, and the core mechanisms of cultural reproduction remained, as for example the use of Yiddish, and the institutions and methods of studying and teaching, so that change in methods and mechanisms has been evolutionary. And so, by a curious contrast, the North African communities, who suffered no demographic collapse, underwent the loss of the institutions which for generations had transmitted their traditions, in the wake of migration to Europe, to the Americas and to Israel. Somehow, the shock of modernity, the shock of migration to Israel—and also, at least in Israel, the shock of powerlessness—cut off their contact with their heritage. This provides a clue to the affinity between the Sephardi renewal, the placing of *t'shuva* at the heart of that renewal and the centralisation of religious authority within Israeli Sephardi Judaism.

The word Sephardi means 'Spanish', and refers therefore, strictly, to the descendants of the Jews who were expelled from Spain in the late fifteenth century, and whose culture, especially their language *ladino*, also known as Judeo-Spanish, was preserved principally on the Northern shores of the Mediterranean—in Livorno, Salonika, Sarajevo, Rhodes etc—but also in élite Jewish families in Northern Morocco. However, since the mid-twentieth century the word has been used in a much broader sense to refer also, and now mainly, to

North African and 'Oriental' Jewry. Indeed, the Sephardim of Israel are principally people of North African, Middle Eastern, Iraqi and Persian origin, whose ancestors' mother tongue was Arabic or Farsi, and whose Jewish dialect in North Africa was Judeo-Arabic, written, like *ladino* and Yiddish, in Hebrew characters.[14] The migration of Oriental Jews to Palestine before Independence came from further East—Bokhara, Afghanistan—and was often connected to trading relations. Its traces are to be seen in the architecture of the Boukharim neighbourhood just North of Central Jerusalem, where numerous buildings date back a century or more. These often ramshackle compounds belong to trusts, the legacy of merchant families from the East (Mussaiouf, Kedourie) who established synagogues which still function, in the heart of a devotedly ultra-Orthodox population among whom the people of Oriental and North African origin are no longer particularly prominent. There is little continuity, save in the name, between the pre-Independence, and indeed pre-Yishuv,[15] Sephardi population, which was somewhat aristocratic (but marginalised during the Mandate by the Ashkenazi Zionist settlers), and the post-Independence immigrants from North Africa and the Middle East. Those from Iran and Iraq were of a more prosperous and educated background, and also arrived in Israel at a slightly more favourable time, but those from Morocco, who are the largest single contingent, were mostly poor and had benefited from limited modern education. They left in the three waves, the first after 1948, while the second, which followed the Suez Crisis of 1956, expanded into a large-scale evacuation, agreed with the Moroccan authorities between 1961 and 1964 (Bin Nun, 2003). Overall 900,000 Jews left Arab and Islamic countries after 1948, of which 600,000 went to Israel. Of those 600,000, 266,000 came from Morocco, twice as many as the next largest contingent, who came from Iraq. In the period 1952–64 200,000 people came to Israel from Morocco. Another 30,000 came between 1965 and 1971. The smaller Libyan and Tunisian communities had departed earlier: 31,000 had left Libya for

[14] Rabbis addressed their congregations in a Hebrew which still bore traces of Aramaic.

[15] The 'settlement' refers to the pre-statehood Jewish community of settlers in Palestine distinct, at least initially, from the longer established merchant communities mentioned in the text.

Israel by 1951 and 40,000 had come from Tunisia by 1960 (*Statistical Abstract of Israel*, no. 50, 1999). The collapse of the Jewish population in Arab lands was almost total: by the 1970s the only country with a noticeable Jewish population was Morocco, where they numbered some 25,000.

The story of Jews in these countries is, inevitably, still surrounded by much controversy, concerning the role of Jewish agents either in fomenting panic among the Jews or in paying off Arab politicians. The extent of historic anti-Jewish feeling and persecution in Arab and Islamic countries is a matter of bitter controversy (Trigano, 2003), but compared with the history of ideological anti-semitism and physical persecution in Europe, and of the Holocaust itself, it is hard to discredit entirely the view that until Jewish-Arab conflict developed during the British Mandate in Palestine,[16] Jews lived in relative peace with their Muslim neighbours for centuries, especially in the more cosmopolitan corners of the Ottoman empire, as has been convincingly and eloquently documented for Salonika by Mark Mazower (2004) and in Edgar Morin's moving autobiographical essay (1989).[17] Indeed, in Israel we have on occasion heard positive recollections and evocations both by Sephardim, especially the religious among them, and by Ashkenazim. Some, but by no means all, recall a life of peaceful coexistence with Muslims who, unlike secular Israel, were at least God-fearing people, while Ashkenazim can remark on the lack of anti-semitism in Muslim countries, noting that the Jews therefore did not have to build defences, and were left vulnerable only when their traditions were threatened by secularism.[18] Certainly this coexistence with Muslims had over the centuries been punctuated by violent incidents, and under Islamic law the rights of Jews, legally institutionalised in the *dhimmi* system, were subordinate to those of Muslims and vulnerable to the whims of a ruler (Choura-

---

[16] Elie Kedourie, in a famous work (1989), describes the mounting anti-Jewish mobilisation in Iraq in the inter-war period in response, apparently, to the growing Jewish settlement in Palestine, and the British complicity in this.

[17] Another recent contribution in this vein has been Menocal (2002).

[18] The contrast with Eastern Europe may be overdone, at least until the late nineteenth century brought doctrines of race into European politics. In the Austro-Hungarian empire too the Jewish communities were tolerated and—as in North Africa—their own leaders (Rabbinical authorities rather than notables) were responsible to the state for tax collection (Katz, 1973).

qui, 1985). The relationship was torn apart by the Jewish colonisa-
tion of Palestine, the creation of the State of Israel, the subsequent
military defeat of an Arab army, and the nationalist reaction to it.
Also, according to Kedourie (1989), Arab politicians did not hesitate
to fuel hatred of Jews in their countries—who showed little commitment to the Zionist enterprise—nor indeed to profit from their
plight. But Kedourie also has harsh words for the Zionist emissaries
to Iraq who created a situation in which Jews had little choice but to
leave. They presented them as 'rescued' immigrants who yearned to
return to their ancient homeland, thus implementing the Zionist
ideology that strove for the inclusion of Jewish communities all over
the world within a national framework (Shenhav, 2004). After this
painful end to more than two thousand years of Jewish life among
Arab and Muslim populations, there is no basis to a notion that the
years of coexistence in North Africa might contribute to a positive
attitude on the part of Israeli Sephardim to Israeli or Palestinian Arabs.
Indeed, Sephardim show no tendency to give electoral support to
the less militantly nationalist parties. On the contrary they have clearly
tended towards the right ever since 1977. The implication of our approach and of our analysis of enclaves is that to interpret contemporary conflicts, ethnic and religious, or even political or economic, in
terms of their duration over time is misleading: the correlation between the depth and the duration of a conflict is at least open to doubt
and often spurious, and its violence or intensity can be sharpened
with astonishing rapidity over a brief period and for largely political
reasons. Thereafter history is written, ancient rubble is dug up, myths
are created and paranoia is fuelled, until later 'revisionist' historians
and archaeologists, explaining how tradition is invented and community imagined, try, with uneven success, to put the record straight.

Some Israeli academics have described the Sephardim from Arab
countries as 'Arab-Jews' (Shenhav, 1999; 2000; 2004). In this they
reflect both the view that Zionist agents were engaged in provocation and scare-mongering to encourage Jews to leave those countries in the 1950s and 1960s, and also the social and cultural cleavages
which later adversely affected so many of them and the next generation in Israel. Shenhav's idea certainly has some merits (as our
analysis itself shows), and could be defended if all such discussion
occurred in a clinical, analytically dispassionate environment. But
such environments do not exist, least of all in the Middle East, and

the fact is that the people concerned, whatever their nostalgia for the world of their ancestors, would in their vast majority recoil from any description of them as Arabs.

The Head of a *haredi* school in the North of England, interviewed in early 2004, was even more trenchant, expressing a current of opinion which sees the issue from a cultural and religious point of view:

... it is a cause of great sadness to me that the Sephardi tradition, a much less tampered with and purer tradition, has been completely destroyed by Ashkenazi aggression across the world. There are few yeshivas that learn in the style of Sephardim... there are yeshivas full of Sephardi people that learn as if they came from Eastern Europe and the same is true of lifestyle and customs... it has been obliterated by the Ashkenazim. They are yuppy and very invasive ... literally upwardly mobile... as in the state of Israel in the 1940s and 1950s and the 1960s when small groups of Ashkenazim set up the political system ...it is a bit like the grey squirrels and the red ones ...they are just so much more aggressive and so much more determined in a sense.

In Arab countries Jews lived in a world where, despite variations in the intensity of religious observance, the central traditions of a Jewish way of life—the rituals of the life cycle, the taboos surrounding sexual relations, the practice of endogamy, the authority of sages, as Deshen (1989), eschewing the word Rabbi,[19] calls them—were respected and unquestioned. Despite the adoption of a European way of life in urban areas such as Casablanca, Mogador and Fez, under the influence of the French Protectorate, 'a remarkably small number of Jews became secular, for the abandonment of religious tradition was still considered tantamount to heresy by most members of the community' (Schroeter and Chetrit, 1996). There was no equivalent of a secularised Jewish intelligentsia developing new ways of being Jewish, as occurred in Eastern Europe from the eighteenth century.[20]

The main criterion of secularisation in Europe is intermarriage, and although in North Africa intermarriage was quite widely accepted

---

[19] He does not explain why, but one might infer that he was wanting to use a term which could refer broadly to persons exercising judicial authority in the community as a whole, and not only in a particular synagogue—a Rabbi then would be attached to one synagogue.

[20] The evidence for this non-abandonment of tradition refers to the very small number of Jews going to balls and running beauty contests, as indicators of secularisation.

for women, Jewish women who married Muslim men would totally abandon their Jewish identity, while in a symmetrical fashion non-Jewish wives would be fully integrated into the Jewish community. There was no secular space. Among the majority 'popular classes' many Jewish men lived a fairly errant life, earning their living from peddling, spending months at a time among Muslim populations, and away from the *mellah*—the Jewish urban quarter or village where observance was the standard form of behaviour. The image presented by Sephardi ideologues today, of an innocent practice of traditional faith, embedded in the rhythms of everyday life, untainted by the institutionalisation of orthodoxy or of non-orthodoxy, has a ring of truth to the reader of these anthropological texts, and indeed replays the nostalgic evocations of immigrants when they first came to Israel (Deshen and Shokeid, 1974: 98). This is not to say that rules were not strictly enforced: marriage and women's freedom of movement were as tightly controlled as they were among the Muslim population and Deshen reproduces, from the pre-colonial period, fairly stringent rulings by sages on these subjects.

However, North African Jews and their Rabbis were less concerned with the letter of the law than their Eastern European counterparts, and tended to follow 'tradition' rather than 'precepts' (to use Shokeid's phrases again). They were able and indeed obliged by the institutional context to preserve a very strong collective identity and institutions, but did not defend themselves by codifying daily life as happened in the East European Hassidic and *mitnaged* society. In North Africa the temptations of modernity were limited and came from foreign powers who, culturally, posed more of a threat to local Islamic élites and tended to protect the Jewish and Christian population (Stillman, 1991). Given that the trend towards ever-greater stringency on the part of the Rabbinic authorities in European Jewish communities was a response to liberalisation from without, in comparison, in Islamic countries the frontiers of the Jewish communities were more secure, especially as far as the core issue of sexual control was concerned. So whatever the variations in behaviour, the communal authorities found it less necessary to rule on anything and everything: they were less fussy than in Europe. Later, when the immigrants came to Israel and encountered a heavy Rabbinic bureaucracy and Rabbis with Diplomas and independent resources, they remembered that in their countries of origin that authority was less egregious, and less intrusive. Hence a retrospective image was constructed of a society in which, because standard, uncontroversial behaviour was broadly observant and respectful of Rabbis, there had been little need for a repressive religious authority.[21]

Their situation also mirrored Ernest Gellner's (1982) description of Muslim society in North Africa: the Jewish population of Morocco was distributed between a class-divided urban population and those who lived in villages and practiced the cult of saints—sometimes even sharing shrines with the Muslims. The pilgrimages and shrines have many characteristics in common with Christian shrines: votos and ex-votos, miraculous or unexplained cures, good and bad fortune associated with unusual occurrences, apparitions of the saints—who were always Rabbis—in real life and in dreams (Ben-Ami, 1998). The veneration revolved entirely around magical events and had nothing at all to do with learning or Torah, so Muslims too could fit in when they were the beneficiaries of miraculous events. In addition, several Jewish saints were said to have mediated in personal disputes between Jews and Muslims to great effect (*ibid.*: 131ff.).

The majority lived in the urban centres such as Fez and Meknès, where the élite, protected by the Sultan and doing business with him and his local representatives or power-holders, co-existed with, and to some extent sustained, a broad class of artisans and traders, a clerical class of rabbis teaching in yeshivas and a near-destitute underclass (Chouraqui, 1985). Deshen's study of a village *mellah*, especially when compared with his account of the island of Jerba in Southern Tunisia (Deshen, 1982) shows also that in Morocco Jewish public institutions—religious, educational, charitable and financial—were quite underdeveloped, that synagogues tended to be private institutions over which the sages had only limited jurisdiction, and that sages, dependent on the notables, had to take the realities of power into account if they were not to make unenforceable rulings (Deshen, 1989). A yeshiva head in Petach Tikva in Israel, scion of a long line of Moroccan rabbis, whose family name appears repeatedly among the saints mentioned by Ben-Ami, told us that in Marrakesh the

[21] Zvi Zohar (1996) makes a detailed comparison of rulings by the father of Religious Zionism and a distinguished Palestine-based Sephardi Rabbi to underscore this reasoning.

yeshiva received boys from the countryside who had to live by the charity of the urban population: the yeshivas themselves could not support them.

However, there is another side to this story, arising from the energetic organisation of a *haredi* network of yeshivas by Rav Ze'ev Halperin, who came to Morocco from Jerusalem, via London, in 1912, the year of the establishment of the French Protectorate (Lupo, 1999; 2003; 2004a; 2004b). The original reasons for his coming are shrouded in mystery, but in Lupo's account he emerges as a man of determination and remarkable organisational talents. Coming from a learned Ashkenazi tradition and schooled in the austere *musar* move-ment of Eastern Europe,[22] Halperin set up yeshivas in various towns on Lithuanian lines, where pupils would engage in full-time study, not just study on festivals as was the local custom. He organised Rabbis into a Society for the Support of Religion and founded a *haredi* association to create yeshivas, print books, raise funds and, not least, to resist the secularising influence of the Alliance Israélite Uni-verselle. Such was the bitterness of this conflict that the Alliance, according to Lupo, denounced Halperin to the French colonial authorities and he was forced to leave. So when today one hears Isra-eli Sephardim describing the Alliance as 'a catastrophe' they may well be reflecting the influence of Halperin down the generations. For due to his efforts there arose a generation of Moroccan Rabbis trained in the *haredi*/Lithuanian system, dedicated to resistance against secu-larisation, and ready after the Second World War to fill some of the enormous vacuum left by the Holocaust in the institutions of Ash-kenazi Judaism: after the war an organisation was established in New York which enabled some 4,000 Moroccan yeshiva students to leave for Europe, and although the trail runs dry, it can be assumed that many became Rabbis and a proportion doubtless ended up in Israel. This episode adds a further twist to the account below which em-phasises the irony of Shas's invocation of a Sephardi heritage even as it promotes an ultra-Orthodoxy modelled closely on the Lithuan-ian tradition. For it would seem there is a continuity between this Moroccan struggle against secularism, conducted by Halperin and

---

[22] A mid-nineteenth-century movement of yeshiva renewal which emphasised introspection and memorising and came to shape much of what is now known as the 'Lithuanian' yeshiva system (Jacobs, 1995).

his pupils, and the Shas project in Israel (Lupo, 2003). When today Shasniks evoke their observant North African tradition they may possibly be referring to a strain in their past which was already heavily influenced by Ashkenazi practices and may therefore have been less 'indigenous' than they believe.

Elsewhere in North Africa, though, indigenous Sephardi institutions were more independent. On the island of Jerba, off the Tunisian coast, community institutions—funding the slaughterer, the schools, the Rabbis, the publication of books and monthly pamphlets—were made to prevail over the needs of the island's numerous synagogues (Deshen, 1982). Jerba is an example of the intricate construction of social capital through multiple obligations to support community over private or family/factional interests. It seems to have been exceptional on account of the sedentary population—as opposed to the reliance on migratory work such as peddling found elsewhere—though the absence of an élite tied in their turn to the political authority, as in Morocco, was also an important factor.

Rav Halperin and Jerba apart, the overall lack of study centres or synagogues under the authority of financially independent Rabbis—such as existed in Eastern Europe—rendered the North African 'system' vulnerable when the population transferred to the more centralised and bureaucratic environment of Israel. Also, the individuals of high local social standing who held North African communities together lost prestige and power when they moved—often together with an entire community—to an Israeli farming cooperative or new town. Their Hebrew was poor, their literacy limited and their authority, as persons of a certain family or a certain age, had lost its basis in land ownership, while others acquired the skills needed to farm or deal with modern bureaucracy.

The process of Westernisation in North Africa did not feed into Jewish nationalism as did modernity in Eastern Europe. European influence had taken root among the self-styled Spanish élite of Northern Morocco, encouraged by the schools of the Alliance Israélite Universelle, which taught secular subjects in French and encouraged a secular, modern outlook. This social divide was replicated in the emigration: the more educated and professional people, precisely from the Alliance schools, tended to emigrate to France and the Americas where many seem to have been very successful in achieving social status in business, politics and the professions, while Israel eventually received the poorer, less educated sectors. (Chouraqui, 1985; Miller, 1996). One detailed and carefully designed comparative study undertaken in the 1970s shows a striking contrast between the socio-economic destiny of Moroccan migrants to France as compared with Israel, and also between Moroccan and Rumanian migrants to Israel: the Moroccan migrants to Israel experienced the most severe initial downward mobility of all three groups, independent of their starting point, and also the greatest difficulty of all three in recuperating the initial setback (Adler and Inbar, 1977). Even today the descendants of the emigrants in Israel quite often evoke the contrast between their successful cousins in France and the Americas and their own position in Israel.

North African emigration to Israel accelerated as a result of the troubles which followed the foundation of the state and the 1956 Suez Crisis. The communities did have historic ties with Israel, through emissaries who came to raise funds and to keep alive the memory and shrines of saints and of the great Rabbinical and Kabbalistic authorities who had lived and worked in the Holy Land, and whose writings—such as the Shulchan Aruch—were revered among Arab Jews. But few people had ever entertained emigration as a concrete project rather than a dream, and they were hardly conversant with the vision of a Jewish state built on modern democratic principles. Today the activists of Sephardi renewal turn this memory against the Zionist establishment, saying that when they left their countries of origin their project was to come 'to the Holy Land, not to a secular modern state'. But once the emigration got under way it acquired the proportions of a panic: already in 1951 the number of European immigrants to Israel was overtaken by those from Africa and Asia. The circumstances of their departure from Arab countries may well have had quite specific long term implications for them compared to other migrations: it was not a planned economic migration, but compared to European Jews they were not refugees—a fact whose denial by the State of Israel is bitterly criticised by the well known French Rabbi Shmuel Trigano (2003). The sensitivities surrounding this issue are highlighted when we contrast Trigano's bitterness with Shenhav's very different, but in its way equally bitter, criticism of official Zionism. Taking pains to distance himself from the slightest nationalistic bias, Shenhav criticises the Israeli authorities precisely for describing the Jewish immigration from Arab countries as 'a "rescue aliya" ...' purporting to have 'saved persecuted Jews who yearned to return to their ancient homeland, after enduring ethnic repression and discrimination' (Shenhav, 2000). They were poorly informed about the sort of society which awaited them in Israel and were not part of the culture which had produced Jewish nationalism and the project of a Jewish state.

The story of these people's absorption into Israel is a source of regret and disappointment, but not of major disagreement, among Israeli commentators (Horowitz and Lissak, 1987; Shafir and Peled, 2002). The government of the time was dominated by Ashkenazim of Polish and Russian birth or descent. Their motivation in coming to Israel was ideological, and their ideology was secularist—to fashion a modern society along social democratic lines, radically different from the society which they had left behind in their own and their parents' countries of origin. The migrants from North Africa, in contrast, had scarcely been touched by the Holocaust. Even the German occupation of Tunisia seems to have had only a limited effect on the treatment of the Jewish population there (Weingrod, 1990; Goldberg, 1996).[23] They had little experience of modern culture, democracy, socialism, capitalist labour markets, or scientific education. Iraqis seem to have been more fortunate in the commercial skills they brought and also in the areas where they were settled: being close to Tel-Aviv they gained rapid access to the country's main economic centre. Some of our interviews contain bitter recollections and reflections of this experience: repeated allusions to how 'they cut the off our sidelocks' and 'herded us into camps', not least from the son of Ovadia Yosef, David Yosef, and similar language appears in the famous 'Deri video', the bitter lament of Shas's fallen leader which helped the party to resounding electoral success in 1999. But we also heard less emotional or formulaic accounts of discrimination, for example from a Moroccan lady who recalled how

---

[23] See the Introduction to Goldberg, 1996; Weingrod (1990) recounts a story circulating among Tunisian immigrants in Israel about how a saintly Rabbi saved his community by skilful negotiation, and even saved the honour of two young Jewish girls by shutting himself up and praying until they were released by their captors. This is Rabbi Hayyim Huri, whose tomb, converted into a shrine in Israel by his sons, became a very popular place of pilgrimage in Beersheva, as we shall see.

in Morocco she worked in a bank and had good relations with Muslims, but that when she reached Israel she was treated as a second-class citizen.[24]

Sephardi immigration tripled Israel's Jewish population in a few short years. Many efforts were made to 're-socialise' them into the dominant culture (Bar-Yosef, 1968). Following what is now widely recognised as a misguided policy, but responding also to overwhelming short-term pressures, the governments of the time settled the North African immigrants, after the initial period in makeshift absorption centres, in large numbers in development towns on the periphery of the territory (Aronoff, 1974), and in *moshavim*—agricultural cooperatives as distinct from the much more collectivist *kibbutzim* which were the vanguard of the 'new society' filled with pioneering Ashkenazim.[25] The research of Adler and Inbar, conducted in 1973–4, again cast light on what they call differential treatment of Moroccans, this time in housing allocation, as people left the absorption centres, usually after a few months. Compared with Rumanians, Moroccans had less choice of housing even at equal levels of education: this was extremely important since the state subsidised housing heavily and location was extremely influential in determining employment and the value of people's investment in a house or apartment (Adler and Inbar, 1977).

Immigrants from Morocco and Tunisia did not change their religious life in a formal ritual sense, but the material and institutional underpinnings of that life were no longer the same: the notion of a privately owned synagogue did not fit in Israel (although there are some here and there), where the Ministry of Religious Affairs pays salaries to many local rabbis and innumerable small synagogues or prayer-gatherings are run on a cooperative or charitable basis. As Aaron Willis states, the identity of Jews from Arab countries was maintained 'by private institutions, or in the private sphere by family, customs, authority' (Willis, 1995). In the North African system,

---

[24] This is a subject that shapes many popular stories; it is told in many languages and on many occasions. For example, a recent film, *Turn left turn at the end of the road* (Avi Nesher, 2004), includes a very emotional scene in which a sixteen year old daughter born in Israel in the 1960s shouts at her mother 'I'm tired of your stories of your past life!! Were you all kings living in gold palaces?'

[25] Further statistical documentation of Sephardi deprivation is presented in the chapter on Social Movements.

which was less formalised, respected individuals would emerge and occupy positions of prestige, but in Israel there were not enough spaces for them all to occupy, leading to disputes. The formally qualified Rabbis who might be appointed were in turn unlikely to practice the Sephardi ritual.[26] We also read of a sense of 'dejection, failure and self-deprecation in religious matters' (Deshen and Shokeid, 1974) and of a nostalgia for the life immigrants had lost. At the same time, there is a hint of coming changes—especially of the more codified Orthodoxy promoted by Ovadia Yosef—when Deshen in several places contrasts the more uninhibited, personalised style of ritual conducted by the first generation immigrants with the more formal version of the second generation (*ibid.*: 108). Of course the majority trend in the second generation has been a drift away from religious observance, which the *t'shuva* movement may have staunched but is unlikely to significantly reverse.

Anthropological accounts of state-managed community settings in villages or very small towns tend, overall, to portray the difficulties experienced by the North African immigrants in adapting to the bureaucratic and competitive ways of Israeli society, but Shokeid, in his 1998 review of the subject (Shokeid, 1998), also emphasises the North Africans' 'stronger family orientation and ... the survival of wider networks of relatives and community institutions', though there is little reason to believe that these have helped Sephardim find their way in Israel's highly competitive economy. Like others, he also highlights the large number of successful places of pilgrimage, which have become sites of healing and thanksgiving, of donations and blessings, centred, as in North Africa, on the tombs of revered sages. These sages included those whose shrines were brought to Israel from other countries, ancient shrines such as that at Meron, and contemporary figures who have died in Israel (Bilu and Ben-Ari, 1992; Ben-Ari and Bilu, 1994). Consequently, Sephardi religiosity became associated in Israeli public space with healing and pilgrimage, superstition and folklore, rather than with religion as an all-encompassing way of life (Weingrod, 1990). Following a classic pattern, the pil-

---

[26] Thus in one case we read of local squabbles producing an impasse resolved by the appointment of a Rabbi who, though of North African origin, did not follow the Sephardi rite, and found himself ignored by the community (Shokeid, 1971).

grimages are the result of the initiative of individuals with no official certification, and annually attract large numbers of people—though unlike the classic Christian pattern they have not been subsequently co-opted by a religious hierarchy. Pilgrims, drawn in each case from particular immigrant groups (Tunisians, Moroccans), participate in ceremonials which have developed with no centralised Rabbinic control (Deshen and Shokeid, 1974; Weingrod, 1990). In addition, several officially recognised folk festivals and *hillulot* (celebrations usually linked to pilgrimages and cures) have grown up starting with the Moroccan *mimouna* on the day after Passover (Weingrod, 1990: 104–5), which came to be an annual fixture with a set date, and later followed by Kurds, Ethiopians and Persians, each following their own traditions. Issachar, in reference to this proliferation of shrines and *hillulot* catering to Moroccans mainly, but also to Libyans and others, describes how the practice has straddled the ethnic divide, with many Ashkenazim going to Meron for example (as we were to witness ourselves) where the supposed tomb of one of the most famous Talmudic sages, R. Shimeon bar-Yochai, is visited on Lag Be'Omer (a day when *haredi* Ashkenazi boys get their first haircut, among other things), and Sephardim going to the Ukraine where the tomb of Nachman of Bratslaw is found at Uman. The first attempt to set up a Sephardi party, Tami, was led by the son of Makhluf ben-Yosef Abuhatseira, who is buried at Ramleh and whose shrine in Kiryat Gat is visited throughout the year by people bearing petitions (Ben-Ami, 1998). And one of the most celebrated *hillulot* is that of the Moroccan saint Israel Abuhatseira (of the same family) known as the Baba Sali, whose home at Netivot, an important site before his death in 1984, has been promoted and developed into a major site for healing and touristic activity by his son since then. It is principally a Moroccan cult, but attracts many others and is also a place with which politicians like to be associated because of the prestige of Baruch, the son of the Baba Sali (Bilu and Ben-Ari, 1992; Ben-Ari and Bilu, 1994). The tensions between these popular celebrations, which are distinguished by an absence of barriers or of uniformity of dress and behaviour, and the religious habits of ultra-Orthodoxy, were highlighted in 1998 when the Shas leader Arieh Deri, a strict Lithuanian *haredi* from his childhood, went to Sfat, probably because it was the place where Abraham Karo composed the Shulchan Aruch, and celebrated Shas's own *mimouna* in an enclosed space—in contrast to the usual open-air festivities with their inclusive atmosphere. On this occasion Deri denounced the other *mimouna* celebrations as 'being forbidden by the Halakha'. The Shas *mimouna* has not, it seems, been repeated.

SHAS AND SEPHARDI TRADITIONS: POPULAR RELIGION AT THE SERVICE OF RELIGIOUS INSTITUTIONALISATION

Shas is today seen by all concerned as the movement of religious and political renewal of the Sephardim: its motto (El HaMa'ayan) announces a return to Sephardi sources—the wellspring—and a recovery of its ancient glories. In Shas's own folk history the description given by the movement's followers of their experience in Israel resembles a black legend, according to which the 'jewel' or 'crown' of the traditions of Sephardi Judaism have been destroyed by a cultural onslaught from secularised Zionist Ashkenazim. Yet the religious practices promoted by Shas yeshivas and *t'shuva* campaigns constitute a clear departure from the religion of those lands: as the *mimouna* example shows, Shas stands against the idea of a tolerant or fuzzy-edged religiosity, and instead promotes stringency and clear lines of demarcation between the acceptable and the unacceptable. Indeed, by penetrating the state and the official agencies which disburse the 'religious budget', the movement has established a hierarchy and a bureaucracy for the appointment of Rabbis and other religious office-holders, in a departure from the localism of Jewish community management in the Sephardi—and indeed European—world. According to one view, Ovadia Yosef's invocation of the 'crown' of the Shas motto—'restoring the crown to its ancient glory'—refers to the codified Shulchan Aruch and not to the religiosity of North Africa (of which, coming from an Iraqi background, he has no personal experience). The 'crown' would thus represent a widely recognised text which, providentially for the project of an Israeli Judaism, happened to be written in Sfat in what is now Northern Israel, and which also is the standard source for the modern insistence on stringency. There are many comparable examples, like Shas's encouragement of full-time study as a calling for men, which is an even more radical departure from traditional practice for Sephardim (or at least for those who remember) than it is for the Ashkenazim.

In one sense these trends are standard features shared with other fundamentalisms: a rationalisation process which tries to transcend popular religion through hierarchical and centralised systems of interpretation and adjudication. Indeed, one interpretation of Shas has drawn on Max Weber to emphasise its 'church-like' character in contrast to the model of a sect (Fischer, 2004a). But rationalisation is only one face of modern fundamentalism: whatever efforts are made to suppress popular religion, be it Sufism in the Islamic case or the veneration of local saints and the like in Christianity, the popular, uncontrolled invocation of the supernatural merely resurges in another form, for example as divine healing or exorcism in evangelical Christianity.

In the case of Shas the creation of bureaucracy is balanced by other tendencies within the incipient hierarchy and by unorchestrated epidemic mobilisation from below: the centralisation of authority currently exercised by the charismatic leader, Ovadia Yosef, who heads a Council of Torah Sages and emits halakhic rulings in profusion, obviously has a highly personalistic element immune to formal impersonality. But also, Yosef himself seems aware of the usefulness of a balance between the world of rulings—the institutional—and popular religion. Thus on the one hand he is said to be in favour of keeping to one's own tradition in *minhagim* (customs) such as matters of liturgy, but on the other he advocates strict Rabbinic control—and thus uniformity—in spheres relating to personal habits, such as food, sex and Sabbath observance, and of course in the crucial sphere of marriage.

The external rituals of everyday life such as clothing, sexual segregation and modesty, serve to draw the community's frontiers and to discipline its members, but they are also promoted, as we show in an account of an Ovadia Yosef sermon in the next chapter, as devices which help to fend off misfortune and gossip—the 'evil eye' and the 'evil tongue'—and to hasten good fortune such as winning a wife, having children and winning elections. Such things are a source of occasional discomfiture in the Shas leadership because they are also ridiculed by the Lithuanian *haredim*, which is the cradle of the Shas leadership, as well as by secular Israelis.

In the media Shas is often associated, and sometimes sarcastically, with the figure of the extremely venerable and very elderly Kabbalist

Yitzchak Kedourie, who has been paraded at election rallies and whose blessings are thought to be particularly beneficial—as well, it is said, as very expensive—at weddings and barmitzvahs. In places where Shasniks congregate, such as study centres, and in their homes, posters of Kedourie and Ovadia Yosef sit side by side. Yet in our interviews his name was barely mentioned. The discomfiture with Kedourie in particular emerged during the lead-up to the 2003 elections, when Kedourie's grandson and manager presented a separate list (with scant success), in protest at the exclusion of himself and his associates from the Shas list.

In the 1999 election campaign Shas tried to defend the validity of Sephardi customs as ranking on equal terms with the dominant liberal judicial ideology. Of course, the arguments were heavily tinged with political point-scoring, but they highlighted what we would call a drive to draw a quasi-legal ring-fence around Sephardi 'autochthonous' practices by recognising them as peculiar to a particular community. The issue had arisen in the elections of 1996 when even a Rabbi adopted by the National Religious Party as their 'spiritual mentor' issued a halakhic ruling against their use. But the Meretz party, who stand for the most liberal, secular and cosmopolitan sectors of Israel's élite, went further than mere imprecations, and took a complaint to the Electoral Commission about the Shas's distribution of small bottles of oil to potential voters. These bottles were of negligible financial, but high emotional, value and possibly of magical power, because they bore a picture of the Kabbalist Yitzchak Kedourie, at that time a cherished figure in the Shas firmament. They also bore the word Shas doubling as an abbreviation for the Hebrew words 'remedy oil'. The complaint was heard by a judge on behalf of the Central Electoral Commission and then, when Shas appealed against his verdict, by the full Commission, which is made up of politicians but chaired by a judge. Meretz even produced an 'expert in the sociology of Jewish religious practices' (probably the anthropologist Yoram Bilu) (Barzilai, 2003), their complaint being that these bottles were 'unlawful gifts' and, unlike the t-shirts or hats handed out by other parties, were a type of bribe. Shas argued that to ban the distribution of the bottles was an attack on their free speech and constituted preference of 'one public over another'—that is, preference of the secular community and their electoral practices over those of the Shas constituency where reverence for a Kabbalist is a standard form of expression, no different from reverence for say David Ben-Gurion (*ibid.*: 271). Barzilai says the ruling, upheld by the full Commission on appeal, by which time the election was a few days away, constituted a 'coercive' use of liberal individualism (*ibid.*: 274). Shas of course benefited enormously from this controversy: the party presented itself as 'feared and persecuted …from inside and outside the religious community', and in any case had distributed most of the tokens before the verdict was handed down.

If Lithuanians ridicule Sephardi superstitions it is on account of their Sephardi, not their superstitious, identity. All *haredim*, Sephardi or Ashkenazi, Lithuanian or Chassidic, litter their conversation with wonders and miracles—coincidences in the sacred text, miraculous escapes from terrorist attacks, providential marriages: an endless list of life's fortunes and misfortunes. In North London's ultra-Orthodox community also, Rabbis (and sometimes doctors) tell people to 'check your *mezuzah*' for any imperfections if they find that medicines do not cure their ills. If a marriage starts to go sour people ask, did you pay the *shadchan* (broker) who helped you to find the husband or wife? This popular religion is subjected to a closer analysis in Chapter 6.

This section has laid out the complex intertwining of ethnicity and religious observance, and the many counterintuitive twists and turns that have accompanied the public face of Sephardi religion and of the *t'shuva* campaign in Israel. It could be seen as an effort to disentangle rather than demystify, for although some of what has been said may seem surprising and might be used to disprove popular misapprehensions, that is not the purpose: rather we hope to have illustrated a more general phenomenon, already hinted at in the previous chapter, which is the distance between social scientists' need to classify, define and demarcate their subject matter, and the promiscuous borrowing which characterises religious practice. Yet at the same time, and as we shall see further in the next chapter, the borrowing across some frontiers does not stand in the way of the central concern of *t'shuva* campaigns, namely to establish and strengthen social boundaries.

3

T'SHUVA AS POLITICAL MOBILISATION

SHAS AND THE CENTRALISATION OF RELIGIOUS AUTHORITY: THE ROLE OF THE NEWLY RELIGIOUS

From the 1950s the ultra-Orthodox Ashkenazim in Israel preserved and developed countless study centres for young and adult alike, while, apart from synagogues in the community and the official Sephardi Chief Rabbinate, the Sephardim had no grassroots religious institutions they could call their own. They were treated like an undifferentiated mass, with no regard for the differences among local traditions from Morocco to Iran, so even in 'their' synagogues they must often have felt ill at ease. Whereas Ashkenazi ultra-Orthodox retained cohesion and exclusiveness by creating neighbourhoods of their own, and even dominating an entire town in Bnei-Brak, the Sephardim, who in any case did not possess a distinct ultra-Orthodox sector, were dispersed, often to 'development towns' where the population was uniformly poor, and consequently lost their community ties. The Rabbis who had officiated in their communities of origin seemed to have vanished, to have gone elsewhere, or to have lost prestige, while Halperin's Moroccan students and their successors were absorbed into Ashkenazi institutions.

Just as Halperin had done in Morocco so now in the new state they took children from the camps in which they had been placed on arrival in Israel and put them in their own yeshivas. According to Lupo (Lupo 2003; 2004) the prominent Ponievitz yeshiva opened a special Sephardi branch in Bnei Brak and some small Sephardi yeshivas were opened in development towns, but in time formal quotas were imposed on Sephardi entry by those same institutions that had encouraged them in Morocco and in the early days of North African immigration. These are operative both in the most prestigious yeshivas, where Lupo estimates them at 12–20 per cent, and also in the Beit Yaakov girls' schools, where Sephardi girls have been placed and sometimes still are placed in separate classes. By 2004 there were signs, in the town of Arad for example, that the Beit Yaakov network was differentiating into separate schools for pupils from different backgrounds, of which one was Sephardi, another Chassidic, another 'Lithuanian' and so on. Nevertheless, in 1992— the year when Deri led Shas into a government with Labour against his wishes—Rav Schach had notoriously said that Sephardim were not fit to run their own institutions. Perhaps the unkindest exclusion barred Sephardi *bachurim* (yeshiva students) from marrying the daughters of members of the Lithuanian community. But this is not often mentioned, and perhaps Sephardim see that particular exclusion—as opposed to the institutional discrimination—differently, less as discrimination than as normal endogamy. Arieh Deri was referring to the institutions, not marriage, when he said in 1997 that 'racism in South Africa is as nothing compared to the treatment of Sephardim in the ultra-Orthodox school system...ultra-Orthodox Ashkenazim have racism in their blood' (Daniel Ben-Simon, quoting Lupo, in *Ha'aretz*, 9 July 2004). On the other hand, in an interview with us in December 2004 his response to the issue was guarded: this exclusion had 'some basis in different customs', he said, implying that though he found it distasteful, even hurtful, he did not want to make an issue of it. And in the yeshiva world this tacit exclusion is particularly sensitive because the custom has been, for generations, that the yeshiva head marries his daughters to promising students who may eventually succeed him, rather than rely on the lottery of father-to-son succession (Friedman, n.d.).

The only Sephardi religious activities to gain any fame, as explained in the previous chapter, were associated with healing and pilgrimage, which in Israel's secular culture means religion as a pastime or periodic diversion, as superstition and folklore rather than a way of life. Eventually, during the tenure of Ovadia Yosef as Sephardi Chief Rabbi (1973–83), something began to change: he himself was infuriated by the contemptuous treatment meted out to him by the Ashkenazi ultra-Orthodox leadership, with whom he sat on various bodies. Despite his own distinguished scholarly record and prodigious knowledge of Talmudic texts, and despite his famously brilliant record as a yeshiva student, Yosef was frozen out and also denied a third term in the post.[1] Nonetheless, as we know, his influence grew and grew, and inside the yeshiva world the Sephardi presence also grew: by 1998 there were almost as many Sephardi yeshivas (462, all 'Lithuanian') as Ashkenazi Lithuanian (488),[2] and between 1980–4 and 1990–3 the number of pupils in Sephardi yeshivas grew by 42 per cent, compared with 15 per cent for the Ashkenazim (including Chassidic and National Religious institutions). Of course, these growth rates are unsustainable in the long run, since in principle none of these students participates in the labour force and all have entitlements from the state.

The political sequel is told elsewhere: here we consider what doctrinal, or ideological path was open to Yosef and his associates when they considered the formation of a Sephardi religious movement. It would be religious because Yosef as leader was a man of *haredi* convictions, and his associates, who convinced him to take the political route, were graduates of Lithuanian yeshivas and therefore practitioners of *haredi* Judaism, but also perhaps for other reasons. The failure of a more socialist, or class-oriented, approach to the mobilisation of the Sephardim—such as the Black Panther movement at the end of the 1960s, or of the only moderately religious Tami party in the early 1980s—may have shown that emphasis on social welfare had a limited chance of success in an ethnic-based movement.

In formulating their heavily religious appeal, the Shas leadership could impose an ideology from above. There was not a network of prestigious grassroots Rabbis or of many direct heirs to a religious authority transmitted from the past, especially the Moroccan past. Indeed, there was a history of disputes and differences between Yosef and those who did exist—including Abuhatzeira, the son of the Saint of Beersheba. The Shas leadership therefore developed a mechanism derived at first from Yosef's tenure as Sephardi Chief

---

[1] Even in 2001, Ovadia Yosef did not attend the funeral of Rav Schach, though Arieh Deri, the former Shas leader, did, along with tens of thousands of others. (Deri was given leave from prison for the purpose.) Word has it that this was because Rav Schach had once said no Sephardi was worthy of being a Chief Rabbi.

[2] In addition to the Lithuanian Ashkenazi yeshivas, the Chassidim had 250 and the National Religious 'Yeshivot Hesder' numbered 282. The total number of students in these institutions had been 148,933 in 1995, and rose to 186,313 in 1998 and 209,000 in 2001 (Lupo interview, March 2004).

Rabbi and then from his de facto prestige as supreme Sephardi authority. Because of the weakness of grassroots Sephardi institutions they had to look to resources provided by the State to develop a religious apparatus, and for that purpose they had to build up a political movement and a presence in the Knesset and in government.

The weakness of grassroots institutions and the rupture with the heritage, as well as the absence of institutions for the education of potential Sephardi Rabbis in a distinctive approach to Rabbinic law and knowledge, meant they had to develop a new system. This of course was based on what the leadership had learnt in the Lithuanian yeshivas, and much could be said about the content of the system, but the crucial innovation was the practice of a centralised religious authority, created to fill the void described above. It should be noted that Israeli Chief Rabbinates are administrative and also judicial bodies, dealing principally with *kashrut* and marriage and other matters of personal status law, such as inheritance, if the parties involved agree to seek their judgment. They are part of the state apparatus, and Chief Rabbis are not ideological leaders nor, even though they are highly regarded, do they have greater authority in matters of Talmudic learning than some others.[3] Ovadia Yosef, in short, is the first person to introduce a centralised theological authority in the history of modern Judaism. He is also the dominant Sephardi Rabbinic authority in Israel, increasingly recognised among Sephardi communities worldwide, and is gradually developing a form of being Jewish—encompassing every aspect of ritual, liturgy, daily life and infinitely more besides—which draws on tradition, but has the overarching new features of being unchallenged and being codified in his myriad of 'rulings'. In other communities people will consult 'their' Rabbi: the Chassidim will go to the head of a particular sect and the Lithuanians to the head of a yeshiva. The 'modern Orthodox' will have theirs and outside Israel the Reform, the Liberals and all the many others will also have theirs. But Sephardim

---

[3] For example, in 2000 the Sephardi Chief Rabbi, Bakshi-Doron, was threatened with ostracism because the most powerful Rabbis said he took too flexible a view on the observance of the 'jubilee year' rules, laid down in Leviticus, according to which fields must be left fallow one year in seven. The other Rabbis opposed the repetition of a casuistic device to get around the rule which had been in force for decades. He backed down (*Ha'aretz*, 5 September 2000). The outcome meant that products grown on land that was supposed to be fallow were labelled 'not kosher'.

in Israel do not have these sub-divisions; if they seek a religious view or ruling, the ultra-Orthodox among them either go direct to Ovadia Yosef or, if they do consult a local Rabbi, expect him either to refer a case to Yosef or to rule in accordance with Yosef's own rulings. Most (though not all) Sephardi Rabbinic offices—i.e. community Rabbis—in Israel are appointed personally by Ovadia Yosef, and thus far they are unrivalled by a caste of yeshiva-based sages. Lesser Sephardi authorities include some in the National Religious movement, which is not part of the ultra-Orthodox world, and the Tunisian yeshiva Al Kisei Harachamim in Bnei Brak, which discreetly propagates a specifically Tunisian mode of prayer and pronunciation, and produces widely used editions of liturgical and study texts.

These delicate gradations and sensitivities of the *haredi* world are important, but it is the campaigning for *t'shuva* and the inclusion of *ba'alei t'shuva* at all echelons including its senior political leadership, which sets Shas apart. *T'shuva* is, and perhaps has to be, the central mission of Shas, an integral part of its institution-building project, and the recruiting ground for the core activists and followers. This stands in contrast to Chabad, who propagate *t'shuva* but do not accept the newly 'converted' as full members—i.e. as marriage partners—for a generation or more.

Shas needed many more people and more diversified talents than could be found among yeshiva graduates: they needed activists, political agitators, teachers and skilled personnel of all sorts to advance their cause. So it is not surprising to find *ba'alei t'shuva* among Ministers, or prominent members of town councils in Jerusalem and Petach Tikva (to name but two). Our interviews with highly placed people in the Shas educational network tell of the great difficulties they faced in getting proper funding for the Sephardi establishments within the traditional ultra-Orthodox apparatus which controlled both state-provided and donated funds for religious education. In the absence of institutions or of a system for the education and training of Sephardi religious personnel, Shas pursued political bargaining power so as to build new ones under the financial sponsorship of the state, and then brought in existing, but dispersed, Sephardi rabbis and learned people to staff them. Presumably, these yeshivas and their graduates were only too happy to escape the oppression and discrimination they complain of in Ashkenazi institutions and start working in Shas institutions. All this constitutes what in French is called *encadre-*

ment, and produces a home-grown religious Israeli Jew as opposed to the secular Jew shaped by earlier Zionism (Almog, 2000).

THE MACHINERY OF *T'SHUVA*

It is now possible to place in context the affinity between the Shas idea of *t'shuva* and the need to provide a set of religious beliefs, practices and processes. One might have imagined that a social-democratic, welfarist discourse, or a straightforwardly primordial ethnic appeal unencumbered by the sacrifices of *t'shuva*, would have been more appropriate for the political mobilisation of an underprivileged mass in a modern democracy, but instead Shas leaders chose the themes of religion and family.

Of course this leadership, emerging from the yeshiva, could hardly have chosen any other discourse or appeal than the religious. They had lived this life since childhood and had no other outlook on the world. The Israeli state was founded by social democratic parties whose leaders had been schooled in a Leninist style of party organisation, so to adopt a social democratic ideology would have been to join the secular enemy. The welfarist discourse had been that of Labour, who had lost their privileged claim on the Sephardi vote in the 1970s. Nor would an appeal for a technocratic programme of carefully planned or targeted benefits have made much sense to them: from their vantage point in the *haredi* world, the welfare state was a corporate system which responded to pressure from well organised interest groups, and also which entrusted its own administration to those groups—viz. the trade union movement (the Histadrut, which ran a vast public sector of industries for decades), and the *haredi* sector, which managed its own education system with resources provided by the state to Agudat Yisrael, as well as the kosher certification apparatus and Rabbinate. They did not, in all probability, perceive Israel's elaborate welfare state as a system of programmes, but rather, as argued, one of enclaves.

So Shas gravitated towards the themes of ethnicity, religion and family. Returning to religion was a way of reconstituting families that had been disorganised by poverty and marginality because so much of religious life was in the family, but also because it was accompanied by a strong rhetoric evoking the lost respect for parents. Secular Israel had undermined this respect with its permissiveness and its hostility to the traditional values which the first immigrants had brought from their countries of origin. The discourse of victimhood still leads Shasniks to blame the secular Zionist élite for this disruption of their way of life, and as if to emphasise their rejection of that élite and its secular institutions they proclaim *t'shuva*, rather than improvements in secular education or similar modern welfare provision, as a remedy.

Adopting the religious discourse did have successful precedents: the small ultra-Orthodox parties which, though full participants in political life, have never fully recognised the legitimacy of the Zionist state, and the National Religious Party, have been ever-present fixtures on the political scene, as successful public representatives of the yeshiva world, defending their enclaves in education and territory, and propagating the imposition of public Sabbath observance and, in the case of the NRP, the defence of the West Bank settlers. The class discourse had been tried by the Black Panthers and other local neighbourhood movements in the 1970s, and a modernist, 'soft' and tolerant ethnic discourse by the ephemeral Tami party (Aronoff, 1974; Willis, 1995), so these experiences might have strengthened Shas's inclination to place religion at the forefront of their political appeal. As Peled (1998) has said, by adopting a religious discourse Shas enabled its followers to integrate further in Israeli society—something which is less surprising in the Middle East than in Europe. But the additional element of bringing the highly dynamic *t'shuva* campaign into politics was new, setting them apart from the standard discourse of defending a traditional status quo and resisting change at all costs.

One can see that if the discourse was to be religious and the party to be a mass party—in contrast to the inward-looking parties of the Ashkenazi *haredi* community—then *t'shuva*, and the creation of a Shas cadre staffed, among others, by *ba'alei t'shuva*, would fit, and might indeed be essential, since the truly observant Sephardim were too few in numbers. Also, by creating an apparatus, the *ba'alei t'shuva* could be attracted by the prospect of obtaining jobs, as schoolteachers, as administrators and as public servants in ministries headed by Shas politicians—as indeed came to pass.

Joining a new community

The Shas method of bringing individuals 'back' to religious observance is proclaimed as 'softly, softly', in contrast to others who might
push individuals towards sudden and dramatic changes. The head
of a Bet-Shemesh *kollel*, who is also a leading political figure in this
rapidly growing town with its proliferating enclaves of Anglos,
Russians, *haredim*, modern orthodox and more, is eager to point out
that Shas does not seek to tear families apart, in contrast to the fears
in the secular world that people who become religious never speak
to their parents again. But however cautious the approach, the
adoption of new habits of dress and eating, new rhythms of waking
and sleeping, will inevitably still lead to a redrawing of boundaries
among an individual's family and social network, and certainly, when
talking about their own return in retrospect, people do not describe
it as a gradual process. The adoption of religious observance brings a
person or family into a delineated group, placing them inside boundaries marked by patterns of behaviour, dress, language and so on.
T'shuva involves joining a different social milieu, with inevitable severe
disruption to individuals and families. This has been interpreted, in
the terminology of Pierre Bourdieu, as rewriting the rules of cultural, religious and symbolic capital, among others, as Shas builds an
entirely new 'field' (Yadgar, 2003).

The change of patterns of daily life, of religious observance through
fulfilment of *mitzvot*—an absolutely fundamental concept meaning
commandments, but also good deeds, or the right deeds—must, if
sustained, constitute a traumatic, albeit self-imposed experience. It is
not one which individuals, or families, pass through alone: once they
have embarked on the process, they are accompanied by Rabbis,
activists, busybodies, people inviting them to meetings, study sessions,
unpaid weekend 'seminars', celebrations, collective activities of a
commemorative or ritual nature, and more besides, all of which
combine to instil in the individual a sense of obligation and, if there
is backsliding, or the temptation to backslide, of guilt. One tangible
form of pressure comes through the schooling of children. Shas
schools are of particular value to parents who attach importance to
keeping their children off the streets, to a longer than average school
day and to transport to and from school. But if their children are to
remain in these schools, especially in those which cater to people

engaged in the *t'shuva* process, parents must take care to observe the Sabbath, the dietary rules and, not least, proper and respectable behaviour; they must banish bad language and streetwise habits. Parents also may learn observant practices from their children; they may indeed be pressured by their children to adopt increasingly observant practices. Teachers are liable to learn of deviations, from the parents' own children, from other children, or from observing how children behave, and school directors may as a result transfer children to other schools, which cater for a less religious clientele.[4] The commitment and involvement of the Shas teachers and school inspectors also leads them, for example, to organise parallel activities, such as the inspector who arranged fortnightly talks for parents on the subject of 'peace in the home' (a favourite *haredi* theme). These inspectors, and many teachers, are committed activists, who transform the provision of a service into an enveloping social network.

The *t'shuva* process attracts numerous organisations and campaigns, pundits, publicists and preachers. They all find different niches, they play complementary roles and, in an essentially competitive context, they connect with one another in all sorts ways, without in any sense following a common coordination: some organise mass meetings, some distribute cassettes, some organise small sessions in private homes, and so on more or less ad infinitum. If you go to a meeting you will have cassettes foisted upon you, you will be offered an invitation to a seminar, and you will almost certainly make a charitable donation. An Ashkenazi ultra-Orthodox pirate radio broadcaster said to us, dismissively, '*t'shuva* is for Sephardim'. But our observations show that the range and variety of evangelical operations on offer in Israel cut across divisions of class, ethnicity, age and location. Some are organised institutionally, others are funded institutionally but operate with volunteers and little institutional control, much of the proselytism is conducted on the air waves by 'pirate radios', described in Chapter 6, and there is something for all classes, ethnic groups and religious tastes, from ultra-Orthodox and Chassidic to New Age.

An organisation of secular people concerned about these activities, Am Chofshi ('a free people') has listed on its Chofesh ('freedom') website the strategies, tactics and devices used to draw people—as

---

[4] Information from Directors of schools in Bet Shemesh and Petach Tikvah.

Chofesh would see it—into the *t'shuva* process. The account divides the *t'shuva* operation into two parts: the penetration of society and, once the new adepts are inside the yeshiva world, the restructuring of every aspect of their lives, language, dress and so on.

The penetration of society is undertaken through public meetings, which can bring thousands into a stadium or a few hundred to a theatre, as well as house meetings which bring a few individuals to a private home. At the big meetings celebrities tell of their own conversion and activists preach the benefits of *t'shuva*, appropriate speakers being produced for different types of audience. In this context the audience is flattered, the future after their 'return' is pictured in rosy colours, bathed in love and family harmony. This is not quite the discourse one hears from Shas, or Chabad, in which there is more emphasis on rejoining a lost tradition, on the obligation of people born Jewish to maintain their traditions and identity, and on the instilling of a sense of guilt if they do not. The organisations depicted in the Chofesh website seem to distance themselves from the repressive, pleasure-denying aspects of Jewish observance and borrow something from New Age: they focus instead on the future, on happiness and love, on the healing, or at least better health, which follows a change of life ('catch people when they are sick'). Group leaders or 'animateurs' look for ways of persuading people that they are already, in their heart of hearts, half-way there.

The document, which confirms—and may even draw upon—a similar account in Mazlish (1984), emphasises the quasi-psychological tricks in which the missionaries of *t'shuva* are trained, and their optimistic, forward-looking, health-oriented promises bear a striking resemblance to those one encounters among Christian evangelical organisations. One difference, though, is that they do not promise the material wealth which is so popular among Pentecostal churches, influenced by the Health and Wealth Gospel.

The techniques used are elaborate: group leaders in role-playing sessions exchange the roles of believers and doubters with seminar participants; people are persuaded that their presence is itself a commitment, and made to feel guilty if they do not continue; in small meetings a participant may be stopped in their tracks with embarrassing questions. The seminars, even residential weekends, are very cheap and sometimes almost free of charge, but this again builds a sense of obligation to attend sessions described as 'marathonic', to remain in touch after the seminar, possibly to make donations, to pass on names of potential converts, and to pass the word around acquaintances in furtherance of the cause. The movement communicates with potential followers more through personal contacts and pirate radio than through public advertisements and announcements.

Once the 'convert' is inside the yeshiva world, the picture changes, as Chofesh describes it, from 'softly-softly' to root and branch eradication of a convert's previous life. By now they have been cut off from their old friends and family and are subject to a 'resocialisation' process. They acquire a different material basis, take new jobs—or none at all if they are studying full time in a yeshiva—receive moral guidance from a tutor or Rabbi, and join a new social network. In a striking phrase, a tutor from the Netivot Olam yeshiva for returnees in Bnei Brak described one of his pupils as having 'well and truly cut the lines',[5] and he used the phrase more than once. It reminds us that the cutting of ties to family, inflicting severe emotional pain on parents, which Shas Rabbis say they take care to avoid, is widely observed among European and North American returnees after leaving their secularised background (Podselver, 2002).

The Am Chofshi account is self-evidently about Arachim. We had the opportunity to observe how missionaries are trained under Arachim's auspices at a three-day Arachim course in Jerusalem. The course was attended by people from a variety of sects and communities—Chabad, Lithuanians, people from Sephardi institutions—all of whom paid a fee of about $30 per day. Expert male speakers included a Professor of Physics from Bar-Ilan University, and they all demonstrated experience and sophistication in their style and content of delivery. They spoke in front of an audience carefully divided by a partition separating men and women, and averted their gaze when addressed by the women. Despite a formal requirement that women present their questions in writing—while men could ask their questions orally—women did in fact intervene in discussions. Those present were almost all dressed according to *haredi* custom—the men bearded and in black, the women in modest clothing and with their heads covered. One speaker addressed the issue of science, explaining

---

[5] The conversation was in German and the phrase used was '*er hat sehr gut die linee geschnitten*'.

notions utterly unfamiliar to an astonished audience such as black holes and the 'big bang'—but when questioning reached a certain point he said he could go no further without consulting his superiors. Another speaker used standard notions from management education, but invoked quotations from great Rabbinic authorities such as Maimonides in support. Several sessions were designed to help the listeners improve their persuasive skills, with titles such as 'emotional intelligence', 'how to speak in public', 'how to give a class', 'the image of an ideal teacher' and 'teacher training'. 'Say you want to "share" not to teach'; 'show love for your audience'; 'look them in the eye'; 'encourage participation and show respect for the audience's traditions—for example by using a Sephardi accent when officiating at a Sephardi wedding.' 'Rely on emotional intelligence: it is hard to convince an audience's head—you have to go for the heart; go for the positive line—do not use scare tactics.' A third speaker focused on how to speak to sceptical academic audiences, an Arachim speciality.

Arachim's 'soft' approach to evangelisation is not an isolated example: there has for some time been a flourishing international pamphlet industry in which guidance is offered in the light of both scientific and Rabbinic sources for living an observant life (Caplan, 2003). In the newly built and predominantly ultra-Orthodox Jerusalem neighbourhood of Ramat Shlomo, Rabbis who dominate the local community council—a non-decision-making deliberative body known as the *Minhelet*—invite professionals such as experienced educators and child psychologists to discuss issues like disciplining children or family problems in general. Sensing that their followers may overstep boundaries of what is acceptable, they invite speakers who can adduce Biblical examples for modern concerns.[6]

Other organisations appeal to different groups of the population, attempting to adapt their answers to their different needs. Yad leAchim (Brothers' Hand) has existed for many years and its purpose is to struggle against Christian missionaries, though it also helps to bring children into Shas kindergartens. 'Malcot David' (David's Queens) is an organisation that attempts to strengthen women's

---

[6] According to the social worker attached to the *Minhelet*, requests from residents for subjects on which they wish to hear these talks focus on family problems and 'limits to beating your child'.

approach to religion as a bridge to their husbands and family. There are also organisations dealing with women married to Arab men, seeking to bring them back to Judaism, and an organisation named Shofar, linked to the evangelical preacher Amnon Yitzchak. Shofar organises his personal appearances and distributes cassettes, CDs and videos—often free of charge in public places such as road intersections, or in people's letter boxes. In contrast to the anonymity of Arachim, Yitzhak is promoted as a unique high profile public figure. He sees his role as promoting *t'shuva*, and then encouraging his listeners to go to a Rabbi or institution to enter the process. We shall hear more of him when we come to the media and popular culture in Chapter 6.

In contrast to Arachim, which as a support organisation provides services to clients of all kinds, the Netivot Olam yeshiva, also created by the Lithuanians, has hardly any Sephardi pupils or students. Sephardi ultra-Orthodox institutions have their own evangelising organisations, of which Or HaChayyim is perhaps the most prominent. It is in principle open to people of varied backgrounds, but the position of its leader in the Shas Council of Torah Sages is but one of many features which identify it with Shas and with Sephardi identity: the form of service in its yeshivas is Sephardi, its students go out to campaign or demonstrate on behalf of Shas, and when Ovadia Yosef visits them he is greeted with ovations, hand-kissing and cries of 'he is the *tzaddik* of our generation'. To these new recruits Or HaChayyim proclaims their North African and Middle Eastern heritage of a religiosity free of discrimination in the search for a marriage partner, or of conflicts between the Orthodox and the secular—indeed free of secularism itself. But these are to some extent minor differences: in the image of established ultra-Orthodoxy in Israel and elsewhere, Or HaChayyim draws its initiates gradually in the direction of stringency, as frontiers harden on all sides.

According, once again, to the Chofesh website, yeshivas for the newly religious begin by wiping the slate clean and pressing a person to renounce worldly interests such as money and sex, devaluing all that has gone before in their lives. Then follow two further stages in which the person identifies with the new way of life and learns what is required of him, and then adopts a new language—what some might call a jargon. This, according to the website, even goes to the extent of a final stage in which the individual communes with God and confesses his doubts and depressions. All this is complemented by provision of living quarters for men in full time yeshiva study and eventually housing in neighbourhoods built for or heavily occupied by *ba'alei t'shuva*. This ability to gain control over people's lives is linked by Chofesh to active campaigning for recruits to *t'shuva* in prisons—like Pentecostals in Brazil and probably elsewhere. Chofesh claims more than a quarter of students in yeshivas for *ba'alei t'shuva* are ex-prison inmates, while the *t'shuva* movement itself often proclaims its success in preventing prisoners who return to religion from reoffending (see also Beit-Hallahmi, 1991).

In Israel, where returnees are becoming a routine feature of the social landscape, all sorts of people will tell with surprise about a relative or friend who suddenly 'turned' to religion. A range of *t'shuva* 'options' are on offer, some 'softer' and others 'harder', some for Sephardim others for Ashkenazim, not to speak of those for Americans (e.g. Or Sameach—Light of Happiness—an early foundation) and doubtless others. There are reports of organised efforts to 'catch' young Israelis on their backpacking tours of India and Latin America. This is almost a standard rite of passage post-military service, and apparently the backpackers find a Sabbath or Passover welcome from missionaries in their regular haunts in Lima, Buenos Aires or Kathmandu. Kathmandu, just as Chabad has a 'house' on university campuses in the US and the UK, in addition, outside Israel, to many other facilities for people to adopt, or readopt, the less stringent Reform or Liberal versions.

In the Sephardi world in Israel, the Or HaChayyim yeshivas for *ba'alei t'shuva* and Shas schools undertake a systematic approach comparable to the training of cadres. The new adepts are proportionately far more numerous in this Shas-related world than in the established Chassidic and *haredi* world in Israel, since Sephardi ultra-Orthodoxy is such a recent phenomenon, as the research of Nissim Leon, described below, illustrates, and also since *t'shuva* is the top priority of the most powerful organisations identified with Sephardi Judaism.

Within this array of options the path advocated by Arieh Deri, as explained to us in an interview, is the 'softer' version, in the sense that he believes people who make *t'shuva* should keep their jobs and stay with their families and neighbourhoods, do their Army service and so on. However, the question which arises is whether this softer version is sustainable in daily life, given the conflicting pressures faced by the individuals involved, as shall be seen in Chapter 6. For Deri also, it is important that such people be available to take responsibility in government and civic organisations.

Mechanisms for transmitting tradition

Contemporary religious renewal and fundamentalist movements instil and transmit liturgy, and what might be called the technologies of the body, through institutions, especially educational institutions of many kinds: for children and for adults, paid and unpaid, more and less formal. They cannot rely on the family to educate the newly converted or those who are reviving traditions discarded by their parents and grandparents. Pentecostal Churches in Brazil train their own people to induct newcomers, for example by leading study groups, and provide newcomers with roles within the church—beginning with the simplest tasks such as sweeping the floor. Likewise, the more untutored people are drawn in to the *t'shuva* process, the more nodes of authority are needed to teach them how to behave, how to pray, how to undertake a myriad of everyday tasks. Shas has, for example, created a women's adult education network, Margalit Em Yisrael (Margalit Mother of Israel), named after the late wife of Ovadia Yosef, which claims to run 400 women's *chugim*, study groups, with some 50 participants in each.[7] The groups' activities include explanations of commandments for daily life (the Halakha), how to humour their husbands, how to keep peace in the family, how to increase their self-esteem, how to help other women to avoid abortion, how to take the TV out of their home, and outings to commune with nature or visit tombs of great Rabbis. Shas also runs youth clubs through El HaMa'ayan ('To the source', not to be confused with HaMa'ayan, 'The source') an organisation founded in 1985 with the aim of developing Jewish values and education.

---

[7] This organisation is evidence of Ovadia Yosef's relatively positive attitude towards women and their role, since he is much more ready than other Orthodox groups to give them a central role in the process of *t'shuva*.

These activities are—or were in 2001—funded by the state under the rubric of religious, social or educational activities, and therefore politics had to be kept out of group discussions. Nevertheless, the unspoken identification of these activities with Shas is not in doubt.

In the *haredi* world, childhood is not, so to speak, what it used to be. Certainly children are inducted into the rhythms of observance, the rituals and taboos of daily life, from the moment they can understand the words 'it is forbidden' (as Isaac Bashevis Singer would say). But parents are overburdened with large numbers of children, with study obligations and with the need to earn a living, so there is an institutionalisation of childhood funded by state subsidies to schools and yeshivas. In Israel crèches and kindergartens are staffed by *haredi* women who themselves are mothers of many of the children under their care: in effect, then, a small group of mothers will be looking after each others' children. Beyond kindergarten, boys spend very long hours in school, mostly studying and memorising Rabbinic texts, and they may also board at their yeshiva from the age of fourteen, after which they are unlikely to return to live for a long time in the parental home because once they are out of yeshiva they get married. The pattern of parental disempowerment culminates with marriage at a very young age, arranged through family ties but also sometimes through the yeshiva heads: in Jerusalem, Petach Tikva and also in Bnei Brak yeshiva heads told us that they regularly arranged marriages, sometimes through contacts with the seminaries attended by girls between the ages of sixteen and eighteen.

The development and maintenance of these mechanisms costs money, and the ambitions of these movements outstrip the financial capacity of their followers, however generously they give. In Judaism the change in the modes of transmission and their funding has already had far-reaching implications, despite the apparently backward-looking or anti-modern content of what is being transmitted. In Eastern Europe and in North Africa Jewish communities sustained a small number of Rabbis, who also could act as slaughterers and circumcisers, and a certain number of educators who taught young children. In Eastern Europe quasi-mystical Chassidic *tzaddikim* established, or inherited, Rabbinical 'courts', and communities of dedicated young men were established around austere yeshiva heads. These distinguished or saintly figures established dynasties and were supported by charitable donations and their students' families. In North Africa, as we saw, religious institutions were maintained by the patronage of leading local families—except in the remarkable case of Jerba. Today these community-based and funded practices have given way to worldwide apparatuses of educators, and prestigious yeshiva leaders teach young men and also part-time adult students—who may be professionals and high achievers in their secular lives—to a standard where they are perfectly able to outshine and overshadow local community Rabbis (Friedman, 1986; Soloveitchik, 1994). In Israel, furthermore, these educational and 'learning' institutions receive state subsidy and bring bureaucracy, and the development of religion as a profession, on a scale unknown in Judaism before the Holocaust.

RECLAIMING A HERITAGE

We have seen how the movement of Sephardi ethnic revival has found its voice in the *t'shuva* movement through a combination of image-building and targeted campaigning, and we have offered reasons why this path has been taken, rather than a more secular path of social democratic demands for what is, after all, a largely secular, or only moderately religious, electoral constituency. But what of the substance of the ethnic religious heritage? Has the *t'shuva* movement, for its part, found a distinctive Sephardi voice, or is the substance of no matter?

Apart from the festive expressions mentioned in the previous chapter, and which by their very nature are not features of daily life, Israeli Sephardim do not exhibit their cultures of origin, in contrast, for example, to Chassidim who wear the uniform of their sect on a daily basis. The ethnic markers are there, to be sure, but they are the markers of *Israeli* Sephardim, not for the most part, save perhaps in accent, of Morocco, Iraq, or other places of origin. So there is a delicate transition or, better, overlap between ethnic markers reflecting the migrations of a person's forebears, and cultural markers which denote or betray an individual's class status as well. These markers signal, for Israeli Jews, an individual's location *vis-à-vis* two very different mainstreams of social respectability: *haredi* Jews on the one hand and Israel's secular establishment on the other. Markers are borne in the way one dresses, the way one walks, the way one talks and of course the way one looks.

This might explain why themes of ethnic identity are by no means always in the forefront of Shas conversation. They are ambiguous and sometimes painful. At study centres such as *kollelim*, and in interviews with activists, our interlocutors were more interested than we expected in talking about *t'shuva*, religious matters, moral issues, the family and the like, and although there is no indication that they were trying to hide or downplay their ethnicity, it is our impression that the theme has tended, at least as often as not, to be introduced by us, the interviewers. In contrast, in explicitly political public spaces, where the audience is both secular and religious, there is no hesitation in appealing to ethnic resentments and pride. One high profile example is the video entitled, significantly, 'I accuse', after Emile Zola's famous declaration during the Dreyfus case. The video, produced after Arieh Deri was convicted for corruption in 1999, bitterly denounces the vendetta of which he has been the victim. Of the country's élite he says, 'they could not face the fact that a young Moroccan came to improve the position of the Sephardim'—a phrase illustrated by photos of left-wing secularist politicians Shulamit Aloni and Yossi Sarid. Elsewhere the words 'this shows a clear tendency to target the people who came from Oriental countries' are accompanied by a clip of a classical music concert designed to typify the cultural arrogance of the secular Ashkenazi-European élite. 'They', says Deri in the video, 'came to build a secular state... we did not form part of their plan, with our Rabbis, our beliefs, they did not know what to do with us... and they cut our children off from their beliefs.... We came to Israel with a spiritual heritage and when we came here they took everything from us ...' During the 1999 election campaign 200,000 copies of the video were distributed for free and contributed, among other factors to which we shall return, to Shas's unexpectedly good result (Bick, 2001).

This is one of many intersections of *t'shuva* and ethnic identity, and its implications turn out to be ambiguous. Shas followers and activists mention as a source of pride and almost of doctrine the idea of an inherited religious culture, embedded in their social relations—alluded to in Deri's mention of 'our Rabbis, our beliefs'—

and they often claim that *t'shuva* is easier for people of North African and Middle Eastern origin, since they, or their parents, did not go through a period of secularisation in their countries of origin. The standard line from informants is that detachment from religious observance is much more recent for Sephardim, as compared with generations of modernity in Europe, and that even if they are no longer practising, they have often had first hand experience of religious observance through their parents' parents, if not their own.

This discourse could be said to invoke a sub-conscious, intuitive religiosity, and a way of life, distinct from the magic-symbolic invocation of the supernatural. We heard of the respect which Sephardim have for their parents and for the Rabbis, and of the way in which ritual observance, for example women's attendance at the monthly post-menstrual bathing ritual (the *mikveh*), which was elsewhere a constraint and a sacrifice, was seamlessly woven in to the fabric of everyday life in their countries of origin. Thus we were told at the head offices of the Shas education network, 'all our grandparents were *haredim*', and the Sephardi tradition of study is the true ancient system, inherited in a line unbroken by the Enlightenment, whereas the Ashkenazi system is 'only 150 years old'.[8] Yet at the same time activists talk of the rupture with their idealised past, of the bitter reality of the disproportionate social problems affecting Sephardi Israelis, especially those of Moroccan origin, and of drugs and family disorganisation. In the propagation of *t'shuva* the merit of a return to observance as a way of confronting these problems is given enormous emphasis, in particular the greater respect for parents that it is supposed to engender. In the words of a lady who came from Morocco in 1963 'Today teachers are afraid of pupils, but it is different where they learn Torah'. And this in the same breath as a remark about drugs: 'All the youth take drugs.' A prominent Shas politician in Petach Tikva again puts the three themes of ethnicity, *t'shuva* and social regeneration together: 'Shas has tried to give the Sephardim their home back—*atarah leyoshna*—[literally restore the crown to its old glory] ...Shas is a religious revolution but also answers to social

[8] This notwithstanding the fact that Ovadia Yosef himself and his senior associates were educated in the Lithuanian system and have disseminated it in Shas-related institutions.

needs…Education is the solution for *chazara bet'shuva* [those returning to religion]: the secular system was falling apart because of violence, drugs, lack of respect for parents… We do not have problems of violence or drugs…the relation between parents and child is completely different. They are not friends: there is a hierarchy.'

However powerful memories of the past may be, and however much they are reinforced or elaborated by Shas rhetoric, they cannot undo the institutional interruption which came in the wake of mass migration. The dilemma is reflected in the remarks of a French-trained educational expert in the Pedagogical Centre[9] of the Shas network, comparing her own generation with those now at school: 'whereas we learnt the traditions from our grandparents, we cannot teach them to our children—and therefore need to send them to schools where they will learn them.' It is not therefore a matter of surprise, let alone of criticism, that when it comes to restoring this ancient crown the outcome is something utterly different.

In the sphere of Rabbinic erudition and legal or quasi-legal (halakhic) rulings by Ovadia Yosef there is little sign of a Sephardi heritage. Studies by experts in Rabbinical style and law show that Ovadia Yosef has made a point of departing from the traditions of Middle Eastern Rabbis to adopt stricter interpretations and rulings closer in spirit to post-war Ashkenazi *haredi* practice (Zohar, 2001). The proliferation of courses teaching codified versions of religious observance likewise testifies to the loss of continuity, as a vast array of newly labelled Sephardi religious practices are developed which may eventually come to be thought of as Israeli practices. Contemporary Sephardi Rabbis have to split hairs to demonstrate differences between Sephardi and Ashkenazi regulation of everyday life, as did a senior administrator in the Shas educational network who explained to us that whereas the Ashkenazi *haredim* tend to err on the side of stringency, in case of doubt, the Sephardim would require proof before prohibiting a practice. On the other hand, he also said that in 'fundamental' issues the Sephardim might be more strict, and gave as examples the case of a diseased lung in a cow: the Sephardi butcher

---

[9] The centre produces teaching materials and encourages educational modernisation and innovation, so its philosophy is somewhat different in emphasis—more advanced, some might say—from what might be practiced by teachers in the classroom. We will return to it when discussing the Shas education network.

would discard the entire animal, whereas the Ashkenazim would discard only the diseased part.[10] When it comes to matters of Torah study there is little concern to emphasise differences; rather we should note the responses of the Director of one of Shas's 'prize' new schools, in Bet Shemesh, who was at pains to insist that, as far as the substance of education is concerned, there is no point in differentiating between Sephardim and Ashkenazi *haredim*. (Of course, in saying this he may also have been trying to rebut any suggestion that 'difference' meant inferiority of the Sephardi schools.) The head of a Sephardi yeshiva told us he did not follow the technique of *pilpul*—a particular approach to Talmudic exegesis associated in his conception with the Lithuanian tradition:[11] but the underlying point is that he could only find a difference in this rather specialised virtuosity. Differences in the core liturgical text are almost non-existent, but there are major differences in musical chant and in liturgical Hebrew pronunciation between Ashkenazim and Sephardim which are ingrained at an early age and are felt as highly sensitive markers of belonging. These have never been a matter of controversy in the sense of one claiming to be 'better' than the other, but the research described below by Nissim Leon reveals that the *t'shuva* process can open the door to the introduction of multifarious combinations, which, although they may appear incompatible from the point of view of those accustomed to the traditional liturgical forms, can constitute nascent Israeli forms of religious practice transcending Ashkenazi-Sephardi distinctions. What is unlikely, if not impossible, is that such innovations could give rise to a single widely followed Israeli Orthodoxy, for the *t'shuva* movement opens spaces for all sorts of bricolage.

The Sephardi heritage, or tradition, seems then to be used less explicitly, less aggressively and more subtly and allusively in the

---

[10] Another example seemed about as far from 'fundamental' as one could imagine: concerning the required level of dilution in wine used for ritual purposes—the Ashkenazim accept only 16 per cent water, while the Sephardim require 51 per cent. The substance of the statement remains obscure to us, but it is an instance in which respondents have to resort to tiny details, 'wracking their brains' to illustrate these differences.

[11] Lupo (2003) seems to describe the Lithuanian method as definitely not *pilpul*. For our purposes the point is that our informant, was trying to find a dividing line.

propagation of *t'shuva* than one might expect from a viewing, for example, of Arieh Deri's video diatribe, or from attending some political rallies. In the eyes of the leadership ethnicity is used as much in the service of the *t'shuva* movement as the other way round. We have listened to a small number of the innumerable cassette tapes which are an integral part of the *t'shuva* movement, and they do not mention the word 'Sephardi' or 'Mizrachi'; the evangelist Amnon Yitzchak barely makes any reference to Sephardi issues or identity, or for that matter his own very evident Yemeni identity, in cassettes. Nor did he in the public appearance we attended in the Jerusalem Theatre, which was also attended by a noticeable number of Ashkenazi ultra-Orthodox yeshiva students, among a varied crowd of ultra-Orthodox, newly religious and secular. The identification is transmitted more allusively, for Yitzhak's *djellaba* robe and his accent identify him clearly enough as a Yemeni, so perhaps he does not need to mention it in his speech. The few elements that, according to Caplan (1997),[12] are particularly characteristic of Sephardi preachers on their cassette tapes, focus on explaining human disasters as punishment for violation of rules of everyday life (*mitzvoth*), but these have nothing to do with a propagation of Sephardi identity, being rather a feature of religious norms in general, as we argue in Chapter 6.

These observations tend to reinforce what has been said by Shine (2003) and by Shafir and Peled (2002), namely that 'the concrete meaning of the slogan [restore the crown to its old glory] is "synagogues, ritual baths, keeping the Sabbath, yeshivoth, torah schools…"', and that 'it would be very difficult to find, in Shas's official pronouncements, political demands that refer specifically to Mizrachi culture' (Shafir and Peled, 2002: 93). At the same time, electoral data as reproduced by the same authors, and discussed in the next chapter, and the non-verbal symbols, expressions and exhibitions to which we have already alluded, show that Shas's social base and appeal is to the Sephardi population. Peled's well founded view (Peled, 1998)

---

[12] Distinctive only, according to Caplan, in the sense that they appear only in cassettes by Sephardi preachers (which presumably means preachers with Sephardi names). The distinctive features related to supernatural sources of punishment and reward, and whether this type of belief is peculiar only to Sephardi traditions, is another matter.

that Shas has found in religion a mechanism of integration for Mizrachim into Israeli society, implies that an ethnic revival which emphasised only the separateness of their own traditions, language and religious practices, would have left their marginal condition unchanged or even worse. For Shenhav too, religion is the only path that allows the Middle Eastern and North African Jews to be a part of the Zionist national discourse (Shenhav, 2004), while Fischer and Beckerman maintain that Shas allows them to return to religion proudly and without apologising (Fischer and Beckerman, 2001), and others see the movement as a protest against the Ashkenazim (Shitrit, 2001). Religious campaigning, of course, hardens the religious secular divide, but cuts across the racial divide. Certainly the integration is largely rhetorical and symbolic, but for more than a few it does have a palpable effect on their ethnic sense of pride.

It is not unusual for a demand for a recognition of difference to be at the same time a demand for citizenship and integration. This is the case in Latin America where indigenous movements demand an end to discrimination and in some cases recognition of their own legal practices[13]—issues which can be thought of as aspects of citizenship (Campbell, 1995)[14]. By demanding that the national state itself recognise their laws and remedy these ills, movement leaders accord a degree of legitimacy to, and express confidence in, the liberal democratic framework, even if some indigenous demands seem to blur the edges of the purest versions of liberal democracy. In this perspective Shas is awkwardly poised: on the one hand it accords much more legitimacy than other ultra-Orthodox, anti-Zionist political forces to the Israeli state, but on the other its discourse is laced with bitter hostility towards the impersonal, liberal and individualist framework of Israel's legal system in particular, and to the secular bias of the state in general. This is another dimension of what, for different reasons, Tessler characterises as the Shas's hybridity (Tessler, 2003).

Although by 2004 they had quietened down, disconcerted by their first relegation to the opposition in twelve years, Shas and its

---

[13] Enshrined in some Mexican legislation for example as *usos y costumbres*—usages and customs.

[14] Campbell describes his study in terms of identity as one of ethnic renaissance, but the demands of the Zapotec movements are for citizenship, especially fair electoral and judicial proceedings.

political leadership are by no means averse to controversy or even provocation: leaders and activists have been known to speak and behave in highly conflictive, even confrontational, ways. When Deri was imprisoned, after many appeals, in 2000, his supporters set up an encampment outside the jail, with twenty-four hour singing, chanting and Torah study. (It was called the 'Lion's Roar Yeshiva'—a play on the meaning of Deri's name Arieh, which also means 'lion'.) Leaders and activists seem happy to fuel the controversy which the movement engenders, as exemplified by Ovadia Yosef's remarks about the judges of the Supreme Court ('they fornicate with menstruating women', *The Jerusalem Report*, 24 April 2000), or Minister of the Interior and party leader Yishay's refusal to implement that same Court's decision on the legality of non-Orthodox conversions in 2002, or denunciations of government persecution, as they saw it, of clandestine radio transmitters. The party's response to the discrimination, of which they complain so bitterly, has been to distribute resources to their followers on a clientelistic basis (which secular people and others tend to describe as corruption). For example they call on people to put their children in Shas schools, and promote adult study centres under Shas control where people can attend while receiving a monthly allowance. For them, there is more interest and advantage in pursuing the *t'shuva* route and in trying to consolidate support through particularistic benefits, a strategy the Israeli political system rewarded handsomely till 2003. Others, like Etta Bick, will say of course that such a particularistic approach merely perpetuates the problems it claims to solve by being segregationist by definition and also because it does not provide an education for the modern labour market (Bick, 2004).

ETHNICITY, HIERARCHY AND MARRIAGE

In Ashkenazi Jewish ultra-Orthodoxy the issue of marriage looms ever larger in their parents' minds as children approach maturity: broadly, boys are expected to marry at about twenty-one, after they finish secondary school level yeshiva, and girls as soon as possible after eighteen to avoid falling prey to a life of disorder and sexual freedom, with its attendant risks of illegitimacy and uncertain parentage. Many *haredi* communities in Israel—including Shas's kindergartens for children from families of established ultra-Orthodox status—do not allow even mixed kindergartens, and encounters between the sexes post-puberty are strictly regulated, confined to processes which could lead to marriage and which are rapidly cut off if they do not. A deep concern with pedigree encourages very young marriage and brief courtships, which are at least carefully monitored and in Chassidic communities simply prohibited. The permissiveness in the outside world feeds the fear that people might not know where potential spouses come from, or who they really are, and, by the same token, the fear of illegitimacy, which in *haredi* circles is a scar on the person and his or her descendants.

Beyond lineage, in the Lithuanian community, scholarly standing counts as well as pedigree: the brightest yeshiva students are a more esteemed 'catch' for the parents of a prospective spouse, and members of Rabbinic dynasties in Chassidic sects, where leadership is broadly hereditary, are more likely to marry a person from another sect than their followers, so long as the marriage is with a member of another dynastic family. As with the ever-increasing stringency of daily observance, so in matters of pedigree—and thus of sexual propriety—distinctions become ever finer and the subject of ever more obsessive curiosity. This in turn links in with a dynamic of power. Rabbis, appointed directly or indirectly to community positions or yeshivas by their senior authorities or Torah Sages, may come to be the repositories of a family's and an individual's most intimate secrets, and are in a position to influence private decisions. Even among the Lubavitch, for all their dedication to bringing Jews back to Jewishness, the unspoken norm is that returnees can only marry other returnees, and the 'mark' of their origin is even transmitted to the next generation. They share with illegitimate children the shadow of doubt over their true origins.

Although some returnees—distinguished academics or professionals for example—will be treated with greater deference than others, the Sephardi-Ashkenazi divide is a prominent one. Outside Israel it would seem that the two traditions keep largely apart in the marriage-go-round: to find them intermarrying in Orthodox circles in New York, Buenos Aires or London, where the Sephardim are very much a minority, is almost impossible. In Israel, with its vast

Sephardi presence, intermarriage among secular people is not at all unusual and barely provokes any comment, let alone disapproval—we already mentioned that in 1980 it reached 20 per cent, and today it is estimated at 30 per cent—but in ultra-Orthodox circles it is a sensitive issue. Unwilling to broach it directly with our Sephardi interlocutors, for that very reason, we heard about it indirectly. A Rabbi who appears frequently on both pirate and legal radio, and on television, told us he only permitted his daughter to marry a Sephardi when he had checked the young man's background and found that his family had been in Israel for many generations: had he been a North African he would not have permitted the marriage. He then elaborated with the following image: 'when someone throws water over you in the street you go to see if it is clean water or has been used for washing the floor—in the latter case you have to change your clothes.' In Ramat Shlomo, the predominantly ultra-Orthodox Jerusalem neighbourhood we have already mentioned, a professional social worker attached to the community council explained to us in almost brutal terms the problem of mixed families: these number about 10 per cent of families in the neighbourhood, predominantly consisting of Sephardi women married to Ashkenazi men: if a Sephardi man marries an Ashkenazi woman, he said, 'he would be mistaken to live here'. He said mixed families would be left in little doubt that when their children were refused entry to a high quality religious school, the technicality adduced in justification was merely a pretext. In a standard, unkind, joke, an Ashkenazi *haredi* who marries a daughter to a Sephardi might be asked: 'does she have a wooden leg or something?'

Perhaps the most sensitive observation we have heard on this subject was from a woman in the Brisk community, an extra-observant offshoot of the Lithuanians, who said that if it was known that she was even merely thinking about a Sephardi partner for her daughter, this would damage the chances of a good marriage for her other daughters.

The issue of getting in to a school, or above all a respected *haredi* yeshiva, is a constant theme: yeshivas operate a quota system, as we have seen, and this extends to the Beit Yaakov network of girls' schools which Lupo, in our interview, described as operating the 'strongest discrimination'. The head of the Shas girls' school in Beit-

Shemesh recalled how in her schooldays the Beit Yaakov girls' schools resisted hiring Sephardi teachers, did not allow Sephardi ritual (melodies for example) in their schools, and also excluded Sephardi girls from their high-achieving stream. In August 2003 the issue came to the attention of the public in the form of a demand from the Association for Civil Rights in Israel to 'put an end to the ethnic quota system' in Beit Yaakov seminaries for 16–18 year old girls. A journalist from *Ha'aretz* (5 August 2003) explained that a 30 per cent quota on Sephardi girls was operated by the most prestigious seminaries, that it was operated in a mysterious way by various seminary heads and Rabbinic authorities, and mentioned spine-chilling cases in which a single Sephardi grandparent, or even great-grandparent, was sufficient to count against an applicant—a practice which, as we have seen, had already provoked Arieh Deri's infuriated remarks in 1997. But as always there are ambiguities and these were illustrated by two apparently contrasting features of the story: that Sephardi *haredi* families had complained to secular institutions such as the Ministry of Education and the Civil Rights Association, and that in spite of these repeated rebuffs they continued to pay homage to the 'pecking order' of *haredi* educational institutions.[15]

Although the political rhetoric emphasises discrimination in yeshivas, ethnic resentment has not turned Sephardim away from styles of religious observance and above all Torah study that draw extensively on the traditions and contemporary institutions of those self-same Ashkenazim. Most striking, the issue of marriage across ethnic lines, which we have already described as the hardest slight, did not figure as a source of Sephardi resentment in our interviews: perhaps it was just too painful, or perhaps they did not see it as a question of discrimination, but merely a feature of the hierarchy of which they were, or were becoming, a part.

Here the cross-cutting character of Israel's enclaves comes into play. The population who are the targets of the *t'shuva* campaign do not have a history of involvement in the *haredi* world and therefore have not experienced discrimination on the part of Ashkenazi ultra-Orthodox; their own experiences, as stereotyped by Shas discourse,

---

[15] The story is reminiscent of the treatment of Oxford and Cambridge Universities in certain sectors of the British media, where the scale of resentment, expressed in almost prurient language, is in proportion to the desperation for admission.

have been of social exclusion in a state dominated by secular and Ashkenazi Zionism. Return to religion is a gesture of dissent against this secular élite and, as many researchers say, the Sephardim who adopt this method of dissent nevertheless become fuller participants in one of the core elements of the Israeli state. Their marriage predicament has to be seen against this background of a positive, and radical, choice to join a different community. In rational choice terms, they are acquiring the benefits of joining the ultra-Orthodox world, although they know that they are not entitled to the same benefits as those born into that world, who, having not done military service, and having few professional skills, are more tightly locked in, have fewer alternatives, and therefore could be thought to be entitled to greater benefits.

These considerations about the place of the ethnic in the call to *t'shuva*, and vice versa, raise complex and important issues about Shas and the Israeli political system. Through the party's tenure of the key spending Ministries of Health, Social Welfare, Religious Affairs and the Interior, Shas placed recognisably and proudly Sephardi men in positions of power and enabled Sephardim to become full operators and beneficiaries of government-funded social and educational programmes. Because in Israel budgets always contain chunks of social and educational expenditure—schools, yeshivas, day-care centres, *kollelim*—allocated by politicians on the basis of relations of political and personal loyalty, these ties have probably done more for the raising of the political visibility of the Sephardi population, their symbolic capital so to speak, and thus for their sense of pride and membership in Israeli society, than would have been achieved by more conventional and transparent—i.e. bureaucratic—means.

Shas's social and educational programmes are all somehow linked to the *t'shuva* process: more or less all have an emphatically religious educational content, which contributes little to socio-economic advance but much to promoting the collective presence in the political arena and in the public space.

The call to *t'shuva* has proved itself a highly effective recipe for the emergence of a new actor in Israeli politics, particularly because religion has broader legitimacy than ethnicity in Israel's tense politics of identity. The Sephardim who embark on this path may be abandoning one hierarchy for another, but for some reason seem to resent the discriminations they face in the secular world more than those they face in the *haredi* world, in the image of the leadership who denounce the discriminations of the yeshiva world but reiterate their admiration for that world's values.

TENSIONS BETWEEN TRADITION AND STRINGENCY IN THE PURSUIT OF A UNIFIED ORTHODOXY

The Shas motto which refers to the retrieval of the ancient crown of Sephardi tradition implies that a tradition has been lost and that religious renewal will replicate it. Yet the research by Nissim Leon shows that not all the traditions have been lost, and that the renewal is certainly not a renewal of tradition. In his study of a town of 52,000 (Leon, 1999), although out of eleven Sephardi/Mizrachi synagogues he could find only one that identified itself exclusively with one Oriental place of origin, he found a widespread identification with the Sephardi or Oriental liturgical tradition—in melodies, pronunciation, certain details of the liturgy—among synagogue members who believed they were following the tradition of their forefathers.

Into this milieu came Shas and *t'shuva*, and life was never quite the same again. In two cases younger *ba'alei t'shuva*, and others in the process of strengthening their religious life, all identified as a new generation, began to take a more prominent part in a synagogue where the old-timers had reigned unchallenged. In one case he describes a complete 'takeover': the Rabbi organised a small *kollel*, and then obtained funds from the Ministry of Religious Affairs to expand it, as well as to provide a kindergarten and Torah classes, eventually building a 'Torani' Centre. In a second case, there was more resistance, as the newly observant *ba'alei t'shuva* became more assertive, bringing in a 28-year-old Rabbi, who had been trained in a *haredi* yeshiva and was a protégé of a senior Rabbinical figure in Shas. In standard Israeli style, even though he was not appointed as the synagogue's Rabbi—a position for which they probably did not have the resources anyhow—the group's mentor created and occupied a space: he began to attend the synagogue, to exert his influence, and to rule on matters of liturgy and daily life.

The old-timers' response, in this second case, derived from a strong sense of religious life grounded in custom, not in rulings or texts, as

Leon emphasises. Consequently they resisted the young Rabbi's attempt to create a religious school for children (Talmud Torah) arguing that it would not be in 'the Iraqi tradition'. Referring to such disagreements, Leon quotes expressions of irritation, even fury, directed against this interloper who wanted to convert them into 'Ashkenazim', to 'take away my house, my customs, my traditions', and who was even pejoratively dubbed a 'Shasnik'. Ironic and amusing as this may be, it reflects the divide between Shas and the traditional religion its slogans seek to glorify, and also explains the movement's attractions for, and perhaps dependence on, returnees from non-observant backgrounds who do not bring with them a baggage of traditional observance. Although the sense of Sephardi identity remains, one can see how, imperceptibly, the new Israeli orthodoxy can establish its authority and how the opposition it faces is so small—since the old-timers in these synagogues may complain but do not have the resources, or perhaps even the motivation, to set up a rival project. This case shows once again how, in the long run, ethnicity offers a framework or vehicle for the consolidation of a distinctive Israeli Orthodoxy, and one which transcends differences between the various Oriental, Middle Eastern and North African traditions.

The young Rabbi's interventions show the inadequacy of some ready-made assumptions concerning Sephardi-Ashkenazi differences and 'tradition-modernity' differences. Invoking the authority of Ovadia Yosef, he is in some ways 'more lenient' in his rulings than the old-timers expect, but incurs the label 'fake Oriental' (*mizrachi*) from an objector. He quotes Ashkenazi Rabbinical authorities, and introduces contemporary Chassidic melodies, which are utterly incompatible with the Oriental musical tradition, since they follow a different mode. In the liturgical reading of the Torah he insists on adopting the 'Al Kisei Harachamin' Yeshiva editions as the only correct ones—a yeshiva which some regard as too concerned to affirm distinctive Tunisian practices.

Where the role of women is concerned the 'Shasnik' practices do little to disturb existing modes in the religious realm. In the communities studied by Leon they are active in charitable work but continue to be excluded from textual study, and of course from taking a public role in synagogue services. They facilitate marriages and help families with health problems, for example by arranging for people to see a healer. They defer, as indeed do the old-timers out of habit, to the 'new' Rabbi, conferring upon him the same 'gifts of the spirit'—*emouna*, here meaning learning and a certain mystical power—that their ancestors have done for generations. (Among Ashkenazim, the diffusion of Rabbinical expertise in the population at large has reduced respect for the person of the community Rabbi.)

On the other hand, outside the synagogue itself and Torah study sessions, Shas women are encouraged to participate in public activities and to study and work. Compared particularly to Ashkenazi ultra-Orthodox women they work in more modern professions outside the home, and also have a prominent political role: we have noted the women's discussion groups and consciousness-raising activity under the aegis of the Margalit Em Yisrael organisation, and we should also add the prominent public roles of Arieh Deri's wife and of certain women in the Ovadia Yosef entourage. They are also regarded as carriers of the *t'shuva* movement in their own right. In this they follow in the path of Chabad whose opening up of spaces for women's education and other activities outside the home is certainly one aspect of its departure from Chassidic tradition.

Many of these innovations are propagated by rationalisation and institutionalisation, whereby authority comes to reside in institutions that are independent of the local community. This institutionalization has been accompanied by the adoption of external markers common to all Sephardi *haredim*. The 'Shasniks', as they are known, wear a particular style of very dark blue double-breasted suit, with wide Armani-style lapels, evidently *haredi* but also different enough from other *haredim* to be distinctive. Their women mostly use hairnets or loose headscarves in place of the wigs prescribed by the Ashkenazi Rabbis. Like other *haredi* communities, they regard the production of very large numbers of children as a '*mitzvah*', an act of piety, justified by the need to hasten the coming of the Messiah and to replenish the millions lost in the Holocaust. In fact, the statistical evidence shows that the rate of increase in fertility among Sephardi *haredim*, in the period since they began joining the *t'shuva* movement, has been so much greater than among their Ashkenazi counterparts, that they are most likely to overtake their Ashkenazi cousins in fertility (Berman, 2000; Lupo, 2004).[16] When Shas activists invade territory and institutional spaces they set up outposts—such as schools—which they then proceed to develop institutionally. The *hozrei bet'shuva* also construct what Leon (1999) calls a 'speech community': they adopt exaggeratedly formal Sephardi modes of expression and a distinctive accent and jargon, accentuating certain features of Sephardi pronunciation, setting themselves and their allies—the 'Rav' which always means Ovadia Yosef—against 'them', the secular, or the *smolanim*, the leftists. Other *haredi* communities draw their legitimacy and their heritage from particular geographical areas of Eastern Europe and particular Rabbinical families which have provided their leaders (Gur,[17] Bratislav, the 'Lithuanians'). They are also inward-looking and enforce their codes of conduct, upbringing and observance uniformly and rigidly among all their members. Shas has had to face a very different challenge, and has constructed an Israeli-based community of multiple ethnic origin, trying to create a unified set of everyday regulations out of the heritage of far-flung communities stretching from Morocco to Persia and even to Bokhara and Kabul, but with a strong emphasis on looking outwards and not inwards and on persuading the mass of Sephardim to return to strict observance. In emphasising this evangelising mission, Shas is creating the division between secularism and observance which had been absent from the North African and Middle Eastern Jewish communities, and is also creating a new, more elaborate type of enclave in *haredi* society—which is itself an enclave within the broader society. Only the core of Shas lead a life like that of the Ashkenazi *haredim*, devoted to full time study and observing every letter of every law, though this core is growing rapidly (Berman, 2000). Beyond them are the missionaries, the consciousness-raisers, who are on the street and on the airwaves, and beyond them are the Sephardim who support Shas with donations or vote for its candidates. They use the political methods embedded in Israel's enclave system, but they are not quite an enclave like any other.

[16] Berman, using data from government statistics, shows that total fertility among Sephardi ultra-Orthodox women rose by more than two and a half children between the early 1980s and the mid 1990s—compared with a rise of 0.89 among Ashkenazi ultra-Orthodox.

[17] Gur is in fact not a location, but is derived from the Hebrew word *ger* meaning stranger, because they originate in migrant communities in Hungary.

THE EXPERIENCE OF *T'SHUVA*

Renewal and renunciation

There is much debate regarding the relative weight of spiritual, doctrinal and practical considerations in constructing a Jewish way of
life, and consequently different sects, groups and even individuals
achieve or advocate different solutions. Some emphasise the mystical, others more 'rational' Talmudic scholarship; the mystical traditions differ between the expressive, corporeal Chassidim of Eastern
Europe, the esoteric Kabbala tradition[18] and the incantations and
charms of varieties of North African religiosity which have something in common with Sufism. There are balances to be struck, or
stands to be taken, on the extent to which *t'shuva* is a matter of day-
to-day observance or of inner transformation, whether it should be
pursued even at the expense of relations with parents or close family,
whether it is in the long run compatible with a secular profession,
and so on. These are pragmatic responses rather than matters of doctrine, which vary between sects and communities and with the social
pressures which come with the *t'shuva* process, and they vary in
stringency. If an adult is returning to religious observance, that person is unlikely to be able to take up full-time detailed study, and may
even have difficulty learning the Hebrew of Rabbinic writings,
or grasping the various languages of Torah study (Aramaic, 'Holy
Hebrew', Ancient Hebrew etc.) so the recommended emphasis is
likely to be on practical, perhaps rigid, observance. Their male children, in contrast, may well be inducted in the full rigours of Torah
study.

The emphasis on moral or spiritual transformation of a person's
inner life can be thought of as an aspect of a mystical tradition within
Judaism. The latter can be heard in talk about the awestruck contemplation of the infinite—the Kabbalah's *Ein Sof* (the 'Infinite' or
'Endless')—but that tends to be reserved for virtuosos, for people
held in very special respect, such as Yitzchak Kedourie, and those
closely associated with them. For the majority, Rabbis preach a mor-
alistic personal transformation involving the banishment of base

---

[18] Recently the Kabbala seems to have been placed on the banner of cult-like
organisations which exhibit classic authoritarian and money-grabbing features:
this is not what is being alluded to here.

thoughts and desires, of bad language and disrespectful behaviour, and the pursuit of a state of faith or trust in God.[19]

In explaining practical everyday Jewish life, preachers at Or Hachayyim's main Jerusalem yeshiva, observed in May 2000, who included the organisation's founder and leader Reuven Elbaz and members of his staff, enumerated the details of ritual: the sentences were formulated in a manner which implied they came from handed-down authority ('it is written' or 'it is said'), even when the subject matter was the minutest detail of how to carry out a particular ritual procedure. Their content was of the kind which would be uninspiring, and certainly not new, to people brought up in a *haredi* home, since they would have imbibed these rules and regulations from their earliest childhood, and might even make fun of newcomers to observance who need to have them explained in a formal manner. For example, if a person is alone at the conclusion of the Sabbath, should they listen to the corresponding prayer over the telephone? The answer is that a sick person may listen to someone saying the prayer over the telephone, in which case their prayer must absolutely be repeated word for word, otherwise the blessing is without value. And if the prescribed spices for the occasion are not available, Eau de Cologne must not be used as a substitute, because this has been manufactured for a quite different purpose.[20] Elbaz's assistant explains the dress code in terms of its contrast to the clothes of non-Jews, of the *goyim*. 'It is forbidden to follow any non-Jewish customs, for that might lead a person to worship other Gods, against the first of the Ten Commandments.' The list is read in a monotone, with no time for elaboration or discussion.

These may seem to be quite straightforward injunctions, formulated in terms of fulfilling a Jewish duty to observe commandments

---

[19] The word used by Rav Eliahu of Or Hachayyim (see next paragraph) is *emouna*, which Nicholas de Lange translates as trust or confidence in God (de Lange, 2001).

[20] At the ceremony for the conclusion of the Sabbath a box of spices is handed round for the participants to inhale: one does not hand them round in a supermarket box, but in a container which, though there is no standard design, has been made and kept for the purpose. Museums sometimes have very beautiful examples. This, as always, is the modal practice: there are *always* variations. Apparently, some very observant people do, if the need or inspiration arises, use bottles of perfume.

and not transgress frontiers between Jews and non-Jews, and to obey
the injunctions of the Rabbis. Note that the frontiers to which they
allude are not only between Jews and non-Jews, but also between
the sacred and the profane—as in the example of Eau de Cologne.
The intuitive absurdity of the example demonstrates the speaker's
anthropological sensitivity, for it is a standard feature of ritual that the
objects it marshals are made specially for the ritual purpose or else
go through a benediction or incantation which makes them suitable:
examples are infinite and would include the priest's prayer over wine
for the Eucharist, or the breaking and blessing over bread at the start
of every meal by observant Jews. The speaker was explaining that the
role of the spices in this ceremony did not depend merely on their
fragrance, but on their fragrance *plus* their ritual preparation. But he
was also drilling his listeners in the practice of obedience to a religious authority figure.

Ritual injunctions in all religions are repetitive and operate according to codes which are to some extent not understood by those who
follow them. Experts—priests, rabbis, diviners—are expected to
understand the efficacy of ritual, because they have, through training
and initiation, understanding or insight which is opaque to the non-
expert. Their explanation of ritual efficacy is never fully convincing,
but neither is it wholly discreditable, because such claims are of their
nature irrefutable. Either the cost to followers or clients of following
their advice is very low, or the cost of not following it is very high. If
the followers and authorities are bound together in some sort of
power relationship, or if the followers are heavily dependent on each
other for mutual support and thus approval, then of course, whatever
the other risks and rewards, the costs of not following the advice are
very high indeed. Chapter 6 returns to this point. Ritual observance
can also be reinforced by its interaction with the randomness of
chance events. Following Pascal Boyer (2001) and before him Evans-
Pritchard (1937): 'things go right, things go wrong', but the mystery
remains as to why they went right or wrong for a particular person at
a particular moment, and explanation of events which are especially
subject to random variation, by reference, for example, to the accomplishment of a ritual task, has the advantage of increasing the motivation for virtuous behaviour without violating our underlying
understanding of the workings of nature. This applies especially to

events like traffic accidents or winning the lottery, or sudden movements in a share price, but *not* a general market crash or boom, or
overall accident statistics, which are more predictable!

If Rabbis or folk wisdom use the observance or non-observance
of one or another injunction to explain a random event, they do not
ask us to violate our intuition or 'folk' science. And since there are
other reasons for fulfilling commandments anyhow, little or nothing
is lost—in credibility on the part of the story-teller or in credulous-
ness on the part of the listener—by explaining or justifying rules and
regulations in terms of the good fortune they might bring, or the
misfortune which might be brought about by neglecting them. It is
therefore not surprising that religious traditions abound in stories
about virtue rewarded and vice punished, in small ways affecting
ordinary people. Ovadia Yosef, at one of his regular Saturday night
appearances shortly before the Jewish New Year in 2000, told a fable
of a man who gave up the chance of a business deal because it was
time to say his afternoon prayers, only later to find out that he had
narrowly escaped a confidence trick. He also spoke against the idea
that men and women should inherit equally, which according to
him is against the Ethics of the Fathers (a frequently cited compilation of Rabbinic sayings and exchanges), saying that equal inheritance might lead to the loss of the inheritance, for example through
illness or some other misfortune. Such remarks and illustrative stories
were interspersed among detailed injunctions about how to pronounce a blessing, how to pray and occasional exercises in numero-
logical wordplay. To recount these *exempla* one by one might give
the reader a misleading cue to analyse them carefully, bypassing the
impact on those listening (whether there and then or via 450 satellite
dishes dotted around the country). The effect on those listening is
determined not just, perhaps not even principally, by their content,
but rather by their number and the cascading effect of their enumeration: the listeners are to be impressed by the erudition and
prestige of the speaker, who puts them in touch with an age-old tradition served up not as history, not as philosophy, but as a stream of
stories and injunctions interspersed with moral exhortation.

These examples show how links are created between the *ba'al
t'shuva* and an apparatus of authority, and also with a world of unpredictable punishments and rewards. In addition, his conscience is also

addressed, for as in most contemporary evangelical movements, conversion involves moral change as well as a change of mores.[21] A *kollel* student in Bet Shemesh asks: 'why did God bring us into the world?—not to suffer, or to work—we are mere tourists in this world—the end of everything is the next world… all material life is of little worth.' The evangelist Amnon Yitzchak—of whom more later—devotes a whole cassette tape to the question 'why are we here?' a stock item in *t'shuva* sessions. He speaks at length about the world to come, about the soul living after the body has died, about reincarnation, about near-death experiences, and above all about earning God's forgiveness through *t'shuva*, and thus obtaining a reward in the next world. The righteous (*tzaddikim*) 'take all their punishment in this world and their reward in the next.' And he recounts stories to 'remind us that there is a next world so that we can prepare ourselves.' In another cassette, this one by Rav Ben-Zion Motzafi, a figure who is close to Ovadia Yosef, entitled 'The supremacy of *t'shuva*', the theme is reminiscent of the Gospel passage, 'there will be more rejoicing in heaven over one sinner who repents than over ninety-nine righteous persons who do not need to repent' (Luke 15:7). Motzafi says God would even be prepared to put a crown on the head of a bad person, even Yossi Beilin and Yossi Sarid,[22] if they make *t'shuva*—he would even receive Ishmael![23]

Occasionally we heard references to heaven and hell and ideas about eternal damnation.[24] At an Or HaChayyim study centre for

---

[21] When the head of a Chabad yeshiva in London was told of the resemblances between Chabad and certain evangelical churches he asked 'but do they change their lives?'—replicating precisely evangelical terminology.

[22] Two notoriously secular, left-wing (in the Israeli sense) politicians, and Ministers in the Barak government.

[23] Abraham's son by his concubine Hagar, regarded as the progenitor of the Muslims. Motzafi is described as 'close to Ovadia Yosef' because, as already mentioned, we heard him precede Ovadia Yosef at the Persian Synagogue one Saturday evening.

[24] One might contrast this with the words of Rav Abdel-Haq, a very learned but highly independent Rabbi who has no links at all with the *t'shuva* movement. He emphasised more the classic Jewish distinction of 'high' and 'low'—the higher referring, in classic Kabbalistic style, to the mystical or the pure, to the head as opposed to the worldly and to the lower parts of the body. Thus he said it is worse to think an evil thought than to commit an evil act—for the thought involved a 'higher' part of the body. In some Chassidic communities men wear a

young French Sephardi men who are in the *t'shuva* process and also planning migration to Israel, Rav Eliahu, the head, laid particular emphasis on the inner world of the person, on the world to come and on the abandonment of this-worldly pursuits. Even bringing up one's children, he remarked, is an ephemeral matter, compared with the world to come. He advised his students to distinguish between doing things for their own sake and doing them for some instrumental or extraneous purpose. In saying this he was referring implicitly to Torah study, and his message was that they should not think there was any benefit to be gained from it other than study itself—they should not devote themselves to Torah for the sake of acquiring prestige or high position. He described a vision of a life of never-ending *t'shuva*, a journey in which every millimetre has enormous significance, even if one never quite arrives at the destination. Indeed, in these times, he seemed to be saying, we are condemned never to reach it. He portrayed a succession of apparitions (*dévoilements*) of the Prophet Elijah, over generations, ending with the revelation to Joseph Karo, who was said to have visions, and to utter sounds which nowadays would be described as 'speaking in tongues'. Rav Eliahu explained that all this came to an end with modernity, or the *haskala*, the Jewish Enlightenment which opened European Judaism up to secularism and modernity. Before modernity, Rav Eliahu said, there were people in the mountains of Morocco (ancestral land of most of his students) who, because of their innocence of modernity, still had these visions. They were the inheritors of a great chain which transmitted mystical experiences down through the generations. After Karo and the great visionaries of sixteenth-century Sfat (Safed), the chain was broken, and all we can do is make constant heavy sacrifice in the pursuit of *t'shuva* and the next world.

The *kollel* Director in Bet Shemesh (mentioned above, p. 81, and also below, p. 152, in the discussion of Shas's grass roots approach to mobilisation) interpreted the *t'shuva* movement as a moment in the spiritual history of Israel. He too dated its beginning to the Yom Kippur war of 1973 (although some date it to the Six Day War). Israel had won the 1967 war with too much ease, and forgot about

---

cordon around their midriff to separate the 'baser' lower part of their bodies from the 'higher' upper part.

God, but was caught out in 1973 when heavy losses were incurred and many soldiers and their families began to ask questions. This is what had led him and his brother to make *t'shuva*, to study with Or Hachayyim and eventually to set up a yeshiva in Bet Shemesh. He was a leading political and religious figure in the town, saw himself as a missionary to the poor and the marginalised, sustaining the social dimension of his interpretation of the movement as a collective response to the crisis of the Yom Kippur war. His brother was at one time responsible for the students in Or HaChayyim's main Jerusalem yeshiva, and became Minister in the Barak government and in the first Sharon government.

The idea of religion, and the return to religious observance and Torah study, as remedies for a life devoted to frivolity or material success, would not be surprising, save for the relative novelty of such ideas in a Jewish tradition where the renunciation of pleasure, and the adoption of a life of austerity, has been reserved in the past for selected saintly figures. But such language has now become standard: an Or-HaChayyim student spoke of being moved to make *t'shuva* by a sense that there was 'something missing inside me' (a very common phrase). A full-time married Torah student in Bet Shemesh talked of a war within himself 'between what I wanted and what God wanted for me'. The leader of his study centre or *kollel* was admired for giving up a career as a professional footballer for *t'shuva* and a life of study.

Side by side with fulfilment of an infinity of constraining norms in daily life, *t'shuva* within the Sephardi renewal movement opens up a range of paths, and many more than would be opened by joining Chabad, for example. Some of these activities are remunerated, though almost always at a fairly humble level: while some may opt for full-time study attending a *kollel* every day, others can work in the educational system as teachers—for which Shas will prepare them in its teacher training college—or as administrators; others can find a niche in social work of one sort or another, funded through Shas and its political tentacles, or in the promotion of women's discussion groups. Some *ba'alei t'shuva* will continue to work in their own professions, while devoting large amounts of their time to helping out in projects, to distributing cassettes, or to volunteering in radio stations, in a yeshiva, or in charitable activities. Others, having lost interest in material success, may change to new, less demanding jobs, so as to free up time for the movement. Doubtless there have been fewer jobs available in the Shas circuit since the 2003 elections, but the number of children in the Shas network of kindergartens and primary schools remained at its pre-election level, or even higher in 2004. Although the state funding obtained through Shas membership of successive governments is invaluable, it would not become a social movement without these informal networks and volunteering.

These people share a discourse which portrays them as participants in a collective enterprise of great significance—a feature which we also find in evangelical movements. They look out for new recruits, they collect donations and the young, especially, campaign at election times. Shas provides its activists and followers with a sense of membership not just in one or another of its organisations, or even in Shas itself, but in a vast movement of religious and ethnic renewal which reaches far beyond the core of true believers who meticulously observe the commandments. The message of *t'shuva* in principle applies to the whole Jewish people, while the ethnic renewal, even if it is not always explicitly invoked, and even if it is 'constructed' with little regard for historical authenticity, is deeply ingrained in unspoken markers, dress and accent, as well as in the music and the details of religious ritual, which make a person feel part of a movement which goes far beyond those who have adopted the path of *t'shuva*.

The core of religiously observant are essential to this enterprise, and one reason for this is the time, labour and skills which they give to the movement. Here we observe the effects of the mysterious economics of religion, which also underlies the enormous success of evangelical churches. As our research, and that of many others (Burdick, 1994; Lehmann, 1996; Corten, 1999; Martin, 2001) has shown, evangelical churches seem able to conjure up organisational talents, rhetorical gifts and entrepreneurial drive from the most apparently unpromising sectors of society: they collect money, build buildings large and small, train people to handle accounts and plan, operate broadcasting stations and so on, in places where the non-religious economy seems to suffer from a severe shortage of entrepreneurial drive and organisational skills. The churches activate reserves of energy and talent which the commodity economy, because of institutional and social structures, frustrates and suffocates. Shas of course is not entirely comparable because it receives so much government subsidy, but its collective aspiration is to expand well beyond what that subsidy would, on its own, permit. People who adopt the path of *t'shuva* are not only moving back to personal observance, they are also knowingly joining a movement in which they will in a sense be citizens and as such obliged to devote a large part of their daily life to it. Even the large number of children they will have, will be a contribution not just to their own families but also to the movement.

The opposite of pleasure

The images of a dissolute life purveyed by the missionaries of *t'shuva* do not contain pictures of multi-millionaires, extravagant Hollywood mansions or the Wall Street treadmill. Rather they are of fairly ordinary people, including the converts themselves, indulging in everyday routine amusements such as parties, merry-making and socialising with women in public places. The pleasures of frivolity are not what they seem—they are superficial in the precise sense of the word, and underlying them there is a sense of danger and a notion of evil. Danger is constituted by sexual urges, by the freedom to dress individually and thus, by extension, to choose one's public persona. TV, the internet and all forms of visual media entertainment are banned. The distrust of sexual urges is linked to the enforcement of uniformity of dress and deportment: clothing is display and a means of attracting attention, giving rise to uncontrolled urges and desires, so religio-political authority becomes involved in regulating clothing as a way of suppressing dangers lurking beneath the surface of unregulated behaviour. The private persona is driven into hiding behind a mask—an archetype subtly modified by each sect or affiliative group with its own markers. Behind the uniformity there is regulation by Rabbinic authority, but we shall see in Chapter 6 that pressures for ever greater stringency come from below as well. And maybe the regulation accentuates the fear of the devil within—the *yetzer ha-ra* or drive to evil—driving bad thoughts and urges underground and arousing suspicions nourished precisely by the efficacy of the mask.

Rabbis, or other persons charged with the care of the soul, thus become very inquisitive and very knowledgeable. They come to know the details of the lives of their students, their students' wives and other family members. The faithful acquire a fear of incurring a fault, and confide in figures of religious authority as Catholics once confided in a confessor—though Rabbis cannot offer absolution. We were struck by a passing remark from a school director to the effect that the school had not asked the head of Or HaChayyim, Reuven Elbaz, to act as an advisor on social or moral matters because he knew too many of the parents already. This shows unusual sensitivity to conflicts of interest, but it also reminds us that Elbaz' job, as head of a vast network of *yeshivas*, is to be personally acquainted with a large number of those involved in his vast organisation. The followers of Chassidic sects say they consult their 'Rebbe'—that is, the sect's supreme authority—on every single decision of any importance.

An unblemished life is a life wracked by guilt. The drive to evil lurks beneath the surface. Also there is permanent uncertainty: rules may change, Rabbis may issue edicts condemning certain acts or habits, rendering a person suddenly sinful. There is doubt surrounding many areas of life and, as shown by the examples above about how a sick person might mark the end of the Sabbath, what the outsider may regard as trivial is not trivial at all. It is in the way of Talmudic knowledge that scholars are constantly on the lookout for areas of doubt, and the newly observant especially will be plagued by this uncertainty, which will always be present at the margins of standard everyday routines. Their lives are open to scrutiny and gossip (the 'evil tongue' in Hebrew, matching the 'drive to evil') and as they get deeper into the life of *t'shuva*, and spend more and more time studying, so they join small close-knit groups who meet together for long periods every day, studying—or just hanging around—in *kollelim*, and having few secrets from one another.

It is tempting to believe that, because of this tightly rule-bound life and the fear and guilt it engenders, ultra-Orthodox Jews—or members of fundamentalist and charismatic churches and sects more generally—are more vulnerable to mental illness than other groups. It seems like a claim which panders too much to secular prejudice, and has been repeatedly tested and refuted empirically. However, Greenberg and Witztum (2001) found during a long period of practice of psychiatry in the longest-established ultra-Orthodox area of Jerusalem, and on the basis of careful, relatively well controlled studies, that although the ultra-Orthodox in general did not exhibit different patterns of psychiatric illness compared with the population as a whole—save to the extent that the form of their illness was influenced by their lives as ultra-Orthodox—the *ba'alei t'shuva* (almost all men) did exhibit a 'higher than expected rate of mental illness', and that a 'disproportionately large number of them' had 'suffered previous psychiatric disturbance' (Greenberg and Witztum, 2001: 162). These findings may carry some weight, but they can also be open to a sociological interpretation which would point to the uniformisation of daily life, the ever-more-restricted space available for private life and the uncertain scope of Rabbinic rulings as causes of a haunting sense of guilt. The individual responds to the risk of infractions in the private sphere by living ever more in the public sphere, opening his life to the public eye and exhibiting stereotyped, low-risk behaviour. Why then do people who 'convert', who in a sense 'choose guilt', choose such a life? The response that it offers a better life 'hereafter' is unconvincing. A rational choice-based answer might refer to various opportunities offered to bring their children up in a highly controlled environment. For those who are unmarried *t'shuva* offers the chance of finding a wife and building a family in a relatively secure social context, albeit, as rational choice theorists explain (Iannacone, 1997; Young, 1997) at a high cost to themselves. The benefits in terms of avoidance of military service or state subsidies can hardly be counted save as compensations for their poverty—and this does not account for the choices made by *ba'alei t'shuva*, most of whom have already done their military service before changing their lives. The 'free-riding' arguments (Berman, 2000), which might explain why ultra-Orthodox remain inside the community, need some modification if they are to be applied to people who are newcomers, although, as suggested earlier, they may be less discomfited by the exclusions which apply to them than secularised observers are likely to assume.

The choice which returnees have made more or less detaches them from the ownership or accumulation of capital, but the prospect of profiting from it is reduced because of the massive obligations involved in marrying one's children and setting them up in a place of their own. Making *t'shuva* means relegating work to a secondary place in one's life. Where once they might have found an identity and even fulfilment in work, people who undertake *t'shuva* put that commitment to one side. For those with a family, it will be hard to cut off totally from the secular professional world in exchange for a $500 monthly government subsidy for studying, but henceforth work will be at most an adjunct to the real business of life, it will be a tool or instrument of survival (*parnasa* in Hebrew), not a vocation or a calling (*avoda*) (Stadler, 2002). Not infrequently, we came across people who had given up quite a promising professional life—as architects and pharmacists. They now lived from work that was much humbler but which enabled them to prepare for and observe all the festivals, and to respond to demands to help their new-found community, and did not bring them into close contact with the opposite sex, or expose them to other temptations.

The counterpart to the uniformity of the life of returnees, and also to the highly limited scope of their private spheres, in the Shas world, is the power of Rabbis organised more or less in a hierarchy under the leadership of Ovadia Yosef, and in Shas-dominated bodies in national and local government across the country. The Rabbis replace the market by providing a mechanism whereby individuals can obtain access to assets and jobs, and, as has already been noted, they also exercise powerful influence in intimate family matters. This surveillance or interference is in effect the price people pay for the security and benefits of living in a community protected from market forces, and of taking part in closely knit networks of mutual help.

The rational choice account explains that tightly knit communities (or 'clubs') have to protect themselves from free-riding by people who might take advantage of the benefits of membership without contributing financially, or without adopting the required lifestyle. This has been applied to religious behaviour generally by Iannacone among others, and the Israeli context offers a particularly appropriate case (Berman, 2000). Here the ultra-Orthodox—Ashkenazim and Sephardim, including returnees—enjoy official, state-funded privileges as well as informal 'entitlements' in networks of mutual aid, in purchasing at very cheap non-profit shops, in a vast number of interest-free credit arrangements (*gemachim*), or in access to charitable donations—for example nappies offered to all-comers

by childless couples as an act of *tzaddikut* (righteousness). They protect themselves from free riding by requiring stringent observance of
codes of behaviour and religious norms, and also by making it
almost impossible for graduates of their schooling system, especially
male graduates,[25] to survive economically outside the community.
But one should not forget that these constraints are the product of a
power structure which defines the tight limits of their lives and the
life-chances of their many children: the *haredi* Rabbinical authorities, not only in Israel but worldwide, decided in the early post-war
period that boys would receive an almost totally religious education,
with hardly any secular subjects apart from basic maths and English;
local Rabbis exercise control over entry to schools and prestigious
yeshivas, and also over the allocation of funds. In Israel these funds
come from the state, and until the Education Minister in the Barak
government, Yossi Sarid, intervened, their use was not subject even
to accounting inspections. Thus the missing factor in otherwise
highly perceptive rational choice analyses, is this dimension of power
placed in the hands of individuals operating with few procedural
constraints in the modern sense.

Commitment to living in accordance with precepts (*mitzvot*)
inserts a person into a demanding clerisy. To the outsider this may
appear grim, over-serious and uncompromising, but the 'insiders' have
adopted a path which not only rejects much of what secular society
takes for granted, it also actively closes that world off, placing beyond
perception and reach its values, institutions and everyday habits. If they
do not close them out fairly early in the *t'shuva* process, then they will
scarcely begin their journey. In the secular world individuals are
expected to forge a path for themselves: personal condition and circumstances heavily influence social acceptability, and people expect
to be free to move between different milieux. A *ba'al t'shuva*, in contrast, is valued irrespective of his or her personal or social qualities,
irrespective of wealth or poverty, race, colour or education. All that
will count, having crossed the line, or 'cut the lines', will be observance of the precepts in everyday life and, for men, their standing as
Torah students, or, more precisely, their children's standing, for no
one becomes a Talmudic genius by starting to learn as an adult.

---

[25] Ultra-Orthodox women have in recent years begun to find work in hi-tech jobs
where they are not exposed to contact with men.

Ba'alei t'shuva become members of a *kollel* like any other except that they are usually on long-term probation, always occupying a position below those who were insiders from birth—and this of course is a major difference. There are only a few high-profile celebrity cases which contradict this picture, whose conversion is advertised as a big 'catch' by the *haredim*. This condition of non-competitiveness (in everything save learning and the fulfilment of the minutiae of the Torah's commandments) is particularly prevalent in Israel where young ultra-Orthodox men have the option—indeed almost the obligation—of subsisting without pursuing a worldly vocation. Uniformity and conformity are much more highly valued, and so an individual can become a type of citizen, a person of recognised standing, by punctilious observance of rules and fulfilment of tasks, in study centres, in fund-raising, in political campaigns or whatever. The holy life, with its more enduring or less ephemeral joys and its uniform pleasures, is this citizenship, this recognition.

SOCIAL CAPITAL?

For all the sacrifices it requires, those who undertake *t'shuva* must surely acquire a portion of social capital, in one or other of its meanings. Perhaps not in Bourdieu's sense of a quota of power projected symbolically (Yadgar, 2003), but in Putnam's sense of participation in a rich associative life (Putnam, Leonardi *et al.*, 1993). This is illustrated especially by the highly institutionalised and public character of the life they will lead, and by access to the benefits of mutual aid, and indeed participation in charitable giving. In the Shas milieu, at least before 2003, there are also the benefits of participation in institution-building, in creating spaces for children to play or learn and in campaigning on behalf of the cause of *t'shuva*. (Since 2003, there is reason to believe that the political energy of Shasniks has been eroded.) But the rational choice approach, and indeed the cognitive one which we will invoke later, could be thought to give a less rosy picture, in which the associative life does not involve participation in decision-making but rather submission to personal authority, and in which living a life in public means gossip and the fear thereof.

Shas rally in August 2002. (Photo © Alex Levac)

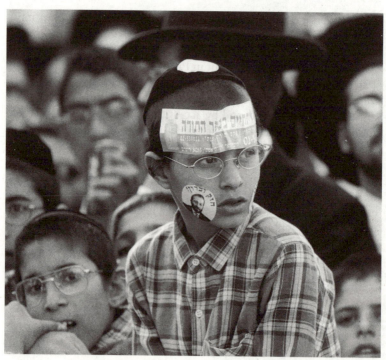

Scene from a rally in August 2002: a picture of Arieh Deri is affixed to the boy's face surrounded by the words 'Strength to him and blessings upon him!' (*Hazak vebaruch*). (Photo © Alex Levac)

Group of Shas supporters holding aloft two banners. The one on the left is inscribed with Deuteronomy 27:26: 'Cursed is the one who does not confirm all the words of this law by observing them. And all the people shall say "Amen".' The intended interpretation is that Ovadia Yosef represents 'the words of this law' and everyone should follow him.

The second placard (on the right) is a quotation from the Midrash: 'The righteous man decreed and God agreed' "The intended interpretation is that 'you should follow Ovadia, because he is a Tzaddik—a righteous man—and even God himself will agree to his decrees'."

Scene from a Shas rally in August 2002: the poster says 'Shas—Kosher and Joyful'. The boy facing the camera raising his fingers represents the first letter of the word 'Shas'. (Photo © Alex Levac)

4

SHAS AS A SOCIAL MOVEMENT

THE HISTORICAL PROJECT AS ENGAGEMENT
WITH MODERNITY AND PUBLIC DEBATE

If a social movement is to be a force of social transformation, at least in a modern society, it needs a project which is something more than a slogan. It needs to gather a range of intellectual activities and groups with a degree of institutionalisation and a degree, therefore, of independence from the political leadership of the movement and from the many factions and branches that contribute to and enrich the movement. Otherwise the intellectuals merely produce propaganda and speak only to the converted.

More than a manifesto, a project is a wide-ranging framework for intellectual debate. Indeed, it could be said to find its expression in a shared culture, or shared set of loyalties and affiliations more easily characterised in emotional terms than in terms of a coherent philosophy, spread across many institutions and fuelling their activity. Somewhat like a religion in fact. Far from being inspired by one doctrine or one set of goals, the great social movements, like major religious traditions, have tended to be riven by doctrinal disputes and competing goals: their unity exists, but it cannot be characterised in terms of a single doctrine. One classic modern example is European Social Democracy which pervaded the universities and institutions of the welfare state, the trade union movement and political parties, spawning innumerable debates and divergences, yet all along retaining a common culture. Marxism also flourished in innumerable institutions in Eastern and Western Europe, but it withered away, and one contributory factor to its demise has been the paralysis inflicted in both Eastern and Western Europe by the entanglement of doctrinal struggles and marxist parties with intellectual debate in

120

academic institutions. The weakness does not arise from the political implications of intellectual disputes in themselves, but from the use of political levers to manipulate intellectual life and the work of research institutions.

The same reasoning applies to charismatic and fundamentalist religious movements: they may have numerous followers, who may represent cultural shifts of various kinds, but they are not successful at bringing about broader change in society, despite their members' claims that they can and will do so by changing personal behaviour and instilling morality. Of course they can mobilise blocking minorities and of course their activities have effects, but they are not the effects their leaders would proclaim, and their anti-intellectualism limits their ability in this regard. Excessive uniformity of thought weakens rather than strengthens a movement—as occurred with Communism—and fundamentalist and charismatic religious movements may also in the end be weakened by their incompatibility with scientific inquiry and the independence of mind that accompanies it. Of course, they have *their* intelligentsia, but these are people working on a tightly bounded set of assumptions, in institutions controlled by the leadership of their movements, and imparting wisdom on the basis of a narrow range of texts and strictly prescriptive interpretations. Pentecostal pastors are trained, but do not receive the type of education in religion that might enable or encourage them to develop independent thought, while the more revolutionary Islamic fundamentalists persecute those who would develop scholarly interpretations of classic texts, and in fact hardly publish anything except propaganda (Beinin and Stork, 1997).

Haredi Jews present an apparent puzzle in this connection because they devote themselves in thousands to a life of study and therefore appear to cultivate an intelligentsia. But this is not scientific study: it sets aside historical, linguistic and archaeological evidence which might contextualise the texts; it relies heavily on the authority or prestige of a name and on the invocation of that authority through disconnected quotation;[1] and it is confined to intra-sectarian criteria of validation. *Haredim* show no inclination to debate or engage intel-

---

[1] In the standard formula, it is enough to say that 'Rabbi such-and-such said...' to legitimise a statement, though it is still permitted to disagree if another authority does so.

lectually with institutions or movements who think differently from them, though they may be eager to convert other Jews to their way of life. For the ultra-Orthodox, the modern scholarly study (the 'higher criticism' as it was known when it was developed in the late nineteenth century) of Biblical texts and theology through the use of archaeological and linguistic evidence and the like is a travesty, even 'heresy' (Jacobs, 1995: 52). For all their erudition, they totally reject evolutionary biology and are as creationist as the most extreme Christian fundamentalists.

The Catholic Church, the Anglican Church and the great Protestant denominations have all found a mechanism, in academic institutions, whereby theological and philosophical reflection and research can take place independently and scientifically, though not always without tension or controversy.[2] In Judaism the same could be said of the Reform and Liberal communities. Ironically, while this arrangement has helped all these religious institutions and their multifarious offshoots to exert influence on society, their influence among their own followers has been diluted in various ways. Roman Catholicism has severe problems of church attendance in Europe, North America and Latin America and is experiencing something like an 'invasion' in the form of the Charismatic Renewal. Pews are empty in many Church of England churches, and although the Reform and Liberal synagogues may be the majority they are constantly on the defensive *vis-à-vis* the attitude of the *haredi* who totally reject any compromise with them.

Unsurprisingly, then, there is a price to pay, because gaining influence in a society by adopting the structures of secularism means losing revolutionary élan. David Martin provides an illustration of the tension between advance and retreat with reference to the headlong growth of nineteenth-century American Methodism and its subsequent stagnation. Methodism's 'primary and original sphere of action was finding the supernatural in everyday life', but eventually it encountered a self-limitation as it 'began to build Gothic churches and to create universities, one of whose objects was to train its professional ministry' (Martin, 2001: 7–8).

---

[2] As exemplified in the difficulties caused, and experienced, by Liberation Theology in the Catholic Church, described in Lehmann 1990 and 1996.

The benefits of institutionalisation arise from the establishment of spheres and boundaries within which rational exchange can proceed on a basis of shared criteria of truth and deductive reason. In this way a movement can reach out to the unconverted and, by taking part in great and small debates, participate in shaping its future social environment. This shift towards the acceptance of impersonal expertise, which is one basis of modern scientific endeavour, involves a difficult balancing act and may be one element that determines whether religious movements can accomplish the transition from sectarian single-issue dissidence to social movement.

The Catholic Church shows how the institutionalisation of scientific debate and rational exchange can establish religious institutions as legitimate participants in the great debates of a secular society, and it illustrates how a specialised theological sphere exists in parallel to, but to a substantial extent independently of, the bureaucratic authority systems which constrain the exercise of priestly or Episcopal prerogatives. Much the same can be said of the Church of England. The experience of Latin America's followers of Liberation Theology is one illustration of religious voices speaking out to society. In Europe, the role of churches in public debate is captured by 'vicarious religion' or, in Grace Davie's phrase, 'believing without belonging' (Davie, 2000): large numbers of people who do not think of themselves as religious in a conventional sense, nevertheless look to the leaders of highly institutionalised churches to make pronouncements on the burning questions of the day.

Preachers and pastors, with their revivalist and moralising rhetoric, may seem, and indeed may be, closely in touch with the sentiments and language of their mass following, but the mere expression of hostility to élite and erudite culture is hardly a guarantee of their transformative role. On the other hand, it can be asked how the establishment of a theological élite and the accompanying liturgical regulation can conceivably enable a movement to engage with society at large.

Answers to this question hinge on what is meant by spontaneous participation, and on the power relations contained within that spontaneity. A straightforward model of religious renewal contains two apparently contradictory assumptions: one about the uniformity of practices throughout the movement, and the other about the absence of bureaucratic structures. How, it might be asked, can such uniformity be achieved without tight bureaucratic control?[3] Uniformity of practices is produced without much bureaucratic enforcement, and preachers who speak for hours without notes say the same things not only from church to church or yeshiva to yeshiva, but also between religious traditions (from church to yeshiva to mosque) and between cultural spaces separated by thousands of miles. Why this should be is an extremely important question (Lehmann, 1998), but it is not answered by reference to spontaneity, let alone to an idea that preachers represent what the people 'truly feel' or believe, and even less what might truly serve their interests or better their material or social lot. It may well be susceptible to the epidemiological approach advocated by Sperber whereby the 'combined effect of countless micro-mechanisms' (Sperber, 1996) is seen to arise from the shaping and reshaping of representations by infinitely or frequently replicated situations, or by factors such as ease of memory and ecological relevance, all of which are independent of local cultural circumstances—which is why Sperber is so dismissive of 'some special hermeneutics giving us access to representations belonging to a culture, yet uninstantiated in the individual heads or physical environment of its members' (*ibid.*: 53).

The production of a project, and of the intelligentsia that goes with it, is as determinant of the long-term impact of a movement as the size of its popular following, since the quantitative spread of what might be called unselfconscious beliefs (those which spread epidemiologically) may remain without historical effect. Of course, religious movements do have an impact, yet we can rarely be sure that the impact is the willed product of their ideologies.

To achieve their aims charismatic and fundamentalist movements would need to articulate not only a hegemonic project but also a framework within which to present, propagate and debate that project with broad sections of society, but this to some extent negates

[3] In addition, though it is not germane at this point, it is often observed that movements, or their component churches, are subject to frequent fissiparous breakaways, which might be taken as evidence of weak leadership control or strong local democracy. However, this is unimportant because breakaways, which usually originate in local ambitions, entrepreneurial initiatives or simply personal rivalries, do not abandon a movement or present a challenge to its top leadership: they just set up another, carbon-copy, local church.

the fundamentalism of their premises, just as the need for an intelligentsia negates their anti–intellectualism.

The sectarian rhetoric and policies of most Israeli religious movements are softened a little by the tempting opportunities offered to them by country's institutional arangements. These can be summarised as the 'enclave system', and a ferociously competitive but tightly regulated arena of proportional representation, with its vault-key in the practice of coalition government. These elements encourage even the most irredentist to join the game, for the benefits from sectarian-style participation are high compared to those of non–participation, and in a small country with very lively media the costs of participation, or entry, are low. Shas has oscillated between Deri's leaning to a broad appeal and a modernizing–populist agenda and the more inward–looking, defensive inclinations of Ovadia Yosef. The movement also owes much to the use made by Rabbi Ovadia Yosef of his position as former Sephardi Chief Rabbi and his overshadowing of his successors, and to the paraphernalia of office which he has managed to preserve, both symbolically in his continued use of the Chief Rabbi's attire, and politically in his continued influence on appointments of local rabbis, yeshiva heads and the like. It is to his role that we now turn.

OVADIA YOSEF: A DEFINING FIGURE

Although since the imprisonment of Deri in 2000 he has intervened more directly than before in the minutiae of politics, Ovadia Yosef remains above all an icon and an emblem, providing a legitimising umbrella for the vast range of references and activities sponsored, patronised, supported, and not least financed, by or through him and the party leadership, as channels for government funds of one sort or another and, since Shas was removed from the government, as owner of a business which also appears to provide funds for the Party. By ceaselessly promoting his name, the various educational, religious and political organisations that have grown up in the orbit of Shas and the *t'shuva* movement have endowed his persona with an aura of unchallengeable authority.

Yosef's biography shows him as an atypical figure in whose life several strands of Judaism and of Israeli history coexist. Though born in Iraq in 1920, his parents brought him to Jerusalem as a child and hence he became part of the pre-state Sephardi Jewish society which differs from the pre-state ultra-Orthodox sects and also from the Jewish society of North Africa. It was distinctive in tradition and in style, spoke a different Hebrew from the Ashkenazi communities, and also followed different traditions of Talmudic study. It was more aristocratic than either Eastern European or North African Judaism, and was connected by trading networks to far-flung communities in Baghdad, Boukhara, Afghanistan and Persia. When General Allenby marched into Jerusalem during the First World War the people in the Boukharim quarter laid carpets on the streets for him and his troops. This strand of Sephardi Judaism was squeezed out in later history, surviving in the Sephardi diaspora in, for example, Geneva, Paris, New York and Buenos Aires, but little in Israel. Its yeshiva, Porat Yosef, originally funded by a Calcutta merchant, was burned down in the Old City in 1948 and later reconstructed in the heart of Jerusalem's traditional *haredi* district, the *Geula*. It is now a mainstream, though very distinguished, Lithuanian yeshiva. It was squeezed out by secular Zionism, by ultra-Orthodox *haredim*, and by the much less aristocratic masses who came from North Africa.

Although Yosef studied in Lithuanian institutions and came to be a master of that tradition, and although he has come to represent and symbolise the reinvented Israeli Sephardi Judaism that we have described, there is still disagreement over where to place him. Thus, whereas Zvi Zohar (1996) regards him as more stringent than previous generations of authorities in the Middle East, others regard him as less stringent, or at least more 'political' or more willing to recognise political or social realities, as when he ruled that Ethiopians could be regarded as Jews, that the wives of long lost soldiers missing in action could remarry, or of course in his attitude to the Jewish state itself. He has had little difficulty coming to terms with the overwhelming demographic reality of immigrant communities who came to Israel during the Independence struggle and after, and who did not identify with the indigenous, Sephardi community in which he had been raised.

Rav Ovadia, as he is known familiarly, came late to secular politics, when he was some sixty years old. Reverence for his person is intense, but he does not possess the rhetorical skills that enabled

Arieh Deri to reach beyond the observant constituency to something like a Sephardi mass vote. Dressed always in the Chief Rabbi's
robes, which he never gave up after leaving the office, his eyes hidden by the tinted glasses he never removes in public, he cuts a gruff
but commanding figure. But he also has a propensity for discon-
certing outbreaks of almost vulgar street language, which he himself
justifies as a way of speaking to the people 'face-to-face' (Chen and
Pepper, 2004). When he appears in a synagogue all those present rise
automatically to their feet, and when he comes to the Or HaChayyim yeshiva for *ba'alei t'shuva* the students stand aside in two lines like
a guard of honour chanting 'he is the *tzaddik*[4] of our generation', and
try to kiss his hand, in accordance with North African and Middle
Eastern custom; they welcome the Or HaChayyim leader Reuven
Elbaz similarly, but without the chant. According to experienced
religious broadcaster Rav Gillis, some 5,000 people listen to the satellite transmission of his Saturday night address in local centres, but
this may well be an under-estimate: a social worker told us 1,000
people from the Ramat Shlomo neighbourhood of Jerusalem alone—
where there is a strong presence of Shas and of *ba'alei t'shuva*—gather
to hear it, and they bring their children along too—though he also
said that the local Rabbis 'rounds them up': some of the audience
may owe the financing of their mortgage to those same Rabbis,
themselves appointed by Yosef. This pattern is repeated across the
country, especially where Shas—as a party in national or local government—has sponsored, promoted or facilitated a housing project
for the truly observant, as we were able to observe in Petach Tikvah
for example. The *El HaMa'ayan* pamphlet, published by the 'Foundation for the preservation of Sephardi Heritage' and distributed in
synagogues and study centres, carries a regular column written by
him, or on his behalf, on a technical matter of halakhic law. He can
order yeshiva students onto the street for a demonstration—though
he does so rarely. In 2002, when the 'commune' outside Ramleh
prison where Deri was being held became too disorderly, and the
intifada crisis was developing, Yosef ordered its disbandment, and
when the government declared an emergency mobilisation of reserve troops, he brought all the students in Sephardi and Shas-related
yeshivas back from holidays, in effect, assigning to himself the autho-

[4] i.e. the saint.

rity of all the yeshiva heads. He has a direct hand in the appointment of all Rabbis in Sephardi communities—even though nominally these are in the gift of the Sephardi Chief Rabbinate, which he left twenty years ago.

Yosef's personal appearances are frequent: he does not hide from the crowds and seems to respond positively to invitations from religious institutions and *t'shuva* organisations: thus he attends a 5,000-strong Arachim rally in a basketball stadium, the anniversary commemoration of the death of a distinguished yeshiva head, the meeting of the council of a Tunisian yeshiva in Bnei Brak, and he goes almost weekly to the Or HaChayyim yeshiva and to the Persian synagogue in the ultra-Orthodox Boukharim neighbourhood in Jerusalem. Each time he makes a speech in his inimitable style, which is particularly suited to intimate settings in synagogues and yeshivas, or to the small screen, and less to large meetings. Indeed, Deri is acknowledged to have had greater crowd-pulling power: in the words of one of our informants, if Deri could fill a public square, Ovadia can only fill a yeshiva hall. Often Ovadia's words are few. Like royalty, he does not need to say anything at all: his appearance is enough to endow an occasion with special significance.

Although in some respects Yosef can be thought of as a charismatic figure, in others he is better described as a figure of reverence, and his role changed somewhat after the removal of Arieh Deri from the front of the political stage. He is charismatic in the sense that he is leading a project ('the Shas revolution') to undo the secularism and the modernist ethic which inspired the founding of the state. That foundation has been under challenge for some time from both ultra-Orthodoxy and messianic nationalism, but with the emergence of Shas in the early 1980s Yosef wished to convert a sectarian phenomenon into a mass phenomenon. At the same time, though, his followers regard him as a protector of the deepest traditions.

So long as Deri was the political orchestrator of Shas, Ovadia Yosef could remain in these roles, uttering delphic pronouncements and restricting his public interventions to the religious sphere. But after Deri's removal, Yosef intervened much more directly, and Deri's successor as party leader, Eli Yishai, a less colourful and imaginative politician, came to be seen as a person of little weight, merely the faithful executor of Yosef's will. The continued tension between the Deri and Yishai factions irritated Yosef, who came to favour the latter, and more importantly to exercise ultimate control over both the strategy and the day-to-day politics of Shas. For example, in November 2002 Channel Two television 'brought to light a tape recording' in which Yosef instructed his Ministers to use their budgetary leverage over local authorities for the purpose of ensuring the building of ritual baths, synagogues and (religious) schools (*Ha'aretz*, 26 November 2002). The tape also showed the closeness of the party leadership's consultations with the Rabbi. Later Yosef obliged the leadership to re-enter the government after their abrupt, but to some extent theatrical, defenestration by Sharon in 2002 over a budgetary issue. At the same time the public became more aware of the court politics of Shas and of the intricate involvements of the Yosef family and other families in the political, charitable and business dealings surrounding Shas. Yudit Yosef, wife of one of Yosef's sons (Moshe) is also Yishai's Chief of Staff and at the same time reputedly the gatekeeper for Ovadia Yosef, capable even of preventing his own daughters from seeing him. She is said to be determined that her husband inherits his father's political and religious leadership positions. In the 'opposite camp' Deri's wife Yaffa, who acquired a prominent public profile after her husband's imprisonment, went public with Shas's internal squabbles after her rival Yudit set up charities to compete with hers. Yudit also comes from the family of the Moroccan mystic Abuhatzeira, whose burial site in Netivot has become, as we saw, Israel's most prominent place of pilgrimage, and is reputed to have used her family's magical powers to 'bewitch' the great man. Yishai's wife also runs a charity (*Kol Ha'ir*, July 2002). The ramifications go further: another son of Ovadia Yosef, David, who is a close associate of Deri, something of a firebrand orator and an active Talmudic scholar, is married to the sister of Eli Suissa, a former Shas Knesset member and Minister, who was demoted from the party's Knesset list after Deri's removal and the marginalisation of his close associates (Bick, 2004).

The interweaving of family and politics does not stop with the Yosef household: the ex-Minister of Social Affairs, Shlomo Ben Izri, once a *ba'al t'shuva* and later a senior figure in the Or HaChayyim organisation run by Reuven Elbaz, who promoted his political career, appointed Elbaz's daughter Secretary-General of the Ministry in 2002. The classic picture emerges of a leadership both tied by kinship bonds and divided by family rivalry, which may have diminished the stature of Ovadia Yosef himself, who is not quite seen, at least in the press, as 'above the fray'. Of course, there are family involvements in other parties—Sharon and his sons in Likud for example—but the Shas leadership is different because the family ties are at the core of its functioning: Deri himself, though not linked by formal kinship, was at one stage a tutor to some of the Yosef children, and thus was a member of the household.

The Shas electorate grew vertiginously with the support of many people who, though not religiously observant, saw the party as a channel for the expression of their identity as Oriental and North African Jews. In 1999 the party also soared in pockets of economic deprivation such as the development towns, where Shas capitalised on disaffection from the Likud, which had presided over rising un-employment, as the 'only group visibly helping to alleviate poverty, providing day-care, bus transport to school, afternoon programmes for children' (Bick, 2001). But the decay of the peace process, the unremitting violence of terror and counter-terror, and divisions in the Shas political leadership, later brought about a return of Oriental and North African voters to the nationalist parties (for example Likud or the National Religious Party) in 2003. Shas Knesset members had even faced ultra-nationalist demonstrations in front of their homes as punishment (Chen and Pepper, 2004). Indeed, fear of a loss of votes back to the more aggressive nationalists lay behind two moves by Shas Ministers: the unexpected adoption in 2002 of nationalist and sectarian rhetoric by Eli Yishay, who as Minister of the Interior be-came the first Minister ever in the history of Israel to take away a person's citizenship;[5] and the resuscitation by Minister Ben-Izri of the defunct Demographic Council to look in to the future of Israel's population balance (implicitly between Jews and Arabs), an issue which was soon to be a shared source of concern among many political currents. Ben-Izri followed this, during the 2002–3 election campaign, with the advocacy of restrictions on the immigration of secularised Jews and non-Jews. Most significant, Ovadia Yosef under-took for the first time a formal official visit to the West Bank set-tlements where he appeared before a public meeting, thus turning his back on an—admittedly discrete—doveish reputation. On the eve of the elections he wrote a letter to the West Bank settlers stating,

[5] It was taken from an Arab Israeli found to have assisted terrorism.

'the Oslo Agreement is null and void', and because of the changed circumstances, even though his ruling issued in the 1970s supporting the transfer of land in the cause of peace remained valid in principle, 'it is apparent that the transfer of territory from our holy land endangers lives.' 'We want true peace, not terrorists' peace' (*Ha'aretz*, 27 January 2003). When Likud members voted on the Gaza uni-lateral withdrawal plan in April 2004, Ovadia urged them to turn it down, though it is unknown how much his advice weighed in their minds, as they rejected it overwhelmingly anyhow. He also pro-nounced a ruling against the plan in October 2004, though in doing so set himself clearly apart from those whose opposition was based on a biblical entitlement of Jews to the land: 'Thirty years ago I said I am in favour of land for peace, but it has to be a true peace, made with someone you can trust, so it can save lives. But now, when there is war, when there is no partner, and when there is no one to talk to, there is no reason to abandon territory' (*Jerusalem Post*, 25 October 2004). In December, however, he was prepared to support Shas's entry into Sharon's coalition on condition that Israel started formal meetings with the newly-elected Palestinian leadership in the fol-lowing month (*Jerusalem Post*, 13 December 2004).

Ovadia Yosef's position on Zionism is clearly different from that, for example, of Rav Schach, who regarded the kibbutz society and all it represented as a sacrilege, because it represented an attempt to create a Judaism without religion. Ovadia's position is innovative in that, unlike Schach, let alone even more hostile groups like the Satmar Chassidim and Neturei Karta, he separates the legitimacy of the state from the religious question. Of the former there is no question, since it is an obligation to obey the laws of the state in which one finds oneself. He also regards Independence Day as an occasion for thanks-giving, but has ceased to participate in the specifically religious ritual which has been developed to celebrate it, apparently in response to unease among his followers (Chen and Pepper, 2004). While others attending the ceremony will sing a sequence of psalms from the liturgy, Ovadia will simply recite psalms to himself.

With respect to the judiciary, and especially the Supreme Court under the activist leadership of Chief Justice Barak, Ovadia is more critical—sometimes, as we have mentioned, outrageously so. In Feb-ruary 1999 Shas joined other ultra-Orthodox leaders in organising a rally of 250,000 people 'to protest against the "encroachment" of the Supreme Court in matters of religion and state' (Bick, 2001). The core of his position is that the secular judiciary should restrict itself to civil, and presumably criminal, cases and not become involved in the regulation of state-religious issues. This is the position of the ultra-Orthodox generally (Chen and Pepper, 2004).

Finally, Ovadia has evidently frosty relations with the ultra-Orthodox Ashkenazi leadership. He was offended by the refusal of Rav Schach to support his third term as Sephardi Chief Rabbi, and was Schach not famed for such trenchant *obiter dicta* as 'the Sephardim are not yet worthy of leadership' (*Ha'aretz*, 4 December 2001)? He is clearly engaged in the development of a distinctive style of Torah interpretation that is not strictly Lithuanian. And he has to suffer humiliations, some petty and some less so. Witness the following account of the famous 1990 meeting at the Yad Eliahu stadium when, exceptionally, Rav Schach appeared in public to address the *haredim*, in order to pronounce his opposition to Shas forming a coalition with Labour—a move he later called the 'stinking manoeuvre'. In the event, of course, the move failed.

At the height of the crisis, Rabbi Yosef was summoned to [a] mass rally at Yad Eliyahu to see what Rabbi Schach had to say about the matter. When he and other rabbis arrived, he was seated next to Rabbi Issachar Dov Rokach, the Belzer Rebbe,[6] who was not particularly esteemed among the rabbis and *roshei yeshivot*.[7] Yosef sat there, facing the crowds of Rabbi Schach's admirers, as a kind of vassal come to express fealty and obedience to his master. Rabbi Yosef could not understand Rabbi Schach's heavily Ashkenazic-accented Hebrew and required Rabbi Rokach's translation to learn that Rabbi Schach dismissed all his efforts as totally invalid. The crowds at the stadium and those listening to the address on the radio and television knew very well that Rabbi Schach's words were aimed at Rabbi Yosef perhaps more than they were directed at the Labour Party. At the height of the event, Rabbi Yosef was forced to bow his head and express loyalty. Just as Rabbi Schach did not consult previously with the Ashkenazic Torah Sages, he failed to inform Rabbi Yosef of the content of his impending address. The Yad Eliyahu incident was thus a humiliating ceremony for Rabbi Yosef. At the time, he could do nothing, fearing that the students and followers of Rabbi Schach would resign from Shas if he does

---

[6] The leader of the Belz Chassidim.
[7] Yeshiva heads.

not obey, shattering his party completely. But he never forgot the incident (Friedman, n.d.).

THE MODERNISING FACE OF SHAS

Arieh Deri, born in Morocco in 1959, came to Israel at the age of nine; his family was not religious and lived in a deprived neighbourhood, but he was a very bright child and abandoned school because 'he was not learning anything'. At this time he was 'picked out' by the prestigious Podnovietz Yeshiva. The recruitment of Sephardim by such institutions goes back to Rabbi Halperin's mission to Morocco (Lupo, 1999; 2003; 2004), and after the Second World War Podnovietz had opened a 'special Sephardi branch' in Israel, not least to save Sephardi immigrants from Zionism: they even took children out of Zionist institutions, and out of the 'absorption camps', and put them in yeshivas.

During Deri's time in the yeshiva Ovadia Yosef came to conduct an examination and was duly impressed by the young student who was applauded at the end of his performance. From there Deri went to the Sephardi Hebron yeshiva where he made friends with Ovadia Yosef's son David, eventually becoming tutor to the Chief Rabbi's daughter. Having become in effect part of the Yosef household, he married and then went to live in the Occupied Territories between 1980 and 1983 taking a leadership role in a community led by Uri Zohar, the popular entertainer who had become a 'celebrity *ba'al t'shuva*'. This was not a political venture, and had nothing to do with any nationalist territorial project. It was, rather, an experimental community with people of different nationalities who invited Deri to join them. In fact, as a community the experiment failed.

In the early 1980s Deri's political ambitions and Ovadia Yosef's project to build or strengthen a Sephardi Judaism joined together under Rav Schach's auspices. But the relationship with Rav Schach was complicated, because there was an underlying tension over the treatment of Sephardim in the yeshivas, over the rejection of Yosef's desired third term as Sephardi Chief Rabbi and over the aspiration of these prospective leaders of the Sephardi Jews to be independent of any tutelage—be it that of the Labour Party, who for so long took the Sephardi vote for granted, or that of Rav Schach and the Lithuanians.

In fact, Shas had originated as a side-product of the supreme Lithuanian yeshiva leader Rav Schach's manoeuvrings in Ashkenazi *haredi* politics. Already in 1973, in local elections in Bnei Brak, Rav Schach, infuriated by a coalition of Chassidic leaders in Agudat Yisrael with the Zionist-inclined Poalei Agudat Yisrael, had discretely nudged his followers in the direction of a local Sephardi list (Friedman, n.d.). Then, in Jerusalem in 1983 he nudged them in the direction of support for a *haredi* Sephardi party. Schach's move was explained by a separate quarrel with the Agudat Yisrael politician Menachem Porush, who in 1977 had extracted from Begin the powerful post of Chairman of the Knesset Finance Committee (which has been controlled by *haredi* parties ever since) and by his desire to distance the Sephardim from what he regarded as the nefarious influence of Chabad, who were trying to gain influence in Agudat Yisrael (Heilman, 1990). The move backfired: the Sephardi party found support far beyond the *haredi* community itself, among the broader Sephardi public of Jerusalem, and gained even more votes than Agudat Yisrael (weakened by Schach's plotting) (Friedman, n.d.).

In the following year the party, now renamed Shas, obtained twice as many votes as Agudat, winning four Knesset seats. Still Rav Schach retained the final say in Shas decisions, but by 1990 Deri felt strong enough to thwart Schach's instructions and attempt to join a coalition led by the Labour Party (the 'striking manoeuvre').[8] Later (when Schach was almost permanently comatose) Deri would atone for this insubordination while at the same time continuing to rant against the maltreatment of Sephardim by the Ashkenazi yeshiva community (as in his *J'accuse* video circulated during the 1999 elections.) In 1996 Deri's political independence was again demonstrated when, as Shas political leader, and despite Yosef's lukewarm response to the idea, he opted to join a coalition led by the right, namely Netanyahu, then the leader of the Likud party.

Deri and Ovadia Yosef may have made public noises of obeisance towards the Ashkenazi yeshiva world, and Yosef himself may occasionally have had misgivings about Sephardi 'separatism', but the

---

[8] Schach and the religious parties had long been supporters of governments led by Labour, save when the right tempted them, but at this point he revealed his detestation of their secularism.

evidence of their actions shows a strong commitment to building institutions for the religious Sephardim: gradually the project of ethnic renewal became a project of Israeli Judaism. Thus within two years of Shas's first electoral successes the network of study groups, women's groups, consciousness-raising activities and so on—El HaMa'ayan—had been created, and two years later in 1988 it already had 350 centres, ranging from youth groups to adult education classes (in religion) and pensioners' clubs. Under Rabin in the early 1990s it had, according to Dayan (1999), '600,000 hours of activities and 80,000 participants'. The project of Sephardi renewal had translated itself, as a result of participation in government and the opportunities that this brought, into an institution-building project.

It was not by accident that Yosef and Deri thought of their mission as predominantly one of building and operating schools and yeshivas, for they themselves were from the *yeshiva* world, in which study is a full time activity. Already before 1948 the Sephardi Rabbinic community in Israel—who at that time were either indigenous or linked to Iraq and Iran, but not to North Africa—had been searching for ways to improve their standing in the eyes of their Ashkenazi cousins: they changed the curriculum at their main yeshiva (Porat Yosef) in accordance with Lithuanian practice, by setting aside the mystical and esoteric Kabbala (viewed with suspicion by the Lithuanians) and placing the main emphasis on the legalistic Halakha, which was necessary if they were to certify Rabbis and religious functionaries (Horowitz, 2000). Scholars and above all students, from Yemen and later from North Africa, were drawn in to the Lithuanian yeshivas, who were hungry for new recruits to add to those they had brought from Morocco. The Porat Yosef yeshiva building was destroyed by fire in 1948, to be reconstructed only in the 1960s.

Both journalistic and academic accounts reflect well the ambiguities and the many layers of the relationship between the largely Rabbinical, yeshiva-based Sephardi élite who have moulded Shas, and Israel's Ashkenazi populations (secular and religious), and make it difficult to see the distinctive Shas mixture of religious and ethnic renewal as even stable in itself, let alone as a predictable or determined outcome of a set of circumstances. Seen from a contemporary standpoint, that is, through the prism of the religious-secular conflict in Israeli society, one might emphasise the 'black legend' of the treat-

ment of mass immigration by the reception and 'absorption' services; yet the people who came to form Shas, given their provenance
and their age group, had only experienced this at second hand. They
themselves are more predominantly Iraqi and Middle Eastern, less
Moroccan and North African, than the children of the mass immigration from those countries, so their hostile rhetoric against Ashkenazi Israel is an occasional rather than a daily phenomenon, and a
message of mixed significance. Having mostly had the good fortune
to be raised in the *haredi* community and educated by the Lithuanians, one might emphasise the disdain, or sometimes worse, experienced by them as yeshiva students. After all, in the 1990s Rav Schach
was saying the same things about Sephardi lack of preparedness for
senior positions as Rabbi Halperin had said when he arrived in
Morocco eighty years earlier! Yet this would have to be tempered, or
perhaps complicated, by an awareness that Deri in particular, though
born in Morocco, was adopted early on by the yeshiva world, and
was as much a 'child' of Rav Schach as of Ovadia Yosef, whatever the
complications of his relationship with the crusty Lithuanian. He also
married the adopted daughter of a reportedly wealthy New York
couple. Furthermore, the Shas yeshiva élite did absorb the *haredi* way
of life and shared the *haredi* sense of threat from secular Israel. This
closeness to the yeshiva outlook is balanced by the Shas leadership's
evidently less hostile attitude to military service and to participation
in the management of the state apparatus—to which they exhibit a
response less visceral, less marked by fear, than that of their Ashkenazi cousins. The brothers of Ovadia Yosef fought in some of the
toughest units in the Independence War (Horowitz, 2000), and, as
we have noted, after his yeshiva training, Arieh Deri briefly went to
live in the Occupied Territories. Deri subsequently held highly influential positions in government with both Labour and Likud, and as
Minister of the Interior even cultivated the Israeli Arab population
who were still voting in relatively strong numbers for Shas in 2003 in
certain areas (Abu Gosh, Haifa). In 1989 he said 'we *haredim* want to
be involved in all the decision-making' (in implicit contrast to
Agudat Yisrael, the traditional *haredi* camp) and that they wanted to
be 'part of the *centre* of the nation' (*Ha'aretz*, 7 April 1989, quoted in
Shitrit, 2001). Such deep involvement marks him and his colleagues
off from the older-style *haredi* politicians who scarcely ever venture
into ministerial positions, preferring to exercise pressure indirectly.

For Shlomo Fischer, Shas has pioneered a stance which, again in contrast to the traditional *haredi* camp, is both religious and completely committed to the State and its legitimacy and does not enter into debates about fundamentals: by 'detaching the legitimacy of the state from Zionism it raised the possibility of a legitimation that is non-totalistic-ideological but is more of a civil sort. Shas does not have a utopian ideal of its own in the light of which it wishes to construct a collectivity which will replace the Israeli one ... they can remain engaged with the "fallen" Israeli reality and take into consideration its needs and requirements.' Fischer admits that this sits uneasily with Shas's model of a totalistic religious life, but he is right to point out that this is an evangelising party whose leadership looks outward rather than focusing on a ready-made, enclave-like constituency. Nor does Shas pursue an agenda of total delegitimation of its opponents (by branding them as sacrilegious for example) (Fischer, 2004a). Since it aspires to speak on behalf of the Sephardi population as a whole, most of whom are only 'traditionally', or culturally, religious, Shas is a party with a difference. In addition to the contrast with the old-established religious parties stemming from Agudat Yisrael, Shas is also quite distinct from the messianic nationalist strand which has taken over the National Religious party, since it has no truck with ideas about divinely granted territory, and from the secular parties of left and right which, as bearers of the mainstream Zionist tradition, draw their original inspiration from European concepts of nationalism, socialism and liberalism. It does, nevertheless, stand out as the first non-Zionist party to clearly proclaim the legitimacy of the state.

During the 1990s Deri took Shas down an increasingly populist road with shrill invocations of Sephardi heritage and resentment against their treatment in the *haredi* world and also the low status of Sephardim in society. He mixed the bitter recall of absorption camps and DDT sprayings that had welcomed immigrants from North Africa in the early days with denunciations of the secular state: '*they* came to build a Zionist state, while *we* came to the Holy Land' was a standard refrain. In 1999 he took the daring decision to make his trial the centrepiece of the Shas campaign, and in the short run it worked. But it alienated potential allies and it heralded a period of aggressive relations between Shas and both left and right. The innuendo about prejudice in the Supreme Court and in the Public

Prosecutor's office, mixing ethnic and social resentments, was a step too far and would eventually come home to roost in 2003 when Sharon took the first opportunity to eject Shas from his government (Bick, 2004).

The Deri case, accusing him of taking 'kickbacks from a yeshiva which received government funds and using them for his personal enrichment', including the 'purchase of a luxury apartment', began in the late 1980s, dragged on throughout the 1990s, and eventually reached the Supreme Court. He was found guilty on 'five counts of bribery, fraudulent receipt of funds, and violation of public trust' (Bick, 2001), and received a three-year prison sentence starting on 3 September 2000, a fine and a ten-year ban from political office. The maximum prison sentence would have been five years. Even outside Shas many people—but not everyone—took the view that Deri was not a serious criminal, that his crime was less severe than those of other politicians who had not been tried or convicted, and that he was the victim of a political élite threatened by Shas. The verdict was broadcast live, further raising Deri's profile a few weeks before the election. An opinion poll found that 19 per cent of the public, but 81 per cent of Shas voters, thought that Deri did not receive a fair trial (Bick, 2001). For months Israeli streets were brimming with demonstrations around this personage, and Shas proffered all manner of insults at the political establishment but most scandalously at the judiciary. The February 1999 rally 'to protest against the "encroachment" of the Supreme Court took place in this context.

Deri was at that time certainly a figure who invited controversy, and maybe he even enjoyed it. After the row about the 'stinking manoeuvre', there was a row about whether he had tried to bargain his party's support for the withdrawal of the army from Hebron in 1997 in exchange for an abandonment of his case by the Attorney-General. At a rally in his defence over this issue Deri reiterated his bitter attacks against secular Zionism: 'Zionism', he said, was an 'offence against God', trying to create an irreligious Jew; nationhood could not be divorced from religion and the Ashkenazi establishment had tried to deprive the Oriental Jews of their Jewishness (Weissbrod, 2003).

Eventually Ovadia Yosef tired of the controversy and removed him from the Presidency of the Party. For Yosef the top priority was to get the party into government in order to pay off the 100 million shekels of debt accumulated by Shas's school system and then enable the movement to continue with its religious mission. It seems that the schools were channelling tax and social security dues into their own expansion, so the need to get into government in order to obtain the funds with which to pay off these debts was a matter of extreme urgency (Bick, 2004). For those whose support for Shas was inspired principally by the persecution of Deri, Sephardi solidarity and demands for social, educational and economic improvement, paying off the debts was not a priority.

After the imprisonment of Deri the Shas leadership concentrated more on religious issues than on an outward-looking strategy that had emphasised sustaining or broadening the party's appeal to the Sephardi population, focusing on their social needs and voicing the rhetoric of ethnic resentment. Deri's successor, Yishay, proclaimed his unwillingness, as Minister of the Interior, to implement a Supreme Court ruling on marriage and as party leader has emphasised almost exclusively religious themes. His associates also seem to have been shifting in a similar direction, for example the Shas Minister of Labour would steer his inspectors to check on Sabbath working rather than abuse of workers' rights. Shas's social demands became inextricably linked to their religious agenda: thus in 2002, during the first Sharon government, the party joined another ultra-Orthodox party to force through a private member's bill (the 'Alter' law) which gave disproportionate family and maternity allowances to families with more than four children—a measure benefiting almost exclusively ultra-Orthodox and Arab families, the latter perhaps to an even greater extent than the former. Later, in the 2002 Budget, the measure was rescinded: Shas left the government, but then, chastened, returned and agreed to conform (Bick, 2004). When he had the chance after the 2003 elections, Sharon swapped Shas for its nemesis Shinui, though eventually in 2005 he swapped Shinui for another ultra-Orthodox party in building a coalition for the Gaza withdrawal.

Yet there are signs on the ground pointing in a different direction: in Petach Tikvah we were shown a series of projects and institutions which bore all the hallmarks of showpieces for a Shas in pursuit of modernity and broad-based recognition: a gym built as part of a school complex with funds allocated during Deri's tenure as Minister of the Interior; an intermediate girls' school whose headmistress was taking it ahead of the Shas average by installing computers—though these had to be funded by parents—and enabling girls to continue studying up to the final secondary school certificate (*bagrut*), at least in Business Studies; projects enabling disabled people, even women, to play basketball. The headmistress of the girls' school in particular demonstrated a strong desire to make her mark on secular society, by accepting an invitation to speak at a seminar in the Hebrew University, and by inviting one of us—as a member of the Hebrew University—to address a prize-giving ceremony. Here the pupils showed their research projects based on non-religious subjects, accompanied by expositions on what scientific research consists of, in front of an audience of parents drawn from both secular and religious families. This is a Shas school, but it aims to attract children from secular families by offering a better quality education than other local schools. We could not but notice the sense of dynamism exuded by her staff, which stood in contrast to the inward-lookingness and defensiveness associated with most *haredi* institutions in Israel. This is, admittedly, an élite school, expressing Shas's modernising and outward-looking tendency, and one of a relatively small number of intermediate schools run by the Shas education network. According to Anat Feldman, a similar school was opened in Jerusalem in 2000 (Feldman, 2001), and in our interview with Deri he stressed his own and his wife's efforts to promote high quality open-minded secondary *haredi* education for Sephardim, but his reflections on the outcome were poignant: she directs two secondary schools with 500 girls and tries her best to raise the standard, but every year girls try to leave for Ashkenazi (Beit Yaakov) schools and the best performers succeed. 'There are many schools for Sephardi girls but "good" Sephardi families don't want to send their girls there.' He and his wife had taken their own daughters out of Beit Yaakov schools, and their son out of an Agudat Yisrael school, to 'give an example', but others did not follow their example: the implication of his remark seemed to be that his daughters had somehow paid a price for this gesture.

This openness to modernity is noticeable also in the Pedagogical Centre established at the Head offices of El HaMa'ayan. It is depicted graphically on the cover of the Centre's textbook for teaching children about *t'shuva*. The book—entitled 'Learning together'—

has a cover with two contrasting pictures: one is a classic black-and-white photo of children in a Cheder or Talmud Torah in Eastern Europe before the Second World War (reminiscent of Roman Vishniac's *A Vanished World*, 1983) with their customary peak-caps and a querulous, slightly intimidated look on their faces, gazing upwards to their teacher, while the other, this time in colour, shows Israeli children sitting around tables dressed in bright colours, using their own books with no teacher in sight. The cover illustration is cleverly designed to contrast a sunny, modern and co-operative teaching approach with the more authoritarian—and also of course more Ashkenazi—approach attributed to the old *shtetl* world of observant Eastern European Jews. This reflects the Pedagogical Centre's educational philosophy which emphasises participation and cooperation more than in the traditional ultra-Orthodox educational system, so as to make school life more attractive. The French-educated person who explained the Centre's philosophy to us used the word *étouffer* (suffocate) to describe traditional yeshiva education; she aspires to disseminate a religion purged of its *vision sectaire*; in place of the traditional approach, which screens yeshiva children from awareness of the outside world in fear of the temptations and risks it brings, she advocates bringing the outside elements into the classroom so as to satisfy their curiosity under the eye of the teacher.

It is often said that parents send their children to Shas schools, especially primary schools, in order that they may become more obedient and remain within the family and off the street. Shas spokespersons, for their part, do not cease to promote their schools as institutions that will restore parental authority in difficult social and economic conditions. But the effect of the philosophy of the Pedagogical Centre, if applied, is somewhat at variance with those expectations, for it recognises the family as having lost its socialising and educational role, which now becomes the school's, replacing the family as the channel of transmission of tradition. This in turn is consistent with a broader pattern observable in contemporary Jewish life and related in this specific context to the large size of *haredi* families, to women's working (while husbands study in *kollelim*) and of course to the *t'shuva* phenomenon: religion as a way of life transmitted increasingly by the book and by institutions, and decreasingly by the family. Indeed, we heard here, as elsewhere, how bringing

children from unobservant or partially religious families enables the
t'shuva message to be transmitted to their parents, stimulated by the
children's insistence, thus inverting the customary inter-generational
transmission of religious practice. Furthermore, conversations with
head teachers in Jerusalem, Bet Shemesh and Petach Tikvah also
confirmed that parents are being brought back to a more observant
life style as a result of sending their children to Shas schools.

Another sphere in which a branch of Shas is trying to engage with
modernity is that of science. At first glance this could appear in
contraposition to what is said in the public sphere. There is a saying
in *haredi* circles that 'it is all in the Gemara' (or Talmud), that 'Ein-
stein, Black Holes, everything' was already foreshadowed in Rabbinic writings. And in the manner of evangelical Christians (or Jews)
citing proven cases of divine healing they quote instances of yeshiva
students who come top in mathematics despite not having studied
in the secular schools. In the words of a young volunteer worker at
the head offices of the Shas education network, 'someone who knows
the Gemara knows everything—he can reason, he has a training
which prepares him for everything.' In support he quoted the example of an employer in the computer industry who, having at first
taken on a *haredi* with some reluctance, eventually began to prefer
haredim as employees, not only for their skills but also because they
have more respect for an employer's property—'they do not use the
phone for personal calls.' In a similar vein, a member of the Jerusalem
City Council said that after studying Maimonides, only a few classes
are required to master mathematics. A rank and file *ba'al t'shuva*
studying in the Or HaChayyim yeshiva stated that the Gemara
already says it is dangerous for pregnant women to smoke—in fact
the foetus makes a movement even when she watches a tobacco
advertisement on television. And Reuven Elbaz, leader of the Or
HaChayyim yeshiva network, writes pamphlets explaining the scientific, medical basis of the regulation of women's sexual activity or
'family purity laws' (Caplan, 2003).

This notion of the universality, and potential modernity, of Rabbinic wisdom has been taken further by the 'Research Institute on
Life-Norms' (Machon mechkar leanagot vechinuch), whose head,
Rav Samgia, Chief Rabbi of the Ramat Shlomo district of Jerusalem
and a person considered close to Ovadia Yosef, aims to renovate

Torah learning in accordance with modern conditions. The idea seems to be a compromise, using modern science to cast light on Rabbinic norms and knowledge, and vice versa, but it responds to what Rav Samgia sees as real problems. Conceptually, he would like to reclassify the sources of Judaism (the Talmud and the Commandments) in modern terms—extracting and repackaging Rabbinic guidance on the environment, for example, or on education, or training social workers in Rabbinics as well as in the workings of the modern welfare state. There is much on these subjects in the Talmud, but it is not classified in modern categories such as psychology or the environment. There is a hint of softening frontiers, and thus of ventures into politically sensitive, and publicly exposed, areas: but Rav Samgia, who wants to differentiate himself from the Rabbis who say 'no' to every conceivable innovation, and who has cultivated contacts with the university, was still obliged to withdraw from an NGO-sponsored inter-community conciliation programme in the face of pressure from a *haredi* newspaper against secularising contacts.

A further rationale for this initiative, as for activities undertaken by Chabad and indeed by all manner of religious organisations worldwide, is a diffuse sense that it can contribute to remedying the ills of the modern world: hedonism, selfishness, promiscuity, compulsive consumption. Rav Samgia would like to turn advertising to the promotion and dissemination of the *haredi* custom of charitable donation, and thus change the image of the *haredi* community. Aware of the difficulty of sustaining a vast society of full-time adult learners, he would like somehow to find a *haredi* economics. He seems to want to develop a modern idea, namely religion as personal or social service, but in that market this quasi-modernised and quasi-professionalised version would have difficulty competing with the more symbolically potent services of exorcists (such as the well known Rav Batzri), or those who propagate the therapeutic virtues of ritual observance, not least Ovadia Yosef himself. But Rav Samgia remains a visionary: he would like to develop a new book of the Shulchan Aruch—the code of Jewish Law written by Joseph Karo, and the pre-eminent source of Halakha—for the modern world; he would like to create a network of religious and secular people to overcome the chasms separating them—for example separating the physician from the kabbalist; he would like to create a new common discourse shared by religious and secular scholars so that the latter can return to religion and to the true sources.

In meeting the challenges of modernity and secularism, Shas leaders must constantly choose between extending their political power and social influence and protecting their religious core, although once they were relegated to the opposition their choices were radically reduced. One illustration of efforts to move this agenda forward was visible at a meeting of the Chairmen of Regional Religious Councils[9] attended by one of us in August 2001. The Rabbis who attended the meeting, mostly linked with Shas, though this was not strictly speaking a party affair, came in many cases to gripe: they wanted more funding, of course, they resented money being paid to Ethiopian immigrants ('there is even a budgetary item for *tefilin* for immigrants!') while they themselves were ignored; one denounced the existence of some localities with no *mohel* (practitioner of circumcisions) while others complained of their low remuneration compared with members of secular municipal and regional councils. But the convenors of the meeting had other ideas: they invited the Director-General of the Ministry of Religious Affairs to explain to the council members how to operate effectively and correctly in their roles. If they wanted resources and projects and more ritual baths (*mikvaot*) they had to learn proper procedure; there should be a separation between *kashrut* inspectors—an activity surrounded by suspicions of corruption—and those whom they inspect; the Chairmen of Religious Councils should not appoint the other members; no more corruption or *protectzia*; internal procedures have to be reviewed; transparency, it was repeatedly stated, must be ensured. And then came the carrot: if they did all these things, then the Ministry of Finance would be more willing to entrust funds to the Councils, whereas at present the tendency was for funds to be denied to the Ministry of Religious Affairs on account of irregularities which had been uncovered even by the Supreme Court. The young Director-General, exuding competence and confidence, was a moderniser, trying to convey the impersonal rules of bureaucratic procedure to Rabbis who wanted only to hear of funds and projects. After the

[9] Religious Councils are appointed by (mostly) religious parties in municipal government to administer personal status law (marriage, divorce, burial), provide public religious facilities such as ritual baths, and administer funds provided by the former Ministry of Religious Affairs for a variety of purposes.

2003 elections, however, these ideas may well be defunct: Shas is out of the government, the Ministry of Religious Affairs has been dissolved and its functions have been redistributed to other Ministries.

These vignettes show that influential people in the Shas movement, with access to resources, are partially aware of the need for a movement with ambitions such as theirs to engage with modernity. They know they need trained cadres and professionals to work in public administration, and indeed they have already managed to place their people in the civil service. So far, however, this is less an intelligentsia than a technical cadre; Shas does not engage in public debate with the scientific and humanistic intelligentsia, and its leaders' remarks about Israeli judges, whatever their political and conjunctural motives, betray a deep distrust of the impersonality of expertise which underlies modern scientific endeavour. Thus the movement denies itself an opportunity to project its message beyond its core religious and Sephardi following. Using its ministerial and institutional power bases for clientelistic and sectarian purposes to benefit the movement's own followers, or to impose the rituals of observance on less willing citizens, has weakened Shas's efforts to bring about its desired reorientation of the whole of Israeli society. This attitude is summed up in the comments of Shas spokesman Yitzhak Suderi during the 2002–3 election campaign, about how he would deal with the challenge of secularist firebrand Tomi Lapid: 'It's enough for us to show the broadcast about non-Jewish immigration to Israel [from the former Soviet Union], the shops selling pork and the churches; and at the end we'll show a horrible picture of Lapid.' (*Ha'aretz*, 9 January 2003). Lapid's militantly secularist party, of course, overtook Shas in the election and replaced its people in the Cabinet. Deri was out of politics, and barely out of jail; his modernising approach and the aspiration to reach out to society as a whole seemed to have lost out.

SHAS AS A POLITICAL CONSTRUCT: THE PROJECT OF ETHNIC RENEWAL

One merit of the project of *t'shuva*, from the protagonists' point of view, is its requirement of little theoretical or even programmatic elaboration. While other movements and parties (except of course the ultra-Orthodox) produce programmatic statements and manifestos, the substantial amount of material published by Shas institutions and by Ovadia Yosef himself, consists of devotional or exegetic texts, or practical advice about the rituals of daily life. The ethnic theme is however implicitly omnipresent; and there is much emphasis on social benefits in the party's day-to-day practice. A prominent member of a Municipal Council, who was regarded as a political figure of some weight, explained to us that his job was to reduce the numbers of Sephardim who depended on welfare programmes, and that the 'Shas revolution'—as it is often called—was to 'raise the abilities of people of Sephardi origin, not just religious people.' Our interviews with David Yosef, Ovadia's son, in 2000, and with Arieh Deri in 2004, placed more explicit emphasis on the Sephardi theme and, indeed, pulled together all the ethnic issues that had otherwise cropped up in scattered conversations.

Yosef began by tracing the grievances of North African Jewry to secularisation in their countries of origin. The Alliance Israélite Universelle's schools, which catered principally to the élite, were neither religious nor Zionist, 'and people were not strong enough to understand that this was not the way.' During the twentieth century Rabbis' influence declined considerably in Iraq and Algeria, to a lesser extent in Morocco and much less in Syria. He then distanced himself from Zionism and seemed to express some nostalgia for the coexistence of Jews and non-Jews in Arab countries, by describing how Zionism produced a 'big hatred' of Jews on the part of Arabs. In this he was sharing the collective memory of other Shasniks, who occasionally even described Muslims to us as religious people with whom they could co-exist more comfortably than with the godless Zionists. He was also reflecting a frequent formula heard among Shas activists, who speak of Zionists as someone else, as 'them'. Thus the same volunteer in the head offices of Shas's Education network who we quoted earlier told us that his ambition was to draw up an alternative history curriculum, drawing in part on the 'new historians' of Zionism (such as Benny Morris; see Morris, 1999) so heavily criticised by right-wing Zionist nationalists, in which he would describe how 'Zionists destabilised the situation of Jews in Arab countries' and how they 'put aside' the culture of the North African Jews when they came to Israel.

Yosef quoted research by the Ministry of Education which showed that more than half of the eighteen year olds in the development towns, which remain predominantly Sephardi, did not have the bagrut—the required qualification for entrance to higher education. Like others, he spoke of how, in their treatment of the arriving immigrants, the Zionists 'stole their self-respect, their Judaism', and thus created a 'social and a religious problem'. Why is it, he asked, that although there are doubtless also some criminals among the descendants of the 300,000 Jewish people from Morocco who went to France, so many of them are doctors, lawyers and the like, while in Israeli prisons 70 or 80 per cent of prisoners are from Morocco, and 95 per cent of inmates are Sephardim? In Israeli universities, he complained, again echoing views we have heard elsewhere, 'there are more Arabs than Sephardim'. And then, to cap it all, they brought the Russians and sent them to live together with the Moroccans in the development towns—as we were able to see in Bet Shemesh. While the Sephardim suffered, the Russians received all the benefits, and then demonstrated their indifference to Judaism by opening pork butcher shops, which are offensive even to non-observant Moroccans. This resentment against 'the Russians' is another leitmotif with its accompanying sense of persecution: some interviewees even claimed that Russian immigration was encouraged *in order* to dilute the Jewish character of Israeli society, since most had lost all contact with their Jewish heritage, many were not Jewish in any sense that Israeli Jews could understand, and, apart from the pork butchers, also built Russian Orthodox churches.

In recalling the founding of Shas, David Yosef spoke of his awakening when he was pursuing his Rabbinic studies with Arieh Deri and they decided 'to make a Revolution'. He realised that even the non-observant among the Sephardi population retained many elements of their religious traditions: they still respected their Rabbis, they still celebrated the principal religious festivals, they had a family and community spirit which the secular people, for example on the kibbutzim, did not have. But they had a 'bitter taste in their mouth', and the two aspiring politicians thought that if they were to teach them, make special clubs for their children for example, they would come again to respect their parents as they used to before coming to Israel.

As a brand new party in 1984 Shas had not qualified for the state funding available to established parties, and had only ten thousand shekels for their campaign publicity. They had precisely ten minutes of TV air time which they used simply to show a picture of a dinner table laid for the Sabbath eve and a Sephardi Rabbi saying 'the problem is keeping the Sabbath and the commandments, that is all.' They persuaded his father to go on the campaign trail[10] and won four seats against Ezer Weizman's three. Weizman, he says contentedly, could not understand how he, with his background as a war hero and a seasoned public figure, did worse than these upstarts.[11] The answer was in Shas's enthusiastic grassroots mobilisation of which the established political parties were no longer capable:[12] in the four years after their first electoral success in 1984 they criss-crossed the country, attending three meetings every night, and formed 300 local Shas 'branches', but they were not branches in the sense of party branches: they were synagogues, ritual baths, clubs for women, for children and for men, and they doubtless owed their existence in part to funds obtained through Shas's participation in government.

Hostility against the secular élite was rekindled when Yosef came to the Deri trial: he said Rabin was against bringing Deri to trial, that Deri was singled out by the newly appointed Public Prosecutor who did not pursue cases against other people for similar offences, that the judges 'hate us', that the media coverage was ferociously hostile, and that the language in the verdict was violent in a manner inappropriate for a courtroom. These views—and they are just views—echo not only those of Shas supporters, but also views frequently heard from members of the secular élite, including some mentioned by David Yosef, who tend to admit that Deri was found guilty of crimes no worse than those of others who have not been prosecuted. These people—generally highly unsympathetic to Shas—readily say that Deri was targeted because his popularity and charisma posed a threat to the political establishment.

These elements summarise well the Shas mental construct as far as the past is concerned, but it was striking that when David Yosef

---

[10] Although he did not mention this, a number of Sephardi religious candidates had stood as independents at the preceding municipal elections as a trial run, and the results encouraged them to proceed with an official list.

[11] Weizman, at the time of the interview, was in the news because he had been forced to resign as President of Israel due to allegations of the improper receipt of $5 million.

[12] See the section on occupying vacant spaces, below.

spoke of the future he did not say very much and he did not use familiar Shas catchphrases. He said the Sephardim need a 'Harvard' to rival the Lithuanians' prestigious yeshivas; he looked forward to making a revolution with women, to reducing their inequality and to preserving the family—remarks which may conceivably have been added to appeal to a visitor from Europe. The mere existence of Shas had already produced far-reaching changes—at a certain point, he proudly said, the media were talking about nothing but Shas. Rather than a vision for Israel his thinking was dominated by pride that this leadership had burst in on the political establishment while at the same time remaining attuned to the culture of an unsophisticated Sephardi public, a public who had not understood his allusion when, in front of the crowd gathered to accompany Deri to prison, he had said 'this is our Bastille day'; and he regretted—at that time, before the renewal of violence in late 2000—that 'our people' were too 'radical' to accept his father's belief that Israel has to give land for peace; but he summed his feelings up by saying that 'we gave people pride… we know their language, we know how to behave to them, how to give respect.'

Despite David Yosef's open-minded and relatively cosmopolitan approach, our account has shown that whereas Shas is able to conciliate with no difficulty the themes of religious and ethnic renewal, it faces greater difficulty in the elaboration of a project which could transform it into a modern social movement, able to engage in meaningful interaction with other sectors of society, on the basis of a common understanding of authority and expertise. One problem for its leaders is, *inter alia*, that their religious culture, rooted in their *haredi* formation, has turned them against these modern forms of intellectual exchange. Much as they sometimes express bitterness against their Ashkenazi mentors in the yeshiva world, after the demise of Deri Shas leaders are far more powerfully moved by resistance to the secular world than by resentments within the *haredi* world.

It may well be that the 2003 elections decided this issue, with the 40 per cent decline in the party's absolute vote (down from 13 per cent to 8 per cent in a declining turnout). The 'burial' of Arieh Deri, both as an individual and as an 'issue', meant the party's propaganda dropped all mention of the injustice of his imprisonment which had been at the heart of their 1999 campaign, but also that the loss of his

charismatic and modernising appeal aimed at the Sephardi population as a whole may have reduced Shas to greater reliance on its religious supporters. The party's increasingly close alignment with the
nationalist right and its increasing emphasis on religious, as opposed
to ethnic and social issues, reduced the distinctiveness of its appeal and
must have led it to lose voters looking for a 'pure play' by voting
either for non-religious parties of the right or for other *haredi* parties.

Finally, the vote was heavily influenced by the abandonment of
the direct popular election of the Prime Minister, which had allowed
people the 'luxury' of voting for their favourite non-Shas Prime
Ministerial candidate while still voting for Shas in the Knesset. The
signs in 2003 seemed to be that Shas was returning to the *haredi* fold
from which its leaders had once emerged at the cost, eventually, of its
wider social agenda.

Deri, in our conversation, framed these issues in terms of self-
respect and self-esteem. His concern was less with the socio-economic advancement of the Sephardim than with their ability to organise.
For him the role of the ultra-Orthodox among the Sephardim was
to act as consciousness-raisers (though he did not use this last term).
But he regretted that in this they were hobbled by an excessive
respect for Ashkenazi institutions which eroded the attempt by him
and others to build equivalent Sephardi ones. Even his own family's
efforts in this respect had been disappointing. The best students, he
said, tended almost without exception, to go off to the prestigious
Ashkenazi yeshivas, leaving the Sephardim without leadership and
above all without pride. And the current Shas leadership had neglected this consciousness-raising aspect of the movement.

THE HISTORIC ACTOR

Supporters' conceptions of Shas

The interviews we have conducted with a variety of people, all committed to Shas and the *t'shuva* movement, reveal a degree of coyness
in talking about Shas as a political phenomenon, even about using
the word. Possibly the coyness was also ours—in order to avoid pro-
voking either a defensiveness, or superficial and ready-made pat
answers, or indeed a reluctance to respond on the part of our interlocutors, we quite often avoided raising Shas explicitly, preferring to

present our work as focused on 'return to religion' and 'ethnic renewal'. Given that our interest is principally in ethnic and religious themes, we sensed it was not worth introducing unnecessary contentiousness at a time when the party was riven by factional disputes and, as always, subject to adverse and disdainful comment in the secular press. Also, many of our interviewees were teachers and as such were supposed to be involved in education, not politics, so certain formalities had to be respected. Of course, we observed how many of these conventions and constraints are honoured in the breach, but that did not dispense us from preserving the formalities.

Both the followers of Shas and its opponents and detractors draw on a battery of ready-made formulae. For Shas followers and activists Shas is cited as giving Israel's Sephardi population a sense of self-confidence, as bringing the Jewish people back to religion and to their traditions, as attending to the problems of the poor and needy, as being in direct touch with the people, and as restoring family values.

The sense of self-confidence is encapsulated in the frequently quoted motto 'return the crown to its ancient glory', and in the names of Shas institutions such as Ha-Ma'ayan—'the source'. The phrase 'Shas has given pride to the Sephardim' is often heard, for example, in the image evoked by a sixty-seven year old Yemeni Jew interviewed in a suburb of Tel-Aviv: 'Shas raised the *keren* (ray of light) of religion; now we can go out with a kippa and pray without shame.' The reference to overcoming a sense of shame is very important, and refers to appearing in public both as an observant person and also as a Sephardi: 'Shas tries to give the Sephardim their home back' (a senior Petach Tikvah political operative); 'The Shas revolution is meant to raise the abilities of the people of Sephardi origin to achieve social progress' (member of the Jerusalem City Council); 'Shas... raised the morale of Sephardim, gave them pride and security when saying "I am a Sephardi".' This person sounded as if he was reproducing Deri's speeches, for Deri himself used very similar language in our interview with him: Shas had enabled Sephardim to do things on their own, its schools 'belong to the grassroots, to people who rose up in society', some of them even joining the political élite of their towns, as in Petach Tikvah: 'if each can feel himself to be the owner of what he does, he can do many things.'

The unstable balance of ethnic and religious themes and revivals is reflected in the words of our interviewees. Those who are drawn to

Shas on account of its religious advocacy may sometimes be uncomfortable with the strong ethnic culture and emphasis among its activists on Sephardi customs as against those of the Ashkenazim: thus observant Sephardim who recognise the prestige of the Ashkenazi yeshiva world and its culture may be embarrassed by 'Sephardi' rulings on obscure matters of, for example, acceptable female dress, or the precise timing and procedure for lighting the Sabbath candles. Also, statements about ethnicity can lend themselves to an interpretation based on a sharper sense of difference or division than the speaker intends. For example, one person who praised Shas for creating an environment where people could pray 'according to their father's song' or 'their mother's Torah'—in the tunes and with the rituals of their own Sephardi traditions—also said almost in the same breath that differences between Ashkenazim and Sephardim should not be 'sharpened'—'there is love; people don't understand.' In other words, the ethnic differences that emphasise an aesthetic or conceivably corporal heritage were acceptable to this person, but not those that divide the Jews by claiming different interpretations of Rabbinic law or wisdom. These sorts of response remind us that outsiders looking for signs of difference and contrasting identity can too easily overestimate the extent to which they reflect felt resentment or friction.

Shas as bodily presence

True to its double identity as a movement and a political party, Shas is described as bringing people back to their customs through its physical presence on the ground rather than by its political or legislative activity in the Parliament and the government. One of our interlocutors spoke of Shas' 'main contribution…in the small and marginal places: they send people who open new roads forward, new contexts and new visions.' Shas's leading figure in Bet-Shemesh, whom we have already encountered as head of a *kollel* where he spends most of his day, even described them as 'in among the people like Moses'. Another member of the same Yemeni family quoted above, a twenty-nine year old air-conditioning technician, twice remarked on Shas's physical presence in the community: 'Shas is the only party we see in the street… Shas does not disappear after elections… There is more "soul" to their work.' Yet, perhaps because of his own Yemeni background, he too expressed a certain discomfort with the Sephardi emphasis, Yemeni customs being quite distinct from the North African and Levantine traditions promoted by Shas. This allusion to a movement which comes to the people and stays close to them crops up repeatedly, even among people who say they do not vote for Shas, and it reflects a sense that Shas is not a party like the others, and even that there is a tension between efficacy as a political party and closeness to the people. Thus a Moroccan lady even expressed her regret that Shas had to use political means to achieve its ends, though she was also glad because Shas had restored 'the very meaning of Israel's existence'.

This physical presence is contrasted with the much less caring methods of other political parties. But there is more, for ritual is inseparable from the body, from physical acts, and if Shas is invoking a tradition of customary religious observance, that means ritual and hence is embodied. The physical presence is not just the presence of people: those activists are dressed in a certain way, they speak in a certain way, they stop to pray and do so in a certain way. Their physical presence in itself, without speeches or indoctrination, evokes memories and associations, notably of parents and grandparents, quite frequently mentioned by our respondents. The physical presence of Likud or Labour activists would not have the same emotional effect.

Shas men wear a *haredi* hat, but it is a Borsalino hat[13] tilted forward—as distinct from the higher hats of Chabad (reminiscent of the Shakers) or the perfectly horizontal style of the Lithuanians. They wear a dark suit, said by some to be dark navy blue, not quite black; double-breasted with wide lapels in imitation of the Armani style. They often wear a black velvet skullcap in public, while other *haredim* tend only to wear the skullcap alone when they are off the street. (Men always wear a skullcap under the hat anyhow.) Shas men also carry themselves differently on the street. The classic Ashkenazi stereotype of a yeshiva *bochur* is that of a somewhat ungainly bespectacled youth[14] with sidelocks blowing in the air as he 'fast-forwards'[15]

---

[13] The most authentic model apparently costs $200.

[14] It is a mystery why such an apparently very high proportion of yeshiva students wear glasses: is it because they grow short-sighted from excessively long hours bent over books, is it genetic, or is it just that their parents and teachers send them to the opticians? We await a statistical study.

[15] This felicitous formulation is owed to Tamar El-Or (El-Or and Neria, 2004).

along the street, squeezing between passers-by, avoiding their gaze and hastening to the next lesson or engagement. Speed is a *mitzvah* for him, for to hang around without studying is *bitul Torah*—an offence against the Torah. His opposite number from Shas is quite different: he does not grow his sidelocks;[16] he walks tall, perhaps because he has usually done military service, especially if he is a *ba'al t'shuva*; he does not adopt the fast-forward gait; his beard is cut to a carefully calculated stubble, rather than left to grow in all and any direction; he looks you in the eye.

Shas women do not dress in quite such a uniform manner, but they are still recognisable, in particular by their headgear. All married *haredi* women cover their hair, at least until they are well into old age, but they do so in different ways. Among the Ashkenazim some shave their heads and wear wigs, others wear wigs and hats, and in some sects they wear nothing except a headscarf tied over the forehead.[17] Sephardi *haredi* women in contrast never shave their heads or wear wigs and have no such tradition—and when the subject has been raised Ovadia Yosef has firmly forbidden such Eastern European practices. They are called upon by Shas, if they wish to be strictly observant, to cover every hair on their heads with a scarf or net, but their hair can be long, allowing the scarf or net to hang down the back of the neck. We attended a women's consciousness-raising group at which a Rabbi's wife explained how to deal with hair in great detail. Sephardi women, if they are observant, seem to be under less pressure to wear dowdy greys and browns, and more readily use bright colours. We attended a Chanukah party with some 1,000 women supporters of Shas and all the singers and actresses who appeared on the stage were dressed in up-to-date modern style. Yaffa Deri, wife of Arieh Deri, always appears very elegantly dressed and is apparently admired for this. Our casual observation is that many of the Shas women also walk differently: they do not seem to exhibit

---

[16] To be precise, sidelocks are not worn by Lithuanians or by Chabad, but they are worn by several Chassidic sects.

[17] Observers unfamiliar with this milieu might be forgiven for concluding that in some sects women do everything in their power to suppress their attractiveness in public, and to exhibit the effects on their bodies of their many pregnancies. To correct the picture, though, attention should be drawn to a new genre, known as *'haredi* chic'.

the accumulated burden of years of pregnancy and child-rearing in the way many of their Ashkenazi opposite numbers do, especially the less well-off among them. That, though, may change as the *t'shuva* process feeds through the generations, and also in the light of the rapid increase in fertility among Sephardi *haredim*.

The body is political in another sense. The often repeated remark that Shas is the only party that does not disappear between election campaigns reflects grassroots activism as well, doubtless, as the party's access to resources when it controlled several major spending Ministries. These resources could be distributed along clientelistic lines, and Shas supporters often speak in quite unabashed terms of the party's clientelism, describing its task in government, especially local government, as looking after individual cases, rather than in terms of developing a policy on an issue. One feature which distinguishes clientelism from more impersonal ways of allocating resources is that it involves personal contact. Shas has used its leverage in such a way as to project itself into the everyday life of the Sephardi *haredim* and the *ba'alei t'shuva*: whereas other parties might promote a policy and leave it to the bureaucracy to implement, the institutions promoted by Shas—the educational network, Or HaChayyim's yeshivas, housing associations, the network of clubs and other activities organised for adults—are implemented by Shas loyalists, sometimes working for free as volunteers. So this is no ordinary state bureaucracy, it is an army of the committed, and many supporters clearly value that commitment and gain a sense of their own worth as persons. Consequently, they feel treated like individuals, not impersonally as 'mere' citizens.

Shas in the eyes of others

Being aware of attitudes towards Shas among other sections of opinion, especially secular Israelis, is valuable, though it is not a subject on which we have gathered information intensively. For many of them Shas has come to represent, variously, an expression of the gullibility of the ignorant, or of the aggressiveness of the ultra-Orthodox, while others, more patrician perhaps, see Shas as a wake-up call for a deserved and overdue correction to social injustices inflicted on the Sephardi population.

Listening to and reading the opinions of members of those secular
élite generations who were the moving force in founding and leading the state, until the election of Begin in 1977, gives the impression that they see in Shas a social, cultural and political threat. They
are usually excellent English speakers and attuned to modern liberal
cosmopolitan values. Although mostly non-practising, or at least
non-Orthodox, they often have a religious erudition as part of their
general Jewish culture, or handed down from their more learned and
observant European forebears. Sometimes they speak as if the country had been stolen from them by Shas,[18] also as people who still
'know best'. For them Shas is led by very clever people—especially
Arieh Deri—but they mock the learning of Ovadia Yosef, and portray Shas followers and activists as ignorant, ill-educated and uncul-
tured, and as superstitious practitioners of quasi-magical religion. Thus
a prominent journalist assured us that if Shas lost the support of the
'Kedourie' wing—with its amulets and kabbalistic legitimacy—it
would suffer significantly. In the event, and although both things did
happen in the 2003 election, the electoral performance of the Kedourie supporters, who ran an independent list, was negligible. Among
this cosmopolitan establishment—albeit one which has lost much of
its influence—the stereotype of Shas's leaders as money-grabbing
and corrupt is accompanied by a sense of unease at Deri's conviction,
for they say quite often that the Shas leadership is no more culpable
than other Israeli politicians, from whom they learnt their tricks.

This reaction is further reflected in a series of interviews with
prominent Israeli intellectuals conducted in 1999 by Guila Flint and
Bila Sorj (2000), exploring intellectuals' opinions about the place of
the religious and the secular in Israel. The secular figures among
them—the liberal politician Yael Dayan, the writer Haim Beer, the
sociologist Shlomo Swirsky—tend to regard Shas as a party that has
succeeded by playing the political game skilfully, but not as an agenda-
setter or as the reflection of broad social or cultural changes; stated
more curtly, they see that it has provided schooling which satisfies
the needs of a marginalised section of the population by providing
hot meals and long school days, and that it has given a renewed sense

---

[18] Note that this is said not of the rise of the extreme right—i.e. the settlers'
movements—but of the rise of Shas, whose first big electoral gains were a shock
even to experienced pollsters. It used to be said also of Begin's 1977 victory,
which owed much to Sephardi votes.

of pride, or identity, to the Sephardi population. Both the secular and the more religious interviewees readily recognise, if asked, the insensitive treatment of the Sephardi immigrants to Israel at the hands of the secular European élite, and see Shas as a response to that mal-treatment—and even secular interviewees say that they deserve the attacks they receive from Shas. Not that they take seriously either the *t'shuva* movement or the possible significance of Shas in reshaping Israeli Judaism, or Israeli Jewish ultra-Orthodoxy: the distinguished modern Rabbinical scholar Moshe Halbertal is dismissive of the idea that religion inspires Shas's following to anything approaching the same extent as social concerns. In his view the success of Shas has occurred because other parties or organisations, such as the Histadrut, the central trade union organisation, abandoned the field and left the Sephardim as an available electoral following for whoever would satisfy their social needs or resentments. These modern intellectuals, both religiously observant and secular, regard Shas as a political group filling an empty space, but not as a social movement, and they interpret its rise largely in material terms. Only one, using the term 'social revolution', grasped the profundity of the phenomenon, but even she, by using the term 'social', seemed to believe the issue could be dealt with by appropriate social policies, thus minimising its broader cultural and religious significance.

A long article by Neri Livneh entitled 'The party they love to hate' in *Ha'aretz* (28 August 2000) reported in detail on anti-Shas moods and moves among Israeli intellectuals. The language of the interviewees was often intemperate, occasionally violent and almost invariably angry—though it should be read with the awareness that Israeli political discourse is on average more direct than that prevalent in Europe or the United States. The emphasis was on Shas's religious intolerance and its racism, although one or two people tried to distinguish Shas's religious partisanship from its role as bearer of the social grievances of an excluded Sephardi population. The historian Meron Benvenisti, in an emotional self-caricature, characterised one standard attitude of the country's intellectual élite: 'We belong to the old Ashkenazi élite, even though I am a Sephardi. These new people have arrived and become the majority, and they are stealing what was ours … I have been living in a bubble since 1977, since the "upset" which displaced us from being "we, the chosen" and "we brought" and "we did" and we, and we and we.' Elsewhere the article quotes people accusing Shas of being racist and fascist, its leadership of being *nouveau riche*, corrupt, ostentatious, anti-democratic, shameless and nepotistic, even an 'ignorant cynical gang', and the secular opponents of Shas of spinelessness, fear, 'bubblism' and impotence. Amidst this torrent, the anthropologist Tamar El-Or tried to take her distance, explaining the inauthenticity of then Prime Minister Barak's attempt to use Shas to bolster his coalition: in her view he thought he could treat them with contempt and turn them to his own purposes and he was proved seriously mistaken. For when he set about building a coalition after his electoral victory in 1999 Barak had ignored his supporters' shouts of 'Anyone but Shas, anyone but Shas', presumably because he thought he could use Shas's support at little cost. In fact, of course, they extracted a very high price, especially in budgetary terms.

These issues were even more prominent in the 2003 election when Shinui raised its Knesset representation from six to fifteen and replaced Shas in the governing coalition. This party is viewed by many commentators as a one-issue secularist party whose leader, former TV personality Tomi Lapid, has built his reputation almost exclusively by campaigning against the imposition of religious norms and the multiplication of privileges for the *haredi* population. Having assured the public that it would not join a coalition with any ultra-Orthodox parties, Shinui's position shifted when in 2004 it looked as if some such Ashkenazi ultra-Orthodox parties might join to replace dissident Likud Ministers. Shinui still continued to veto Shas, however, leading Shasniks and others to accuse Lapid and his followers of racial prejudice against them.

Other sections—or perhaps other generations—of the intelligentsia, though extremely sensitive to the social grievances which Shas reflects, still remain ambivalent. Recent academic papers on the treatment of Shas in the press illustrate admirably—and in some ways subconsciously—the contradictory impulses provoked by Shas's political success. The authors of both papers, one on articles appearing in *Ha'aretz* between 1994 and 1999 (Helman and Levy, 2001), the other on articles appearing in the more popular *Yediot Aharonot* in the six months leading to the 1999 elections (Lefkowitz, 2001) express no sympathy with Shas's religious agenda, but are incensed by the patronising treatment of the party in the country's press.

Ha'aretz is shown to criticise and patronise Shas in a variety of ways: Ovadia Yosef is presented in its pages as a 'sorcerer' and 'magician' and his followers ridiculed for their superstition and faith in amulets and the like. The party is compared to the Iranian ayatollahs, who also were pioneers in the use of cassette tapes for propaganda purposes (see Chapter 6). The newspaper lumps all Sephardim into a single cultural category, and conjures up an implicitly ethnocentric Israeliness which the children of Shas will not fit into because of their *haredi* education. *Ha'aretz* sees Shas as a departure from this Israeliness, transforming its character through education programmes and symbolising this shift by taking over buildings previously used by Israel's founding secular institutions such as Histadrut. An underlying irony to this indignant polemic is that the authors take the post-modern view that Israeliness is itself a fiction or a construct imposed by a hegemonic élite. *Yediot Aharonot* is accused of labelling the Mizrahim as 'quintessentially Other, as criminal, violent and emotional, and as poverty-stricken and backward', as 'hypocritical, corrupt and backward', even 'primitive'.

So much for the secularised middle classes and the intelligentsia— but what of the ultra-Orthodox world? Although, as with secular opinions, we did not actively seek out views of Shas in other sectors of the *haredi* world, it did come up in a separate inquiry when we met the *mashgiach* (roughly: 'Senior Tutor') of the yeshiva Yekiri Yerushalayim. This is a distinctive institution because although all its students are Sephardi, it does not use Sephardi music or prayer customs and identifies one hundred per cent with the Lithuanian tradition, revealing a separate, hidden Sephardi ultra-Orthodox world from which Shas is absent. In other words, it is a Sephardi institution ethnically but not in any sense politically. And the word 'politically' is apt here because the *mashgiach*, when he heard we had been working on Shas, delivered a furious tirade against Shas and especially against Rabbinic office-holders in the pay of the state—not because he was against the state but because of his contempt for their ignorance and opportunism. 'They are worse', he said, 'than Tomi Lapid [leader of Shinui] because they use the Torah falsely for nonreligious ends', by which he meant to earn money or gain some personal advantage. 'Maybe they have more influence in society', he admitted, but even the most famous, within themselves 'know the difference' between their world and their worth, and the world of the yeshiva which is devoted to the 'highest, purest qualities of the Torah'. Shas for him was a purely political phenomenon, and he found it distasteful in the extreme.

These vignettes illustrate the range of responses evoked by Shas among the cultural élite and, indirectly, the press. However, the account of *Ha'aretz*'s representation of Shas is tendentious, and reflects the influence of certain intellectual fashions in international and Israeli social science. During this research we have followed *Ha'aretz* on an almost daily basis and although opinion pieces may be very hostile to Shas, they are clearly demarcated from reportage, while analysis and opinion, though occasionally ironic or patronising, are never virulent. Overall, popular response to Shas outside its sphere of influence remains largely undocumented, while the élite response is marked by varying combinations of guilt, fear and disdain, as the above paragraphs show.

Ethnic disadvantage, mobilisation and voting

One version of the birth of Shas was recounted to us in September 2000 by a thirty-four year old man who was working in the head offices of the Shas education network. He recalled that when he was still a teenager there had been various Sephardi Talmudei Tora (schools for young children concentrating exclusively on religious study), but these were totally dependent on Agudat Yisrael, the dominant Ashkenazi ultra-Orthodox party, whose leading political (as distinct from religious) figure had been Moshe Porush and was now his son Menachem. Porush had denied the Sephardi institutions what they regarded as a fair share of the extra resources which had flowed to the *haredi* community after they joined the Begin government in 1977. The heads of these institutions were jacks-of-all-trades who had to act simultaneously as school heads, janitors and night watchmen and were always short of cash. Eventually they called for advice from Meir Ze'ev, an experienced political infighter who was then Deputy Mayor of Jerusalem, and later became a Shas Member of the Knesset. The action which resulted was in effect the rubbishing of a Porush campaign meeting at a school in the Boukharim neighbourhood where all the leading Sephardi Rabbis had studied under Porush's father. When Porush spoke he reminded them 'all you have you owe to me', whereupon one after another various yeshiva Heads stood up and complained about unanswered letters, unsatisfied needs and so on, and Porush became more and more flustered until the audience all produced Shas posters from under their seats. In the end, Porush called the police who helped him escape in a jeep! Porush, we may recall, was also unpopular with Rav Schach, and the story recounted here should be seen against the background of our previous account of the Rav's manoeuvres against Porush. The Shasniks may have been pawns in a mysterious game, but in the end they did well out of it.

Another leading theme of Shas's collective autobiography is the severity of the social problems which have affected the Sephardi population since the 1950s: poor social services, high youth unemployment and (reportedly) drug use, against a background of discrimination and resentment. In 1973 the Sephardim accounted for 51 per cent of the population but for only 10 per cent of the MKs. Five MKs were elected on a Sephardi list in 1949 and two in 1951 (Peres, 1977). In the late 1960s several grassroots movements had emerged among Sephardi youth in Jerusalem, of which the 'Black Panthers' were the most famous, though others, such as the Ohalim, were equally important. Their leaders were largely 'unattached and delinquent' and had not done military service (Cohen, 1972; Sasson, 1993). Some of their followers had scarcely had any education even in Israel, and 40 per cent of those (excluding those in military service) aged 18–26 were not even looking for work. Their action was a shock, accentuated by the introduction for the first time of the language of class conflict into Israeli Jewish life, as the Panthers described relations between the Ashkenazi establishment and the Sephardim as exploitative. They sometimes adopted a 'social bandit' style, distributing the fruits of supermarket raids among the often embarrassed poor. The establishment of course reacted badly, though Golda Meir seems to have been more the aggrieved mother figure, calling them 'disagreeable' (Berenstein, 1979). While some explain the movement in terms of growing social inequalities between Ashkenazim and Sephardim, accentuated by the entry of Palestinians into the Israeli labour market after the 1967 war (Grinberg, 1991), others attribute it to a small social group whose ethnic identity and common class position had been shaped by government housing

policies. The state, using wide-ranging powers over physical planning, had determined both the crowded housing conditions of the
Sephardi families and also the gentrification of adjacent non-Sephardi
neighbourhoods (Sasson, 1993): their apartments were small and
they could not afford to buy them, so they remained dependent on
the state for support. The Panther leaders, who were supported by
some academics and left wing activists, made a bid for a role in
national politics, gaining one Knesset member for one parliament,
though some of them were co-opted and became MKs for other
parties (Berenstein, 1979). The 'Ohalim' focused more on grassroots
action and participation in urban renewal. They criticised the channelling of resources to West Bank settlers at the expense of the urban
poor already in 1979, and tried to 'do a Gush Emunim' (i.e. a land
seizure) in the city (Sasson, 1993: 75).

By 1977 the national Sephardi vote had shifted enough from
Labour to the right to give Menachem Begin an electoral victory. In
the Black Panthers' neighbourhoods, significantly for our subject, a
local election in 1982 brought a resounding victory to traditionalists
as against leftists, but to traditionalists with local roots and grassroots
organisation (*ibid.*: 107), foreshadowing the view of contemporary
Shasniks, that the failure of the Black Panthers was due to their secularism, which overlooked the traditional respect of religion among
their potential followers. In the early 1980s a renewed effort at
Sephardi political mobilisation got under way, in the shape of Tami, a
breakaway from the National Religious Party led by the son of the
revered Abuhatzeira, which achieved three Knesset seats in the 1981
elections but fell to one in 1984 (Shokeid, 1998). Finally, Shas was
formed under the leadership of Ovadia Yosef and Arieh Deri, gaining four seats on the Jerusalem Council in 1983 and first entering
the Knesset in 1984.

Despite Shas's subsequent electoral success, there is little sign that
Israel's Sephardi population in general has improved its position
since the 1970s. Although it is not easy to construct direct and sensitive indicators of Sephardi deprivation, not least because of high
rates of intermarriage between Israelis of differing origin, the uniform pattern of indirect indicators which all point in the same
direction provides ample evidence that Sephardim, especially those
from Morocco (who are the largest single group) have been left

behind in Israel's economic development, though not as far behind as the Arab population. We have already seen data for the immediate post-immigration period, but still in 1998 households in which the head's father was born in Asia or Africa (as opposed to Israel, Europe or North America) lived in relatively more cramped conditions, measured in terms of persons per room (Statistical Yearbook 1999, Table 11.14). Table 12.15 of the same Yearbook shows consistent under-representation of persons whose father was born in Asia and Africa among academics, professionals and managers, and over-representation among unskilled workers. Among students and applicants to universities they were also under-represented, though once admitted Sephardim performed as well as other groups.

Among the Sephardim, Middle Eastern Jews seem to have been at a smaller disadvantage than those from North Africa (Shafir and Peled, 2002: 78–81). They arrived (mostly from Iraq and Iran) in the early 1950s and were settled in areas in the centre of the country where property rose in value. North Africans came later, after the Sinai War in the late 1950s and early 1960s, and were sent to development towns, though we have also seen that substantial numbers went to outlying areas of Jerusalem at a time, before the Six-Day War, when Jerusalem was itself somewhat marginal. The concentration of Sephardim, and especially of Sephardim of North African origin, in the development towns, until the large-scale Russian immigration of the late 1980s and early 1990s, was extremely heavy: 75 per cent of their population was Sephardi, and they accounted for one quarter to one third of the country's Sephardi Jews. In 1987 these localities stood 'below 70 per cent of the entire population' on a socio-economic index calculated by the Central Bureau of Statistics; in 1983, 53 per cent of their workforce was in 'traditional' low-paying industries, e.g. 27 per cent in textiles. College graduates were only 10 per cent of their population, compared to the national average of 14 per cent, and 63 per cent were without high-school diplomas compared with the national average of 56 per cent (*ibid.*: 81). The development towns accounted for 40 per cent of the country's unemployed in 1987, and in 1989 their rate of unemployment was double the national average. However, there is one indicator that by the late 1990s things had improved slightly, since in 1998 their average income was 83 per cent of the national average, which seems better, even allowing for the different measure, than the 1987 finding on socio-economic status.

The data are ecological and, as has already been said, the classifications are necessarily crude. The development towns are only proxies for the Sephardim, and the quasi-ethnic categories conceal, most obviously, differences between people of Middle Eastern, North African and Yemeni origin. Yet denying the indications of inequality is hard, because they all point in the same direction and they are particularly pronounced in the professional categories and in university admission (although David Yosef's statement that 'there are more Arabs in the university than Sephardim', presumably intended as hyperbole, is not correct).

In considering Shas's electorate it must be recalled that even at the height of its success the party has only received the support of a minority of Israel's Sephardi population. The right-wing Likud party received above average Sephardi support in the 1970s and 1980s, summoning up resentment against the Labour-Zionist élite whose 'left wing' parties had previously been considered the 'owners' of the Sephardi vote, harvested through their control of the immigration and absorption process. But this Sephardi support for Likud waned, perhaps because Likud adopted severe neo-liberal and stabilisation policies, and Doron and Kook (1999) have shown how there was a clear switch of votes from Likud to Shas in the 1990s. Shas gained six Knesset seats in 1992 and nine in 1996, when it became the third largest party in the Knesset. In 1999, fuelled by the anger at Deri's conviction, Shas caused a major shock by winning seventeen seats. During this period, the party has been in government from 1984 to 1992 and again under Netanyahu, Barak and Sharon, variously occupying key spending Ministries, namely Interior, Social Welfare, Health, Labour and Religious Affairs. The party's success was attributable in no small part to a change in the election system: Netanyahu and Barak, and Sharon in his first government, were elected under a separate direct vote for Prime Minister, which enabled Shas sympathisers to vote for the party for the Knesset without 'wasting' their say in the Prime Ministerial election. The decline to a perhaps more 'normal' eleven seats (out of 120) in 2003 still leaves Shas as the fourth largest party, and certainly the leading *haredi* political force, as well as representing a strong long-term advance since the party's arrival in 1984.

Shas's vote is, unsurprisingly, heavily ethnic. Doron and Kook (1999) demonstrate that however much the Shas leadership may emphasise religious themes and *t'shuva*, and however much that may be the main objective of Ovadia Yosef and his close associates, it was the ethnic rather than the religious appeal that accounted for most of Shas's electoral growth between 1992 and 1996. Just as Shalev and Kis, with a more elaborate statistical analysis, would show for the 1999 elections. Herrman and Yar's compilation of opinion poll data in the 1994–9 period shows that Mizrachi (i.e. Sephardi) voters, who accounted for 38 per cent of voters in general, provided three quarters of Shas votes (Herrman and Yar, 2001). An analysis of the Sephardi vote subdivided by region, separating people whose origins lay in North Africa from those who had come from the Middle East and Persia, might if possible, have cast further light on the ethnic identity of Shas voters.

However, even the ethnic vote is sensitive to socio-economic factors. Shalev and Kis show that 'Mizrachim' vote for Shas strongly in poorer districts, but their support collapses in richer ones (Shalev and Kis, 1999: 78), whereas the party's few Ashkenazi supporters show religious/ideological commitment by maintaining their proportion irrespective of income factors. Shas, then, appeals to poor Sephardi voters, but seems to have difficulty holding on to them as they climb the socio-economic ladder. In other words 'the vote in Mizrachi areas was substantially more sensitive to class differences' (*ibid.*: 82). Herrman and Yar likewise find that half of Shas voters fall below the average income level, compared with 28 per cent of all voters, and that voters with incomplete secondary schooling are far more numerous among Shas voters (22.6 per cent) than among voters as a whole (14.9 per cent).[19] Not that Mizrachim move to the left as they move up the social scale: a graph in Shalev and Kis (1999: 78) shows only Ashkenazi support for the heavily secular and pro-Peace party Meretz jumping significantly in wealthier districts, while the Sephardi vote is much more resistant to that trend: if prosperity

---

[19] The Herrman and Yar data are from a series of telephone polls conducted with successive samples of 500 people by the Tami Steinmatz Centre for Peace Studies during the 1994–9 period. Shalev and Kis use real election returns (hence the ecological analysis) by district, and socio-economic indicators taken from government statistical sources.

shifts Sephardi voters it is in the direction of Likud or other right wing parties.

Herrman and Yar also find that exactly one third of the Shas vote is contributed by *haredi* voters, and only 8 per cent by people described as secular (*hilonim*). The highly significant remainder are 'practising Jews' (*datiim*) and 'traditionalists' (*masoratim*) who are respectful of tradition but not necessarily observant, and certainly not strictly so, and this confirms our previous claim that these are the key to Shas's difference *vis-à-vis* the other *haredi* parties.

It is important to note that the Shas leadership did not try to mobilise those 'intermediate' votes by softening their stance on religious matters. The earlier experience of Tami, and even the Jerusalem mobilisations of the 1970s, had already shown—though they may or may not have been influenced by it—that to address a wider audience successfully, especially perhaps in the formative period of a movement, does not necessarily imply adopting a softer stance. Whereas Tami had preached tolerance of the less Orthodox and also recalled the peaceful coexistence between Jews and Muslims in North Africa, Shas has had much more success by calling for strict observance in a style which owes little to the North African tradition, by attacking the secularism of the state, and by ignoring, at least in public, a narrative of Jewish-Muslim co-existence in their countries of origin which would hardly find a favourable reception in their instinctively right-wing constituency.

The impact of these qualitative, symbolic and allusive elements in political discourse is hard to interpret, and the studies we have mentioned on Shas in the media are not extensive or profound enough to answer these questions. For example, Ashkenazi religious parties undertake part of their campaigning away from television, inside the tightly knit networks of the *haredi* and *t'shuva* community, where turnout routinely reaches almost 100 per cent even in local elections: we do not know whether, outside these boundaries, their ethnic image would have an effect parallel to that of Shas, given the apparent similarity of content.

To say, with Doron and Kook, that after the Oslo agreements of 1992 the Israeli Jewish population turned away from peace and war to issues of identity, may appear simplistic as an explanation of the success of Shas in the 1990s, but it is consistent with the decline in the Shas vote in 2003, when those issues were once again at the forefront of people's minds. This drew people away from Shas and back to Likud, evidently, but the underlying tendency, whereby Shas attracts a heavily Mizrachi vote but has difficulty in holding on to the vote of the better off or less poor Mizrachim, remains (Shalev and Levy, 2003).

Pronouncements made by Shas leaders in the party's early stages seem to have touched little on ethnicity and overwhelmingly on religious observance. The party's stated objectives were: 'to create educational institutions and *haredi* cultural institutions; to provide an umbrella for educational institutions; to create and manage organisations in support of those in need; to publish and distribute books by "our Rabbis", as well as pamphlets and Torah news; to draw up lists of candidates for local councils and the Knesset; [and] to create a Council of Torah sages to govern kashrut and financial issues' (Feldman, 2001: 55). The words '*eda*' (ethnic group) or 'Sephardi' do not appear; and although the Sephardi theme was mentioned in Jerusalem's 1983 local election campaign, the main demands continued to be *mikvaot*, synagogues, religious schools and local Rabbinic appointments (*ibid.*: 55). The Sephardi theme was present, without a doubt; but it was present by allusion: in the physiognomy of the activists, in their accents, in their style of prayer—in short, in the atmosphere surrounding them.

After the success in those elections, though, when the inexperienced yeshiva boys found that they had a much wider audience among the population of Middle Eastern and above all North African origin, things changed, as we have shown in our account of Deri. In a television advertisement right at the end of the 1999 campaign, Deri, framed by posters of Rav Ovadia and Rav Kedourie, attacked the 'secular left' for currying favour with the Russian vote, which of course is also highly secular, and spoke of their enmity 'against all that we brought with us from the diaspora, against our spiritual inheritance'. He described Shas as 'the only party which belongs to the common people... Shas, a strengthened Sephardi Judaism, is the real answer to the secular left' (Bick 2004).

Here Deri pulls together all the strands: religion, class resentment, and ethnicity—but note the reference to the Russians. This arose, according to Bick, from fierce rivalry which had polarised the depressed development towns, whose large Sephardi populations now encountered competition from newly arrived Russian immigrants (Bick, 2004). As a result, Shas's voting increase in the development towns in 1999, which was quite disproportionately large, may have owed much to local reasons relating to labour market conditions and pressures on social services.

Shas and the other ultra-Orthodox parties also did themselves no good when, in 2002, they obtained approval of the 'Alter' law, which favoured the *haredi* community so egregiously. The possibly con-sequent overtaking in 2003 of the Shas vote by the hyper-secularist Shinui party, whose leader Tomi Lapid has said things about Sephardim and about *haredim* which in some countries would merit him a conviction for racial incitement, may be a kind of mirroring of Shas's 1999 overshooting. Perhaps local elections reflect more accu-rately the party's implantation in civil society, for Shas's performance in local elections later in 2003 shows that the party was able to preserve previous gains: in the cities they now have 132 representa-tives, of whom thirty-two are Vice-Mayors, one of them in Jerusalem. Outside the cities, Shas candidates stood in eighty-nine localities and achieved representation in almost all of them, reaching a total of 156 seats, representing only a four seat decline with respect to 1998.

5

SHAS'S PENETRATION OF STATE AND CIVIL SOCIETY

MECHANISMS OF REPRODUCTION

Shas's involvement in institutional structures

Many of Shas's aims are in the same institutional spheres as those mentioned in the context of other religious movements: to change family life; to change the institution of marriage by restricting as much as possible those not authorised or recognised by ultra-Orthodox Rabbis; to promote its own brand of education. In addition, Shas has tried to change the actual mode of operation of major institutions, especially education, but also local government, by placing rabbis or people close to them in key positions, and by openly using religious criteria in public decision-making: for example, the Petach Tikvah town council allocates different apartment blocks to observant and secular people. These tactics are new for ultra-Orthodox parties in Israel, where traditional *haredi* parties (Agudat Yisrael in particular) confine themselves to pressure group politics, extracting resources and then applying them within their own communities. Shas's disarming partiality would not be unusual in Israel's system of enclaves, save for the open application of religious criteria which is shocking even to many Israeli observers.

While it had a seat in the Cabinet, Shas was able to steer the institutions under its control in favour of more orthodox positions—as in examples we have seen relating to the Ministries of the Interior and Labour. The party also used its position in government to strengthen the presence of the ultra-Orthodox 'on the ground' and in the built environment, most notably through its education network and, for example, by building or expanding neighbourhoods catering to the ultra-Orthodox, and, in accordance with a repeatedly stated objective, by building baths (*mikvaot*) where observant women can perform their monthly bathing ritual.

Like the *haredim* in general Shas sponsors and promotes building activities and housing policies that change the physical appearance of Israel's urban panorama. Shas and the *haredim* refashion localities with their concentrated physical presence, their uniform style of dress and their induced demographic growth. Although the streets of Jerusalem's old religious quarter teem with activity, in more recently established *haredi* areas there are no cafés, clothes shops are invisible from the street and houses have no TV antennas. Ever-increasing numbers of *kollelim* scatter throughout the country, often housed in air raid shelters and other 'temporary' premises, sometimes in synagogue annexes.

In addition to its educational network, the component parts of Shas's network include synagogues and local Chief Rabbis, Or Hachayyim's yeshivas and other educational ventures, a medical insurance scheme, various yeshivas identified with Sephardi customs and the 400 women's *chugim*. But the most important core mechanism of reproduction for the development of Shas and the spread of its message is, of course, education.

The Shas education system (HaMa'ayan)

The Shas education network was created in 1986 and received *ad hoc* state funding from about 1988. This allocation was institutionalised when Deri led the party into the Rabin government in 1992 and negotiated regular annual funding. One effect of Shas's presence in the government was that sums allocated from the budget were released in good time; when the party left government in 2003 there were almost immediately delays in the release of these funds (*Ha'aretz*, 31 March 2003). Statements about the number of schools and students in the HaMa'ayan network are always vague, not least because the numbers form the basis of its funding and are therefore provided by one or another interested party. For example, according to Arieh Dayan (1999), during the Rabin government the network had 40,000 pupils and 3,000 workers, and an informant at the HaMa'ayan HQ in 2000 told us that they had 550 kindergartens, 100 primary schools and 3 girls' high schools. The most official figures we could obtain, provided by the Department for Unofficial State-funded Education (or Office of Recognised Unofficial Education) in the Ministry of Education, showed 13,934 pupils in Shas primary schools (i.e. excluding kindergartens) in 2000, rising to 14,899 in 2001 and 15,896 in 2002, well short of the standard figure, used in reports at the time, of some 27,000. Ministry of Education officials in addition estimated that the kindergartens would account for a further 9,000–10,000, but not for all the discrepancy between the sets of figures. The figure given by the Adva report (Swirski, 1998) for 1998 is 83 institutions with 1,700 teachers and 10,600 pupils, which is also consistent with the pattern of growth indicated by the other sources. Though the Shas school pupil numbers have grown from nothing in fifteen years, they are still not large compared to the numbers in the *haredi* education sector overall, which were about 130,000 in 2003 (Tessler, 2003) having been only 48,000 in 1990—a growth of 70 per cent—and that is without counting a further 31,000 post-secondary yeshiva students aged seventeen and over. According to the Adva report, funding of *haredi* education multiplied by a factor of 6.3 between 1980 and 1999 while, as we see, pupil numbers grew by a factor of 4—double that of the secular state system. Shas did particularly well, according to Tessler, in increasing its school payroll, multiplying the number of teachers by three and raising the budget by 53 per cent, while pupil numbers apparently grew by 43 per cent. Yossi Sarid, former Minister of Education who had had difficult relations with Shas, observed in our interview that Shas's pupil numbers are not large, especially when compared with the 430,000 votes they received in 1999 and the 258,000 they received in 2003. But the numbers have not stopped growing: an overall assessment based on government statistics shows that in elementary schools the share of ultra-Orthodox children rose from 7.6 per cent to 23.6 per cent in the fifteen years up to 2001, due to 'high birth rate..., the huge growth of the Shas educational network...and the establishment of schools for the newly religious', so that in the school year beginning in the autumn of 2004 'one out of every four Jewish students will be ultra-Orthodox' in elementary education (*Ha'aretz*, 26 August 2004). Since Sephardi ultra-Orthodox now make a major contribution to the high birth rate, and since schools for the newly religious are likely to be in some way the fruit of Shas-related campaigning, this shows the party's continuing and growing social and cultural influence whatever its electoral fortunes.

The disproportionate number of kindergartens and kindergarten pupils indicates that about half of the children are removed from the Shas system after kindergarten. Also, when taken in conjunction with the claim that Shas ran 550 kindergartens, it would seem that the average size of a kindergarten is less than twenty children, which is the same as the estimate given by officials in the Ministry. This number is obviously notional, but it is very small, and reflects the dual role of the teachers who may themselves be mothers with large numbers of children, and the children in their care may very well often be their own or their close kin's children. In short, the kindergarten is an amalgam of family and communal responsibilities, enabling the mothers/teachers to earn a small wage while overseeing their children. This nexus is accentuated by the observation from Ministry officials that, unlike those belonging to the state system, Shas kindergartens are often located in rented apartments, which may also mean space rented in private apartments belonging to members of the Shas following, or even to the teachers/mothers themselves. (Note that in Israel free kindergarten places are provided for all pre-school children.)

During the Barak and the first Sharon governments, Shas politicians, using their parliamentary and ministerial leverage to the full, have successfully argued that they cater to an underprivileged and neglected, even discriminated, sector which needs and deserves more. At least until 2003 they obtained more funding per pupil than other types of school and the highest discretionary allocations for 'extra hours': the value of these per pupil is NIS1.3[1] for Arab schools, NIS1.4 for secular state schools, NIS1.6 for Ashkenazi *haredi* schools rising to NIS2.2 for Shas schools. These were called 'political hours' by officials, because since the Director General of HaMa'ayan provides no basis on which they are allocated, it is assumed they are done so according to political convenience of some sort. It is recognised that the Shas schoolday is longer than in the state secular schools, and this makes Shas schools attractive for working mothers in particular. In Bet Shemesh the Shas schools kept children till 4.00 p.m., the state secular schools till 1.00 p.m., and the National Religious

---

[1] 'New Israeli Shekels', the standard abbreviation for the shekel.

schools recently extended their day by two and a half hours to 3.30 p.m. three days a week with 'enrichment' activities—in response, according to a teacher, to the competition represented by Shas. According to Tessler (Tessler, 2001), Shas's budget growth for its schools and kindergartens outpaced the growth of pupil numbers, enabling the network to fund these extended activities. So in 2001 the Shas network was obtaining almost twice the funding for current (non-capital) expenditure per pupil allocated to state schools: the coefficients applicable were 1.3 to state schools, 1.5 to the Agudat Yisrael schools and 2.4 to the Shas schools. Tessler remarks, however, that the trend is volatile, with no consistent annual pattern of growth, and this may have just been an exceptional year. The network's need to raise resources is reflected in the recourse to Shas-related (but probably government-funded) NGOs to plug deficits—as in 1999 when the deficit reached NIS 80 million—and also in Ovadia Yosef's periodic fund-raising trips abroad (Tessler, 2003). One such NGO was closed down by the regulator in August 2004 due to 'accounting irregularities'.

Shas had begun to garner state funding after 1983 when its leadership saw—or claimed—that funds they had obtained from the government for their yeshivas were being witheld (hence the 'riot' against Porush). Gradually the Shas educational network was prised free of the control of the Agudat Yisrael. In 1992 it was agreed that the network would be funded through the National Religious side of the state education system, but eventually, apparently in 1997, it came to obtain its funding directly from the office of the Director-General of the Ministry (a political appointment), which according to Tessler, enables it to escape controls established for either the Agudat Yisrael system or the National Religious schools. The information we obtained was that the Shas schools in 2001 were, like Agudat Yisrael, accountable to the Office of Unofficial Recognised Education, though to describe them as being under that Office's supervision might give a misleading impression, since their inspectorate was not drawn from or appointed by the Ministry. It meant only that the Ministry was able in principle to check that the monies allocated were being spent correctly—a major bone of contention during 2000–1 in the last months of the Barak government and the tenure of secularist Yossi Sarid as Minister of Education.

In view of its budgetary advantages, it is not surprising that Shas also had a much lower average class size: nineteen as compared with thirty-five children per class in the state secular schools according to Ministry officials. In addition, the system receives funding for transport to school and for school meals, and possibly for other supplementary items not provided to the other school systems. These advantages—prevalent in 2001—will almost certainly have been pared back in the wake of the 2003 elections.

Much of the controversy over the Shas school network has been about accountability. In state secular schools teachers are state employees and are therefore paid by the state. Teachers in the *haredi* system in principle receive the same pay as in secular schools, but they receive it from the school system they work in, which means they may not receive the full salary, or that moneys allocated to teachers' pay are spent on something else, or maybe just on extra hours by other teachers. Yossi Sarid, who has already appeared in Shas's demonology, as Minister of Education in the 1999–2001 Barak government, held up the disbursement of funds for a long period while trying to obtain proper accounting of expenditure from HaMa'ayan—even at a time when Shas held several important Ministries in the same government. (On our visits to Shas schools we were repeatedly told how staff had continued to work without pay throughout the period, said to be nine months.) In 2001 there were interminable negotiations about the funding of transport for Shas schoolchildren, which, we were told in the Ministry, was related to Shas's exemption from the standard location criteria for placing children in schools, and also its apparent exemption from the Ministry of Education's criteria of local need in establishing schools. Thus we were given the example of a locality where the Shas representative demanded and obtained 'one school for each Rabbi', even though this breached Ministry guidelines on the minimum school size. In an interview in 2004 Sarid told us the real issue was that the Shas leadership had insisted the transport contract be awarded to a particular firm or individual, who was charging exorbitant prices for the service, and that they refused to change the individual or the contract. He viewed the claim that the teachers had worked for nine months without pay as an exaggeration.

Political leverage is used to reclassify teacher qualifications and establish equivalences so as to promote the status and income of *haredi* teachers. Shas inspectors are employed by HaMa'ayan, while the Ministry employs directly only one single inspector for all the Shas schools. As mentioned, secular schoolteachers are civil servants, but the Shas network employs its own teachers, and both our interviews and Tessler's account show that their commitment is to some extent ideological and also that they are expected to invest their time and energy beyond the formal teaching role. HaMa'ayan officials told us they were very anxious to upgrade teachers' qualifications so that schools would pass tougher inspection tests, not least because this would entitle them to more funding. Likewise, the more qualifications teachers receive the higher their remuneration, especially if they obtain a senior teacher's certificate. The pressure to raise teaching quality, and the financial advantages from its improvement to both schools and teachers—and pupils—create an incentive for Shas to attract *ba'alei t'shuva* to their schools as teachers, because they are more likely to have completed secondary schooling and to possess the full secondary school certificate. HaMa'ayan has one teacher training college of its own which qualifies its graduates to teach only in its schools, and there are many other religious teacher training schools whose courses are recognised as diplomas for teachers even though they do not constitute full academic qualifications. In addition, Shas has found ways of raising the qualifications of those teachers who have had a predominantly religious education, for example by obtaining recognition of some Torah study as equivalent to secular qualifications: thus although they have not studied in a university or a secular teacher training college, they can, by obtaining a Rabbi's qualification plus a year of part-time Torah study, achieve a BA equivalent. Likewise, outside the education field, an arrangement seemed to exist in 2002 between the government and Touro University, the Israel outpost of a New York institution,[2] whereby as little as a part-time two year course in management can lead to a BA equivalent and thus qualify its holders for civil service positions. The Director of the Shas boys' school in Bet Shemesh (see below) was doing a part-time Masters course in Educational Administration at Touro University.

---

[2] An institution catering predominantly to the more observant sections of the New York Jewish Community, named after a financier of the American War of Independence.

The Shas school curriculum

We had the opportunity to observe a number of schools ourselves, and received varying opinions from officials and other informed persons on the curriculum. This variation may have reflected a degree of local autonomy, or perhaps a lack of systematic oversight on the part of the network's managers or inspectors. The same local variation seems to exist in 'streaming', which follows religious and social—rather than academic—criteria where it is adopted. The lack of systematic overview has facilitated the creation of a variety of institutes and schools that open a wide range of possibilities to different children, especially to girls seeking some kind of training for the labour market (such as vocational schools that we visited), as an alternative to the more secular/academic bagrut qualification.

At first the Shas schools had to use didactic materials from the National Religious or *haredi* school systems, but now their teachers proudly tell how they have developed their own more modern materials—as we saw in discussing the Pedagogical Centre.

They also are eager to show how computers and video equipment helps them in their jobs. Nonetheless, the Shas school curriculum is heavily dominated by religion. Even in secular subjects the examples are often drawn from religion, and the History which is taught goes 'up to the Second Temple' (68 AD), and focuses only on the Jewish people, with little if anything even about the Zionist movement and the establishment of the Jewish state—subjects about which *haredim* feel uneasy of course. A volunteer worker in the Shas HQ spoke of 'a little about the Inquisition and a little about the Holocaust'. We noticed that unlike National Religious and secular state schools, Shas schools were devoid of any Israeli national emblem. The head of the flagship Bet-Shemesh boys' school, which only takes pupils from established religious families (not newly religious *hozrei bet'shuva*) told us that secular subjects—which he described as 'the human body' and 'sums'—are taught for three hours a day during the first eight years of education (up to age thirteen), and even then material relating to 'daily life' is excluded. The aims of education, he told us, are 'respect for God', good behaviour and Torah. Its sister girls' school next door has a different balance, giving more time to secular than to religious subjects. The Director of the girls' school reiterated a phrase we have already quoted and which we heard frequently: the Gemara sharpens people's wits and also contains much science, perhaps all science: Pythagoras is there, and the great modern sages like Hazon Ish—founder of Israel's post-independence *haredi* community—astonished specialists like doctors with their knowledge. So if the girls are doing more secular subjects, this is not because their teachers take a different view of their importance, but rather because *haredi* girls are not expected, indeed not allowed, to undertake studies of Rabbinic texts for the purpose of learning or legal development—these are only for boys to study. Girls in their study of religion learn how to manage a Jewish home, the rules and regulations of food and also of bodily rituals, especially the *mikveh*. They also study the Pentateuch, the Halakha—that is, the practical rules and regulations of Jewish daily life—the daily, weekly and festival prayers and the significance of the Sabbath and Festivals. In their secular subjects girls study history to a more advanced stage than the boys, and also sewing, domestic things and a little music ('rhythm'). We were told they follow the same curriculum as the Beit Yaakov schools, which were founded for girls' education in Eastern Europe, and are the leading *haredi* institutions for girls in Israel and worldwide, and paved the way for the breadwinner role which has now fallen to so many *haredi* women.

The Directors of both the boys' and the girls' schools in Bet Shemesh placed much emphasis on their role in moulding their pupils' behaviour. Families are visited at the start of the school year and sign a contract with the school committing themselves to common aims and cooperation, and if the commitment is broken, the pupil in question may be expelled. In addition, close touch was kept with the families and repeated use of bad language, for example, could entail sanctions. In Ramat Shlomo, in slight contrast, an informant told us that although there was not an explicit division of children by religious observance, informal pressures were brought to bear on parents to remove their children where observance did not live up to the school's expectations. We often heard that Shas divides schoolchildren, like the population generally, into those who are born into strictly observant families, those who are in need of 'strengthening' and the *hozrei bet'shuva*, whose families are returning to religious observance—but again in Ramat Shlomo we were told this did not apply. In the two Bet Shemesh schools the pupils are almost exclusively drawn from established strictly observant families, but evidently many other schools take pupils from all three categories—otherwise the *t'shuva* rationale would be lost. The Bet Shemesh schools have perhaps been designated to produce future members of the movement's core of male religious professionals, or at least full-time Torah students and eventual Rabbis, and the women who as breadwinners, housewives, teachers and informal organisers will complement these roles.

But, as we have seen in our account of the Shas project, some of the Shas leaders have been concerned to develop ways of dealing with a modern state and with the development of an outward-looking cadre, as well as with bringing its followers to strict religious observance. For example, one of Ovadia Yosef's daughters has for some time been promoting the idea of a higher education institution where *haredi* women could acquire professional skills without abandoning their way of life. The Shas girl's secondary school we visited in Petach Tikvah, which has already been mentioned, was also a showpiece for the movement, but had a more varied intake. According to the Director, herself university-educated, it was highly selective academically but not religiously, and she was clearly anxious, in her own phrase, to 'build bridges' with the secular world, and to demonstrate that a strictly religious school could achieve high academic standards—whereas the Bet-Shemesh directors placed less emphasis on methods of academic assessment associated with the secular education system. At the prize-giving ceremony of the Petach Tikvah school only two of many projects exhibited by the students were on religious subjects.

Yeshivas for returnees

The Shas school network caters almost entirely to children up to thirteen years of age, after which the boys go either to yeshivas or to National Religious schools, and the girls to either National Religious or, if they get through the quotas limiting Sephardi entry, Beit Yaakov schools. It is unclear how much yeshiva study Shas, or Shas-related institutions, can provide, or whether there is enough Sephardi, or Sephardi-style, yeshiva provision in Israel to absorb all these young men. However, older students who are returning to religious observance do attend the various *t'shuva*-related educational activities in very large numbers, notably in the Or Hachayyim network. We were told that Or Hachayyim had 200 branches throughout the country, employed some 800 people and expended a million dollars per month—but if the former figure is correct the probability is that the latter figure is a serious underestimate. Its activities are funded more by the (now defunct) Ministry of Religious Affairs than by the Ministry of Education, though it also engages in private fund-raising, notably to construct an imposing headquarters in the heart of Jerusalem's religious neighbourhood of Boukharim—under construction for three years at least.

While the new building is incomplete, Or Hachayyim's main yeshiva in Jerusalem operates out of a disused basketball court nearby, on the edge of the Boukharim neighbourhood. It consists of a vast hall in which 200–300 men, mostly in their twenties, are studying in pairs. A tutor sits at a desk to one side and is available for all sorts of consultations, textual, religious and personal. The students with whom we spoke received a monthly allowance from the state of about US $300 and often their wives worked to keep the household going. The yeshiva provided board and lodging for those who were not married, and also arranged marriages where appropriate. The content of their studies was no different from other yeshivas but, in the words of the Director of the Bet Shemesh boys' school, a yeshiva for people returning to religion, who had not had a religious education in their childhood or youth, will not achieve the same standard—or at least not the same recognition—as those who were brought up in *haredi* families: aspiration to that level is reserved for the next generation.

The Or Hachayyim enterprise is not easy to classify within the Israeli system: although many of its establishments are called yeshivas, they take people who are much older than standard yeshiva students; on the other hand they do not fit the model of *kollelim* that accommodate only married men. By forming returnees who have experience of the secular world, they provide cadres for the *t'shuva* movement, as exemplified by those Or Hachayyim graduates who have become very prominent politically. There are puzzles: for example a *kollel* we attended in Bet Shemesh had the Or Hachayyim sign and the name of Elbaz on its entrance, but in fact turned out to have no links with him because 'the money had run out'—while the boys' school in

Bet Shemesh was in the Or Hachayyim system, even though primary schooling is not the organisation's main priority.

To the above activities one could add a variety of other undertakings which are more or less closely linked to Shas and look after adults, for example, the proliferating *kollelim* often set up in bomb shelters, the women's clubs which we have mentioned, and groups of people meeting regularly or occasionally in local synagogues under the guidance of a Rabbi. All this—and in many ways also the more formal establishments we have described—testifies further to the grassroots initiative which drives Shas mobilisation, its low level of institutionalisation and also its reliance on political connections to 'keep the show on the road'. For however much voluntary activity may be involved, the connections are still needed to ensure subsidised water and electricity for the bomb shelters, premises for schools and yeshivas and salaries for Rabbis, activists and hangers-on.

In the late 2005, two years after Shas's exit from government, a flourishing expansion of Shas schools at all levels, fuelled by grassroots mobilization on the part of t'shuva activists, was still being reported. Sub-networks created from the ground up, notably in towns on the outskirts of Tel Aviv, were developing a variety of agendas and inching their way towards adoption, and funding, by the HaMa'ayan network. One striking feature of these networks, consisting of say 15 kindergartens and primary schools, was their modernist and undogmatic character: although they were operating clearly under the sign of t'shuva, some were teaching English in first grade and there was a clear commitment to employing fully qualified teachers, to prepare the children for the labour market (*Ha'aretz*, 18 November 2005). The modernizing agenda of Shas was not dead, or at least not at the ground level.

Élite Sephardi yeshivas

The examples of educational institutions we have seen so far have in common a broken link with the Sephardi past. They are home-grown Israeli operations which, despite a strong ethnic identity and the use of Sephardi ritual and musical motifs, derive their educational methods from the dominant Lithuanian tradition which formed the Shas leadership, and rely for their mass support on doses of popular religion. However, we also visited two yeshivas whose links to the North African learning tradition have not been broken, and which seem to some extent to preserve a degree of independence with respect to Shas and the Israeli state. By independence we do not mean they have anything but excellent relations with Shas and above all with Ovadia Yosef, but rather that these institutions represent what might be called Sephardi high culture and erudition in the midst of a movement where learning is modelled on the Lithuanian system and Sephardi religious identity expressed in the popular religion of everyday life.

The yeshiva Al Kisei Rachamim (On the Seat of the Merciful) was set up by the Mazouz brothers in the *haredi* town of Bnei Brak after they fled Tunisia for Israel in 1971. They had fled because, despite Tunisia's record of good Arab-Jewish relations, their father had been assassinated. Their family had come from Jerba and their father was a judge of the Tunisian High Court, appointed by the country's first President, Habib Bourguiba. He was a scrupulous man who never sat in judgment on Jewish cases in the court because he could not apply Jewish law in the civil court. In the yeshiva the boardroom's glazed cupboards contained their father's library and his formal courtroom robes, with manuscript books in the script of Maimonides, which the students now learn to use.

This yeshiva is devoted to preserving a pure version of Sephardi learning, script and ritual. It publishes prayer books and Torah volumes in which the pointing[3] is revised letter by letter to conform to the Sephardi tradition, and which are acquiring the status of standard texts. Rav Tsemach Mazouz expressed his devotion to the Sephardi tradition in terms not of music or respect for Rabbis, but of the correctness of the Sephardi approach to learning. In his view the two traditions were the same until, some 200 years ago, the Ashkenazim deviated from the correct path—presumably a reference to the Enlightenment. The students, many of whom come from abroad, are admitted by competitive examination unless they have been there since before the age of fourteen, and only 25 per cent of applicants are successful. They all live in the yeshiva and are not allowed to receive telephone calls while they are studying—that, according to Rav Tzemach Mazuz would be *bitul Torah*. The yeshiva aspires to producing not

---

[3] Pointing refers to the signs denoting not vowels but melody when chanting the texts.

just Rabbis but scholars and Rabbinic Court judges, and is proud to count two members of Israel's Rabbinic Court among its graduates. The method of study, as it was described to us, is based less on memory than on the development of understanding and skill in interpreting Rabbinic texts and laws. Students are taught to write their own interpretations and to decide between different ones. Computers connect the yeshiva to Bar-Ilan University's 'Responsa Project' (a vast electronic compilation of the Bible and all the main Talmudic texts) and the teachers help students to find material there. The teachers seem to arrange marriages for many of their students (a not unusual practice), who then remain in Bnei Brak and continue studying in the *kollel* after marriage for a further five years.

This is not a yeshiva maintained by the good offices of Shas politicians. Its students are fee-paying, and the institution has many sponsors in France and elsewhere, although its Israeli students probably receive study grants like those in other yeshivas. Our conversation with the Director was notable, in comparison with others, both for the absence of invocations of the supernatural benefits of Torah study, either in this world (health, good marriages etc.) or in the next, and for the detail of the information given on methods of study and different interpretative approaches. This is an institution which aims to produce an intellectual élite.

The other example of an élite yeshiva is that of Rav Pinto in Petach Tikvah. Pinto, whose lineage counts many venerated saints, is more of a political figure than the Mazouz family, having built his own yeshivas and other institutions in the town, and having been appointed a Rabbi of the town through the good offices of Ovadia Yosef. He was also present at the gathering of members of religious councils described earlier and was Chair of the Petach Tikvah Religious Council. The yeshiva we visited is built to replicate his father's yeshiva in Marrakesh, with an internal courtyard and open corridor on three floors and a domed roof (nicknamed a *kippa* or skullcap). This evocation of the Moroccan past is reiterated and reinforced in the defence of the method of study, and of separate Sephardi and Ashkenazi institutions of learning, though he has Ashkenazi as well as Sephardi teachers in his yeshiva. His yeshiva also takes students from New York and Montreal, and he himself goes abroad to give lectures, speaking in Arabic to North African-born audiences who do not know modern Hebrew.

Like those of the Mazouz brothers, Pinto's students take a competitive entrance examination. They enter at age eleven and stay through to marriage. The Rav also arranges marriages for his students, through a nearby girls' school: it is unheard of for a boy to graduate from the yeshiva without getting married. Also like the Mazouz family, he takes a systematic approach to Talmudic study: he speaks of the Marrakesh method, which he also describes as the 'theoretical Talmud': a conception of the 'basis', namely the text of the Gemara, of the original Rabbinic commentaries, which a student analyses and then, having made an interpretation, compares this with those of sages, such as Rashi, the medieval French authority. The student asks himself why his own interpretation is different from that of Rashi, and then 'returns to the basis'. The precise meaning of this explanation is less important to us than Rav Pinto's emphasis on constructing a rational edifice rather than, or perhaps as well as, treating study as a ritual. This rational emphasis is again illustrated by the absence of exaggerated this-worldly or other-worldly promises of felicity. Even so, he could be said to be slightly more inclined to popular religious beliefs than the Mazouz family: he told us that Hebrew will come naturally to a child—any child—who for some reason is not taught a language, and that 'even the Catholic Church' sees Hebrew as the 'original, primary language'. He also had the popular view of science in the Torah—did Maimonides not discover this foundational character of Hebrew 800 years ago?

These two institutions are distinguished by their pursuit of a distinctive Sephardi approach to Torah learning, or at least to certain aspects of Torah learning. But there are other variations. For example, the 'Lithuanian' yeshiva Yekiri Yerushalayim, founded on the basis of a religious elementary school (Talmud Torah) in the late 1990s, and numbering some 1,000 pupils aged between three and twenty-two, admit readily its exclusively 'Oriental' intake of boys of North African, Middle Eastern and Yemeni background. They will have nothing whatsoever to do with Shas, or indeed with any governmental agency, as we have seen, but occupy an imposing building, with modern boarding facilities, funded by student fees.

These examples can be interpreted in two ways: on the one hand they indicate that there are niches in Israeli society which enable institutions with a Sephardi religious 'brand' to flourish. But they also show that there are many ways—ritual, Talmudic and ethnic, to name but three—of being Sephardi and religious, and that the frontiers thus constructed can cut across one another. And this does not take into account the secular and political ways of being Sephardi, or the less religiously punctilious traditional resources, such as pilgrimages and festivals.

Shas's use of government funding

According to Ricki Tessler (2001), Shas in 1999 had 3,500 party branches and 250,000 activists—of whom 50,000 were militants in receipt of salaries! This may be an exaggeration, but the party has followed a determined strategy of placing true believers in a wide range of institutions, not only in those concerned with religious matters, but on a variety of elected bodies. Thus in 1998 the party doubled its representation on Municipal Councils, as well as its presence on Boards of State Enterprises and other public institutions. The arrangement between Shas or Shas-related bodies and Touro University is designed in part to enable Shas to place its nominees in such positions. Touro courses in Public Administration or Management seem to be packed with Sephardi *ba'alei t'shuva*.

In addition, Shas has taken advantage of Israel's distinctive NGO regime, which is an important device for channelling government funds to interest groups and designated clienteles. NGOs in Israel are, in strict legal terms, no different from elsewhere, but the system whereby they gain access to government funding is different, as was explained to us in 2000 by an experienced lawyer in public service: in addition to $200 million a year from local authorities, NGOs receive a billion dollars a year from the government, a sum that had grown by 40 per cent in five years. Although there are doubtless many examples in which Ministries, having decided what they want to build or achieve, call for proposals, for example to provide a social service or build a power station, there is also a much more political mechanism, whereby, despite reforms introduced in the 1990s, ministers personally receive proposals from NGOs, religious and secular, and practices familiar to us through the model of the enclave system come into play.[4] In 1985 the Supreme Court ruled that the criteria

[4] Other hidden subsidies to special interests, and by no means all religious or polit-

for these allocations should be published, but then Parliament decided it could exempt named organisations from the ruling. As a result, every 31 December, just as the Finance Minister was finalising his budget, MKs would approach him with requests for funding their favoured causes and organisations, threatening either to vote against his budget or to abstain, and therefore obtaining rapid approval. Nevertheless, in 1992 the practice was banned by Parliament, at least in principle. However, still in 2001 the Attorney-General had not adopted the practice of publishing funding criteria, and also some Ministries used criteria so restrictive that they were obviously ill-disguised subsidies to known organisations. So the adoption of impersonal practices did not occur overnight.[5] Recently, the Supreme Court issued an instruction reiterating the obligation of the government to publish criteria for projects, and generally follow proper procedure when allocating land. There are also no clear criteria to specify organisations whose activities qualify for tax-deductible charitable donations—a category which seems to extend to West Bank settlements.

Monitoring of expenditure is just as light as the oversight of fund allocation, so that funds allocated to the Shas school network and 'left over' for after-school activities are spent at the discretion of school managers. According to Tessler, who does little to disguise her hostility to Shas, Shas has exploited weaknesses or little known loopholes and niches in government budgets: 'unspent allocations' or 'reserves'; inattentive procedures in some areas which enable a single institution to make multiple funding applications, or to claim multiple entitlements under different names. In 1996, she claims, 100 NGOs linked to Shas were receiving funds from three different sour-

---

ical ones, were also explained. For example, 170 Army personnel seconded to the Society for the Protection of Nature, or to teaching Hebrew and 'basic child-rearing' to immigrants, though this last has apparently been dropped. Women Army volunteers can be assigned to social work, and religious women, most of whom do not do military service, are instead assigned to work in religious institutions. Other examples mentioned ranged from *haredi* neighbourhood building projects to youth hostels.

[5] For example, when a settlement was finally reached on the funding of the Shas school network in 2001 some names of teachers themselves were published in the official announcement.

ces, implying that they were telling different stories to each. Additional areas of expenditure such as 'special needs' or 'urgent special needs' are found; the creation of new Departments is demanded whereupon they receive budgetary allocations; and finally there is the apparently common practice of inventing phantom students on whose behalf allocations for full time adult study are made. Thus Tessler finds strange data according to which participants in courses offered by an organisation providing religious education to secularised farmers are mostly aged over eighty or under seventeen!

Tessler also found 956 organisations which, since 1992, have been identified with Shas, ranging from youth and women's groups to low-price supermarkets and of course schools and yeshivas. Shas has been able to mix social and religious themes, obtaining funding from Education, Social and Religious Affairs Ministries for what one might call quasi-political activities: as we were able to observe, a political connection can be evoked, even if not a word of politics is openly spoken, by activities which are tinged with *t'shuva* and sponsored, 'animated' or managed by Sephardi Rabbis or simply by people who have a particular mode of dress or accent, or sing to Sephardi tunes—for example, the sports hall in Petach Tikvah, built thanks to the intervention of Arieh Deri when he was Interior Minister. In the public mind, where Shas politicians have a high local profile, such activities and projects are associated not with 'the government' but with Shas.

This section has explored how Shas has intervened in the reproduction of society, especially in various forms of education, and also how in doing so it has found niches in the institutions of the state. Education has provided a convenient umbrella for many different activities and a justification for obtaining government funding in Israel's neo-corporatist machinery. It also enables Shas to link up with a variety of social milieux, from the disabled basketball players of Petach Tikvah to the learned Rabbis of the Mazouz family, and to do so through networks of personal contacts which may often depend on crucial individuals like Arieh Deri and Ovadia Yosef himself—and his many honorific or quasi-honorific positions which provide access when needed—and through political entrepreneurs. The next section explores further the quality of this network.

TIES THAT BIND: THE CULTURE OF SHAS AND
THE SOCIAL NETWORKS OF ITS LEADERSHIP

A movement's culture operates in very public ways through rituals, ceremonies and demonstrations and through styles of dress and identification with certain locations; it also operates in the private sphere, in the multiple and cross-cutting bonds of friendship, courtship, marriage, educational experience, leisure, social gatherings and much else, which are a feature of life in a movement, and especially of the life of its more active members. No account of the international Communist movement, for example, could avoid the importance of the endless round of meetings and marches, the banners, the paraphernalia of militancy, of the Communist press and literature, even its music and art, and also of the boundaries constructed within and around the movement—the core nucleus of full-time cadres, the activist militants, the rank-and-file members, the fellow-travellers— all organised like concentric circles, each more distant from the centres of decision-making. In addition to these public manifestations, and perhaps more important, account must be taken of socialisation, of family relationships among militants, of a shared language or jargon. The Zionist movement likewise brought together a vast array of organisational and cultural devices and spheres: the kibbutz was designed to create a culture of a wholly new kind, even a distinctive secular Israeli style of music and dance opposed in every possible way to the village culture of the colonisers' countries of origin in Eastern Europe—though in some ways it also borrowed elements from that culture; the common experience of war and the institution of the Israeli Army likewise created distinctive cultures (Almog, 2000). Bonds of friendship and solidarity formed by growing up together on the kibbutz and by the political and military experiences of the early generations prolonged themselves in the tight party organisations of the two dominant parties in the early decades of the Israeli state and in its intellectual and political élites—those very élites some of whose members later came to feel that Shas had 'stolen' the country from them. Further examples abound: the anti-globalisation movement thrives on a myriad of local networks and friendships with their own jargon, codes of dress and dissident symbolic paraphernalia. Those networks in turn link across national, linguistic and geographic boundaries without, it seems, any central direction save in some almost professional organisations like Attac.[6] Cases of religious revival illustrate the points with particular force: fundamentalist groups create what Scott Atran (2003a) has called a 'family of fictive kin' which drowns the individual; Pentecostal churches in Latin America—and doubtless elsewhere—make persistent and invasive demands on individuals' time, money and emotional resources which also fit the same concept, though with different political implications. Conversion movements, like *t'shuva*, some more drastically than others, cut people off from their families of origin, arrange their marriages, and operate a fairly quick and drastic change in many aspects of their lives—from their professions to their most intimate activities. The next chapter will return to the implications of this feature.

It is important to emphasize these shared cultural practices because the interpretation of social movements tends to focus on the instrumental, the structural and the material at the expense of the 'ties that bind'. Yet these ties are all-important, for they create commitments on which the movement can call in mobilising support. They must not be confused with, and can almost be opposed to, the standard catch-all explanation of mobilisation, namely 'identity' as propounded by Castells or Melucci (Melucci, 1989; Castells, 1998) among many others. For to use the word identity is to invoke some kind of common origin or primary loyalty—ethnic, religious, chthonic, whatever—whereas the ties described here are created between individuals, not between individuals and an imaginary collective, and as the enumeration of 'shared cultural practices' above indicates, their content is of the most diverse kind. Movements gain strength from the variety of their followers, not from their homogeneity. If, as observers do not cease to point out, a fictitious identity is created, there is correspondingly greater reason for looking to non-identitarian bases for individuals' practical loyalty to a cause, a movement or an organisation, as distinct from the indispensable rhetoric of identity.

The variety extends also to the intensity of the ties which bind individuals to each other, to organisations and to the movement. A movement which is no more than a very tightly knit organisation—

---

[6] An anti-global group which specialises in running training camps and consciousness-raising. The name originates in their advocacy of the 'Tobin tax' on foreign exchange transactions.

a terrorist cell, a conspiratorial revolutionary party, a religious cult—may do things, and may have effects, sometimes frightening effects, but it will not achieve social change unless it develops a penumbra of mass organisations, militants, sympathisers and so on, whereupon its structures will most likely become more open.

The intensity of ties varies both in and between movements. It is not by accident that the inner circle of the Shas leadership, gathered around Ovadia Yosef, is bound by the many blood and marriage ties we described earlier. Within a movement such commitments are likely to be most intense among the core cadres, who, as their ever-deepening involvement closes other options, find themselves unable to say 'no' to an organisation's demands on their time and energy. Also, within a movement there may exist myriads of organisations and some will be more demanding than others, but even relatively passive involvement is carried by networks of personal connections. Shared habits and lifestyles are not only acquired by the totally committed: they can be transmitted even through quite incidental contact. The *t'shuva* movement does not demand total commitment from all new adherents immediately: on the contrary, as explained in Chapter 3, its evangelists carefully adopt the 'softly-softly' approach, at least to begin with. In the same vein as our understanding of Arieh Deri's outward-looking style and appeal, so it has been important to the success of Shas, and to its future recovery, that the network does not close in on itself and gravitate too much towards the classic *haredi* model of a largely closed society. This has been described as the three circles of Shas (Bick, 2001): a core of some 60,000 ultra-Orthodox faithful; a 'second circle' of 'traditional' voters who identify with the spiritual leadership of Shas and even, according to some polls, support the idea of a state based on Rabbinic law, though they are by no means ultra-Orthodox; and a 'third circle' who are motivated more by ethnic identification and a 'quest for greater Sephardic political power', though they may also hold on to the folk religion of their ancestors.

Movements can devour the lives of the core activists. We observed how Rabbis and officials active in Shas would spend long evenings out, returning home at 11 o'clock or later; how they spend endless hours in meetings, how they are constantly available on the telephone late into the night, and how politics encroaches on, even dominates, their family life—if only because it would be impossible for a Shas activist to be married to someone who is indifferent to the movement, let alone opposed to it. We observe the same in London and elsewhere among Chabad missionaries: they seem to be forever in a hurry, and their family and professional lives are indistinguishable. In *haredi* life, as in Pentecostal churches, it is taken for granted that the pastor's wife or the *Rabbanit* (the Rabbi's wife) is fully integrated into her husband's role.[7]

The *t'shuva* movement, like other social movements, brings people together in their daily lives: they attend study sessions daily and often full time and they may, if they are young, unmarried and male, live in collective accommodation. Several interviewees told us how they had broken off a marriage commitment as a consequence of their 'conversion', while one said that subsequently the yeshiva found him a wife. Rabbis' wives in the *t'shuva* movement not only provide backup for their hyperactive husbands but also, for example, run women's clubs (*chugim*), give talks to women thinking of 'returning', or engage in ventures of their own to bring people back to observance.

The creation of ties extends also to the movement's leaders, even if these have been elevated to almost saint-like status, like Ovadia Yosef. Whereas in many contexts leadership is almost defined by the leader's remoteness and inaccessibility, in these religious movements one constantly encounters individuals who have come into personal touch with the movement's leaders. Chabad made an elaborate ritual out of this during the lifetime of its Rebbe: he held regular audiences at which individuals would come to ask advice, would receive it, and would also receive a dollar bill. People who wrote to him received a hand-written response, often with advice about their inquiries. Accessibility was his trademark—and pilgrims continue to visit his grave, sometimes saying they are 'visiting the Rebbe' (implicitly denying his death). In fact, although the Chabad case is the most celebrated because of its distinctive ritual aspect and its high public profile, in most Chassidic sects people consult their Rebbe on every important decision, from business to politics to personal life, and the men who occupy these leadership positions must be assumed to employ a large staff to answer their abundant correspondence.

---

[7] Interestingly, this was not at all true in the case of the Lubavitch Rebbe: he and his wife had no children and by all accounts she kept well away from the organisation.

Ovadia Yosef is similarly generous with his public appearances, at the Persian synagogue, at yeshiva occasions, and also at public meetings proclaiming *t'shuva* or promoting Shas and its election campaigns. Often he is either inaudible or, on account of his accent and delivery, incomprehensible, but this does not matter. In addition many people speak of having obtained his advice or having committed themselves to *t'shuva* after meeting him. In one case a boy, who became so obsessively religious that he ceased to have any social intercourse at all, had to be taken to Ovadia himself, who, we were told, convinced him that he was taking his zeal too far. Stories also abound of unexpected blessings received after meetings with him. Other examples of the physical availability of the Shas leadership include the appearance of Yaffa Deri, during her husband's imprisonment, at school functions and *t'shuva* campaign events, and the attendance of Reuven Elbaz at his yeshivas, where like Ovadia Yosef himself, he is mobbed by the students, requiring a protective group to open his path. The famous Kabbalist Yitzchak Kedourie was, at least in 2000, visible daily at services in his synagogue in the Boukharim district.

Amidst this wide range of considerations related to the 'ties that bind', the following pages will dwell on two aspects: the personal links among militants, activists and cadres, and the ways in which Shas and the *t'shuva* movement have penetrated society's interstices. The cases, though, are of 'core' activists, and that should be kept in mind.

REACHING OUT: OCCUPYING INTERMEDIATE SPACES

The spinal chord of Shas, and by extension of the *t'shuva* movement, is composed of dedicated cadres, true believers available for a range of tasks teaching in yeshivas, advising the young and caring for their souls, as civil servants in Ministries under Shas control, as political articulators in local government, as tutors in yeshivas and much besides. But the spinal chord is not the whole body, and we know from many examples that even the most radically separatist religious sects and movements have many worldly involvements—from Chassidim who deal in the international diamond trade to fundamentalist preachers who broadcast influential political messages, or Mormons who open up the Utah desert. Almost all have to become involved in politics because politics gives access to 'free' goods. Activists and pastors themselves talk endlessly about 'the world' as a vast pool of temptation and unbelief, but that of course is their vocation, their ideology, so one should not assume their bipolar vision properly describes the structure of their movements, and one should also recall that such rhetoric may conceal a fascination and a certain engagement with the world.

Outsiders tend to be complicit with this rhetoric, and may exaggerate their own distance from the world of sectarian and renewal movements, as a way of sharpening fear or hatred of the 'other' or, in the case of social scientists, empowered by our cosmopolitanism and our command of a scientific discourse, as a short-cut to the construction of neat, coherent models and even perhaps as a reaffirmation of the rationality of our own worldview. Of course, tightly drawn boundaries are a reality in many spheres, especially in the social life of the grassroots follower, as can be seen in the spheres of marriage, of dress, in the use of space and time and in education. But, given that there are 'vested interests', some conscious, many unconscious, in accentuating the walls, or the abyss, separating the movements and their surrounding social world, it is important to give due place not only to the forces that create and sustain the 'break' but also to those that maintain and strengthen lines of communication and exchange with the broader society.

We have already seen the machinery for outreach, in the examples of the Arachim organisation and of Amnon Yitzhak's operation, that act as gateways through which potential returnees are invited to enter, and we shall also see how the pirate radios contribute. Once through the gateway, some returnees 'graduate', so to speak, to study groups, local community organisations, or to the care of local Rabbis, while others doubtless return to their daily life little changed. There are numerous gradations among these multifarious organisations: while some do not have an organic tie to Shas, and indeed barely refer to Shas in their activities or pronouncements, even if many of those who attend their meetings may eventually gravitate towards Shas, others, like Or HaChayyim, may identify quite publicly with the party.

Through these alliances Shas fills an intermediate space between the ultra-Orthodox world and the secular world from which it draws its new adherents and where it needs to make a sustained impact if it is to prosper politically, gain and preserve access to state-controlled resources, and bring Israeli society back to religious observance. There is also a 'built-in' pressure to keep up the recruitment of *ba'alei t'shuva*: a steady supply of educated people, with Army service,[8] even with higher education, returning to religion, is very useful in providing Shas ministers and municipal council members with trustworthy staff.

This reaching out is illustrated by a range of agencies and outreach activities, of organisations, initiatives and ventures, all devoted to evangelising among secular people which we came across in our fieldwork. We reached them through Shas-related contacts, but although they probably benefited Shas electorally, they could hardly all be described as part of a Shas apparatus. These instances exhibit several features which illustrate the way in which outreach can operate: volunteer commitment and involvement; intervention in a secular milieu; occupation of an unaccustomed physical space by people exhibiting their religious belonging; an almost omnipresent educational dimension; and the inevitable shoestring budget.

One classic method whereby activists occupy space is through seizure of caravans on building. Israel is littered with building sites, and the sites have offices in caravans or temporary accommodation. When, for example, a project is completed, activists have, by stealth or by seizure or perhaps with the connivance of a sympathetic municipal councillor, gained control of the huts and started up youth groups or kindergartens which then operate without official or financial support, sometimes for months and years. In Bet Shemesh the Shas council member and Deputy Mayor showed us some caravans that were being vacated now that schools had been built, but added that new occupants would immediately replace them with classes for other groups of children. This could continue for a very long time, since Bet Shemesh is the scene of continuous building activity, mostly for *haredi* and modern orthodox communities.

---

[8] Army service is almost a requirement of citizenship in Israel. Apart from positive benefits, there are costs to not serving. A person without Army service has difficulty getting certain sorts of positions, for example in the civil service. Obviously some are exempt on medical grounds, apart from the exemptions of full-time Torah students and *haredi* women.

Seizures of building sites might, elsewhere, provoke a response in the name of the defence of property, but in Israel, in an urban landscape which often resembles a vast nationwide building site, land occupation is a time-honoured tactic. In a country where, moreover, all land belongs ultimately to the state, land seizures attract little negative attention. Thus activists can establish a physical presence in the name of the movement and rapidly provide a service, usually something to do with children, and always for free.

This sort of approach, willing to improvise wherever necessary even if there are no premises available, is characteristic of the numerous organisations and activities promoted under the name of El HaMa'ayan, Shas's network of non-political NGOs. Many of these are subsidised by the government as social and religious activity and are engaged in various types of informal education oriented to *t'shuva*. They reach an estimated 35,000 young people, and feature religious festivals, sports and outings and summer camps for small children, peppered with the promotion of moral and religious norms of behaviour. Other offshoots include Torah classes organised for adult men and Margalit Em Yisrael, the organisation for women which imparts the proper religious way of life, but also concerns itself with issues of family poverty and welfare.

There is also a symbolic dimension to this campaigning activism: occupation of an area stakes a claim to a vacant space between the secular and the religious domains, by implanting emblems of religious observance. The young men who lead such invasions with their neatly cut beards, dark suits and white shirts, spare no time in establishing a rhythm of prayer and study in the spaces they occupy. They offer a 'different' version of an ultra-Orthodox Israeli: they engage in physical work, they know how to talk the language of 'the street', and so they embody a receptive face of the *haredi*, as opposed to the inward-looking, almost frightened deportment of the stereotype Ashkenazi *haredi*, who sometimes acts as if contact with the secular might corrupt or pollute him. This sense of engagement at the grassroots receives further confirmation from an Israeli TV documentary about the 1999 election campaign in the northern town of Kiryat Shemona, entitled 'Children of the Revolution'. The contrast this time is with the established parties, notably the Labour Party, whose activists are depicted as ageing and discouraged, while a pair of young Shas yeshiva students are busy on the street, as always with their Borsalinos, white shirts and dark suits, going from house to house and making a campaign with few resources save themselves and a loudspeaker. They ended up with a surprising surge in votes. The following sections present some examples of how this approach is translated into more institutional activity.

Social entrepreneurship and voluntarism

Voluntary contributions of time and energy to evangelising activities deserve as much emphasis as the state subsidies. They offer a fast-track opportunity for individuals to make their mark without having to apply for a job or wait in queue: indeed evangelising would be impossible without voluntary activity because the sort of commitment it requires is not easily priced in terms of working hours. Rather, and especially if there is access to government funding activism may lead to obtaining a wage of some kind, or to some form of religious entrepreneurship, and involvement in the movement is itself part of an individual's personal capital. Also, however generous the state funding, a movement cannot develop without an exhibition of personal sacrifice on the part of leaders and activists, as Scott Atran has shown (Atran, 2003b). It is therefore not entirely surprising that we were so often told that one of the attractions of the Shas school system is that, in contrast to the conflictive and corporatist image of the state-controlled secular and national religious school systems, its teachers never go on strike. Shas and the *t'shuva* movement may depend on state subsidies, but these come with all kinds of hazards: once allocated they may be delayed for numerous political and administrative reasons and, more generally, with their requirements for accountability, they can be a hassle. So, while a project waits for the wheels of bureaucracy to turn, momentum needs to be sustained and promises need to be kept—it cannot be held in suspense.

Our firsthand observation from the period when the party was still in the government, provided many examples of social entrepreneurship, and of a 'can-do' culture. The following cases illustrate the variety of NGO-type initiatives which are so central to the *t'shuva* movement.

Zeev   The NGO Ma'yanot Hityashvut ('Sources of the settlement process') is the brainchild of Zeev, a characteristic social entrepreneur, who has had a varied career in and out of religious institutions. He undertakes campaigns in agricultural co-operatives (*moshavim*) with yeshiva students who give their time for free—the only subsidy is for transport and administrative costs. Born in Israel of parents who came from Morocco and Libya, he had a national religious and then yeshiva-based schooling and attended a *kollel* after his marriage, while also going to teacher training college and working in a religious school for very small children. He has a painful memory of taking an examination to enter a prestigious Ashkenazi yeshiva and being rejected, despite excellent results: the head of the yeshiva simply told him that only 5 per cent of places were allocated to Sephardim. His career has included a few months in Buenos Aires, employed to check the kashrut of meat exported to Israel. For a time he owned a clothes shop in Boukharim, but moved on when his marriage, and his business partnership, fell apart. After that he divided his time between following a course at Touro University and running the NGO: when he found himself without a job he went to work for Shas as a volunteer and was offered this work with the *moshavim*. So long as Shas was in the government he funded this by receiving payment as a government adviser. Hence, even in the brief period when Shas dropped out of the Barak government he was without funding. Zeev describes himself as an inveterate self-improver, and says he is always trying to 'open myself up to the world'.

The NGO grew out of the revival of the practice of the Jubilee Year. According to Leviticus 25:3–7 the land should be left to rest every seventh year, but this practice had fallen into disuse and those Israeli farmers who wished to observe it were allowed to nominally pass ownership to a non-Jew for a year, until in the late 1990s the Rabbinic authorities began to take a stricter line. Shas sponsored an initiative to encourage farmers who did give up working the land to attend Torah study centres, and arranged payments of 300 shekels a month to them, attracting some 1,800 people. On the back of this success the new NGO was organised to send its teams to *moshavim* (whose members are predominantly Sephardi) where they found disused synagogues and a complete lack of religious observance. Aiming to gradually reintroduce a taste for observance, the teams would begin by cleaning up the synagogues, then they would install themselves there for study, invite the inhabitants to join them, conduct services, teach elementary Torah to the children, run activities for the women, and organise visits to holy places such as tombs of saints. Of course, the teams were not always accepted—if they were not, they would return five months later to try again. In addition, since the *moshavim* suffer from widespread poverty and governmental neglect, the organisation obtains charitable contributions with which it distributes food parcels for the Passover, school equipment packages and clothes for the needy. The scheme has operated, according to Zeev, in 180 of the 540 *moshavim* in Israel, but its survival depends on Shas's presence in the government. At the time of the interview the organisation was in crisis because of Shas's aforementioned brief exit from the Barak government.

Zeev is one of many social entrepreneurs who can be found operating in the ambit of Shas. One comes across frequent examples of charitable activity linked somehow to the propagation of *t'shuva*: in Petach Tikvah we were told that non-profit organisations help people to keep the Sabbath, to reorganise their home life according to religious norms; where appropriate they even leave packages at the houses of the poor—anonymously, so as not to create feelings of shame. To do all this they raise funds or obtain donations from synagogues, from individuals and from public and non-profit sources. This activity is discrete but not disinterested: it is all designed to create an atmosphere in people's lives that might bring them back to religion. The anonymous donations may not create feelings of shame, but their contents—kosher food, religious accoutrements—will leave little doubt in the recipients' minds as to their provenance.

Kol Hachesed Another example of social entrepreneurship, which has nothing to do with Shas but much to do with *t'shuva*, and receives no subsidy from the state, is that of a NGO led by activists from the Bratslav Chassidim,[9] which runs a pirate radio out of Netanya called Kol Hachesed (the Voice of Piety). The NGO is in

---

[9] The Bratslav Chassidim are different from other Chassidic sects because they have no leader, and are really a loosely-knit network of followers of the Rabbi Nahman of Bratslav, whose tomb in Uman, Ukraine, is a major pilgrimage site. Nahman's reputation is that of a mystic and a seer.

the early stages of setting up a school for 120 yeshiva drop-outs. Volunteers provide their services as teachers. The premises are rented out for private gatherings to fund the operation and converted into a *kollel* in the evenings. The project takes yeshiva drop-outs who, having never served in the army, fall between these two pillars of Israeli society and find themselves unequipped for making their own lives. The intention is for the students to serve a type of apprenticeship, but with one important condition: they must study Torah for two hours per day. Together with other organisations, Kol Hachesed claims to provide food boxes to 1,000 needy families, train orphans for their barmitzvah, and help young women who might be thinking of having an abortion—where necessary, and possible, by arranging marriages for them. Through the organisation fifteen doctors provide weekly free medical attention—and benefit from the advertising of their work on the radio station. They put needy people in touch with charitable individuals and help people buy and sell second-hand equipment. In all, this small group told us of six different activities undertaken by them.

Political entrepreneurship

Rachamim   A more explicitly political example is that of Rachamim, a significant party figure who has been on the Shas list as a Knesset candidate, and is the key Shas operative in Petach Tikvah, the major urban and industrial centre contiguous with Tel-Aviv, with 430,000 inhabitants. Born also of Libyan parents, Rachamim had a more religious upbringing and education than Zeev. His *haredi* identity was strengthened by serving as a founder member of the Nachal Haredi, a unit in the Israeli Army in which orthodox men who do not avail themselves of the exemption for yeshiva students can serve together. Rachamim became a senior officer, thus gaining impeccable credentials of citizenship. His education, his experience as an apprentice and later a manager in the diamond industry, which is mostly controlled by Chassidim, gained him a wide exposure to ultra-Orthodox Judaism, while not cutting him off from secular life. Rachamim has seven children, who have attended various types of religious institutions, while one son has done Army service and another is due to join. Another son is a high-flying yeshiva student who gained admission to a prestigious Lithuanian institution, despite the quota. As a prominent Shas politician, Rachamim has divided feelings about sending his son to a non-Sephardi institution, but he says 'people understand' on account of his son's special qualities. His daughter also attends a school identified with the Ashkenazi Orthodox, but which is more 'integrated'. He also professes to take a liberal view of his children's life course: 'I do not pressure them because what counts is respect for God, not the particular way they run their lives.'

For Shas, Rachamim is an ideal—though certainly not typical—'catch'. He has an exemplary family life, knows Torah and has extensive knowledge of different sections of Israeli society, as well as army and managerial experience. His formal status sounds unassuming: he was the Deputy Head of the Religious Council of Petach Tikvah. But Rachamim is in fact a full-time politician. He is a familiar figure all over town. He co-ordinates a committee of Shas office-holders, civil and religious, from different municipal departments, and together they allocate housing and much else besides. Housing is very important because of state subsidies and because the municipality has a hand in allocating housing in new building projects. The housing is distributed among different constituencies, with some set aside for *haredim*—no TV aerials—and some for others. He is on close terms with Rav Pinto, whom we have already encountered as a prominent Rabbi and head of a *yeshiva* in Petach Tikvah. He was a key figure in the allocation of resources to build a school, funded through the good offices of Arieh Deri when he was Minister of the Interior (and thus of local government). According to Rachamim, Deri insisted there should be a sports facility annexed to the school, which we visited on an evening, set aside for use by disabled basketball players. The trainer was not a *haredi*, but he was full of praises for Rachamim and Shas who had ensured that people with a disability could use the facility to send a team to the 2000 Paralympics in Sydney. He explained at some length how this was good for Shas but that such beneficial works were not the reason why he voted for them, as if to say his vote was not 'bought' but given for objective or impartial reasons. Rachamim for his part simply takes the line that Shas members of the municipal council look after and keep in touch with the people, without considering their ethnic or religious affiliation—but he readily says that his ultimate goal is *t'shuva* for the whole of Israel.

Individual initiatives

The disposition to *t'shuva* even inspires individuals to undertake lone campaigns, finding a vein to tap among colleagues or neighbours which draws on, though it is not controlled by, the wider campaign. At Touro University we met Shas supporters or activists looking to combine a secular career in support of the movement with their stringent religious commitments. Among them there were two individuals who again illustrated how *t'shuva* activism brings people into contact with religious institutions, education and politics at the local level and sometimes beyond, as they develop their entrepreneurial and networking activities. One of these was a landscape gardener, born in Israel of Tunisian parents, who had a secular upbringing on a *moshav*, went to the Army, but later met Ovadia Yosef and decided to return to religious observance. In the process he abandoned his girl-friend because although she had drawn him to religion, he then became too observant for her. He married someone else and has seven children. Since then he has founded, with others, a religious settlement on the West Bank called Itamar, where he became the Shas secretary and a member of the Regional Council. When we met him he was studying for a degree in Business Administration at Touro, funded almost certainly by or through Shas, while continuing to work as a landscape gardener.

A second case is a man who had devoted himself to setting up a school against all the odds. For fifteen years he worked in various capacities in schools for orthodox and handicapped children, but his involvement with Shas was intensified when he fought to set up the first permanent school structure in the new neighbourhood of Ramat Shlomo. In accordance with the scheme of mobilisation 'from below', he responded to a demand from parents, became involved in a factional struggle within Shas, appealed to Ovadia Yosef, and had the support of a group of teachers who taught for four months (once again) without a salary. In 2001 he was a member of the local Neighbourhood Council and of the Jerusalem City Council. He is studying at Touro for a school principal's certificate. (The article in

Ha'aretz, 18 November 2005, quoted above p. 180, describes similar sequences.)

In another example, a retired nurse from a 'soft' religious background came into contact with Shas when she was looking for voluntary work. Gradually she began to form a worldwide psalm-reciting network that ensures there is always someone reciting the day's psalm. In addition, she has become a prominent personality in her apartment block and her neighbourhood for her campaigning and also for forming 'consciousness-raising' groups.

These are all people of North African background for whom the Shas movement has opened up opportunities. In the first two cases the opportunities also brought mobility—political rather than social. They have not become rich, so far as we could tell, and they are not intending to turn their children into lawyers and accountants, but their activism has brought them, as well as the retired nurse, status and prominence in the community. They have carved out roles for themselves by bringing about incremental social change and participating in political mobilisation aiming to provide religious-cum-social services to Sephardim. Their Sephardi identity is not expressed in bitter or sectarian language, but, for the two men, their awareness of the exclusion of young Sephardim from the élite Ashkenazi religious establishments is a prime reason for setting up institutions serving the Sephardi population, and Shas's presence in the government evidently provided access to some of the resources necessary for this institution-building.

The main purpose of this exposition has been to show how multi-faceted and multi-levelled the Shas movement is, and how it has to be understood as a multiplicity of individuals and groups operating in a variety of institutional settings, exhibiting an intuitive militant or activist fellowship which is conveyed as if epidemiologically among them. Shas does not have a system for producing ideology or a party line, yet the dual goal of *t'shuva* and Sephardi promotion is shared by all, even when, after Deri's imprisonment, they are split between his supporters, who have hoped he would eventually return to lead them again, and those of Yishai. The diversity of their involvement in all sorts of nooks and crannies of Israeli society made Shasniks appear ubiquitous, especially during its heyday: not only were they present between elections, they seemed to be everywhere, all the time, making their point, making their presence felt. And Israel provides a receptive environment for interstitial mobilisation of this kind, full of available spaces because opened up by a culture of activism, organisation and grassroots pressure.

6

KNITTING THE STRANDS
OF POPULAR CULTURE

HOLY PIRATES

The genius, or good fortune, of Shas's founders was to link ethnic and religious renewal, so that it is now hard to choose between a description of Shas as embedded within a broader *t'shuva* movement, or of *t'shuva* as embedded within the ethnic renewal led by Shas. In common with social movements generally, the *t'shuva* movement uses multifarious means of communication and organisation, adopting a capillary approach to social mobilisation as opposed to the hierarchical methods used by conventional political parties or trade unions, or by the Ashkenazi *haredim*, whose communal activity has been much more subject to Rabbinical control and therefore, with the important exceptions of Chabad and Bratslav, leaves less space for initiative and entrepreneurship. Shas, on the other hand, lives by trusting its emissaries, and by drawing them from its 'target population'.

A movement spreads epidemiologically by capitalising on points of commonality with a range of constituencies as much as by broadcasting a message. Thus the emissaries or activists of Shas have a language in common with the second and third generation Sephardim, but they also share a taste in Middle Eastern popular music with some, and in Sephardi liturgical music with others; with some they may share a hostility to the secular establishment, with others to the *haredi* establishment; they develop characteristic ways of dressing, characteristic headgear (black velvet skullcaps) and, as Nissim Leon explains, a characteristic language, so that gradually people find multiple ways of joining, of becoming part of the flow. In all these niches of social life the movement's activists introduce an unfamiliar innovative set of signs, symbols, emblems and markers, by joining a *haredi* motif with elements of secular Israeli culture that have been kept at arm's length by the Ashkenazi *haredim*: they bring in Army slang, they bring in the jargon of *t'shuva* (with special expressions for the newcomers, the ones who need strengthening—*mitchazkim*), they adopt slight but significant variations in speech, and in songs, accentuating Sephardi, or conceivably pseudo-Sephardi, pronunciation (Leon, 2001). Yadgar also emphasises language as a tool of dissent, namely the deliberate positive charge in Shasniks' use of the customarily ridiculed Mizrachi accent which serves 'as a label for lower-class stereotyping within Israeli televised sitcoms' (Yadgar, 2003).

A complicating feature of this apparent bricolage of modes of speech, of prayer, of rhetoric, of music and of communication, is that, to the outsider, they seem not to fit together, they evoke apparently incompatible cultures and political alignments. How can people be at once obsessively devout in the regulation of their daily life, yet at the same time use street language? How can they deploy the music of contemporary secular youth culture in the propagation of rigorous ritual observance? In this chapter we illustrate the construction of Shas's version of Israeli popular and religious culture by examples from two spheres, namely broadcasting and invocations of the supernatural. The former represents an evidently modern face of the movement, and the latter an apparently traditional one, and their juxtaposition brings to the fore the superficially counter-intuitive bricolage mentioned. But the counter-intuitive elements, the syncretism, do not signify incoherence or implausibility. The different elements of a group's symbolic, affective and imaginary appurtenances are not structured hierarchically, nor ideologically, but through allusion and inferential processes which (via mechanisms which remain little understood) become habitual and institutionalised.

Social movements, like concentric circles, with hard centres (the 'cadres') and ever-softer peripheries, conform social spaces linked not by organisational structures but by inferential symbols reproduced in language, posters, iconic figures and much more besides. Shas, as a social movement embodied in a distinctive, open-ended set of cultural practices, conforms its identity by creating innovative symbolic and behavioural allusions across pre-existing boundaries. They break the rules, as, with their glitzy roadshows and garish outfits, do some Christian fundamentalist and evangelical preachers. In facilitating boundary-crossing, clearly the broadcast media can play a major role, even though television is excluded for reasons of propriety and radios are mostly shoestring operations which rely heavily on phone-in programmes and have a limited range. Radio and cassette distribution networks provide more markers for the movement and its followers. The regularity of programmes, the consistent tone or content of programmes broadcast at certain times of day on certain frequencies, the differentiation of the audience into *t'shuva*-defined segments, and perhaps above all the bridge provided by these media between public and private spheres, all bring the message into the intimacy of home and encourage its spread by word of mouth.

The use of media characteristic of popular culture, namely radio and cassette tapes, of itself provides an interface between religion and the ethnic group most identified with 'the popular' in Israel. In appealing to Sephardim, and among them often to young people whom they regard as mired in the frivolities—or worse—of consumer culture, the broadcasters could not but adopt a language and a style unfamiliar to traditional ultra-Orthodoxy, more street-wise, less hidebound, less weighed down by the somniferous tones of the yeshivas, a trend reinforced by the intervention of free-booting social and religious entrepreneurs in media previously ignored by ultra-Orthodoxy. The notoriety of these activities led us to carry out some interviews with their operators in 2001.

Pirate radios in the broadcasting system

Until 1999 the Israeli state had direct legal control of all nationwide radio and TV stations through the Israel Broadcasting Authority. Only in 1995 were private commercial radio stations permitted, and exclusively at the local[1] level operated under a franchise arrangement with the Israel Broadcasting Authority. Unofficial 'pirate' broadcasting, however, had begun in 1973 when dissident political groups, campaigning first against the country's occupation of the West Bank, later in favour of settlers in the self-same West Bank, broadcast from ships offshore. By 1995 'more than 50' active pirate stations were

---

[1] The Israeli term is 'regional', though it is better rendered as local, given the small spaces involved.

identified, rising to 132 in 1999 and some 150 in 2002. In the late 1990s they were mainly broadcasting music and entertainment (Caspi and Limor, 1999). Thereafter pirate stations transmitting the *t'shuva* message have proliferated, and their unmistakably Sephardi style of speech and music associates them with Shas in the mind of their audience and several, probably the majority, do indeed identify with Shas, notably Kol HaEmet (The Voice of Truth), Radio 2000, MiKol HaLev (Giving with all your Heart), Radio 10 and Kol HaNeshama (Voice of the Soul). After some resistance from Rav Schach, the Ashkenazi *haredi* community began to broadcast on radio stations, though they remain controversial in this prickly constituency, and there seemed in 2001 to be only one pirate station broadcasting specifically in the idiom of the Ashkenazi *haredim*—Kol HaSimcha (The Voice of Celebration). However, radio transmission enables people to cross boundaries without doing so too publicly, and in fact Arieh Deri broadcast frequently on Kol Simcha during the 1999 election campaign, and there is no reason to believe that Ashkenazim and secular people do not also listen to the many Sephardi-run religious pirate stations.

The Sephardi appeal of these radios, conveyed even in the streetwise language they use, can also be understood as a compensation for the very limited presence of Oriental music and culture in the official stations over many years. Those stations only broadcast one hour a day of Oriental content until a few years ago, but even now, though the amount has increased, the content, though possibly more in keeping with the music of North Africa and the Middle East, is not in tune with Israeli popular taste, let alone with the religious tastes of the *t'shuva* movement or of Shas followers. Official radio's secular bias, and its emphasis on high culture and educational themes,[2] plus the monotony of its diet of news, leaves a space for more popular—and therefore more Sephardi—modes of communication and enter-

---

[2] There are seven official stations: two belong to the army, of which one is a mainstream news and current affairs channel and the other transmits mostly music, in both cases with an eye to a highly secular, youthful audience, especially soldiers; Programme Aleph consists largely of high culture; Programme Bet consists mostly of news and politics; and Programme Gimel concentrates on Israeli music of all sorts, including Oriental; Network 88 broadcasts jazz and 'world music'; and Kol Hamusika (the Voice of Music) specialises in classical music. It is not hard to see that this leaves plenty of room for alternative stations.

tainment, and also for religious themes. State radio may give token space to programmes for minority ethnic and linguistic groups, for example the Russian and Ethiopian communities, but it offers little to that segment of the public which can be regarded as popular, yet drawn to religious themes and traditions.

Today, most of the pirate stations seem to be religious, and although they sometimes like to call themselves 'Holiness channels' (*arutsei kodesh*), they are happy to be known as *piratim*. There are also pirate stations devoted to popular music, while yet others serve the West Bank settlers, the vast Russian community and the Arab population. But the religious stations, whose central theme is *t'shuva*, are now so numerous that people find themselves listening almost by accident as they turn the knobs on their car radios or in their kitchens. During 2002 it was noticeable that they were going beyond their core audience and penetrating the secular world, and were also becoming the subject of debates on the mainstream channels' chat shows and political discussions. Their number and proportion are inevitably matters of political controversy. In a Knesset debate on 20 October 1999, a Shas member stated that there were 150 between 1996 and 1999 of which only fourteen were religious. Yet he also said that in 1999 the authorities closed down ninety stations, of which forty-eight were religious, and that in the two months prior to the debate twenty-one of the twenty-eight stations closed down were religious. Any conclusions drawn from these numbers should keep in mind the fact that stations routinely reopen after being 'closed down' and that many so-called closures affect offices but not the transmitters themselves.

Until about 2002 there had never been a prosecution or conviction, but the issue came to the fore again in 2004 when it emerged both that the radios' capacity was far greater than had been thought and also that the authorities were taking a harder line against them: a document submitted to the Knesset's Economics Committee by the Deputy Director of the Communications Ministry stated, 'from the beginning of that year until mid-July, 154 stations were shut down' of which 117 (76 per cent) 'were ultra-Orthodox'. The station with the most closures was Kol HaEmet, correctly described by *Ha'aretz* as 'associated with Shas' (see below). If, as reported, this station had twenty-two offices shut down in eighteen locations, it must have had an 'almost complete nationwide network'. Radio 2000 also had nineteen offices shut down. An eight-and-a-half month jail sentence with a $40,000 fine had also been imposed (*Ha'aretz*, 19 August 2004). Shas MK Shlomo Ben Izri (a Minister in the Barak government), the radios' 'political patron', took these figures as evidence of discrimination against the religious stations, and even claimed in 2004 that competitors divert ultra-Orthodox station broadcasts to the transmission channels of airplanes in order to prompt their closure for endangering air safety—a perennial issue.[3]

The degree of indulgence or repression by the authorities has varied with the colour of the government of the day, but the standard line among *haredim* is that they suffer relentless persecution. The tougher line taken in 2003 may reflect Shas's removal from the government after that year's elections. The Shas MK quoted above in the 1999 debate declared that the persecution of the pirate radios reminded him of when the authorities in his native Georgia sent tractors to steamroller their synagogues in 1953 and the people lay on the ground to stop them. It was clear, he said, that 'they' want to 'shut up millions who have no other station' and that the Prime Minister (then Ehud Barak) 'wants to destroy Shas' (his coalition partner). Even though 20 per cent of the population were observant Jews, religious broadcasting accounted only for 0.5 per cent of broadcasting time on legal channels, so pirate activity was justified.

Knesset debates on this subject were held on 12 March and 28 May 1997, 18 February 1998, 20 October 1999, 20 June and 23 July 2001, during which period they seemed to reflect a shared de facto toleration of a semi-legal situation. The debates have a tone of polemical banter, and end inconclusively as the participants fail to decide to which committee the issue should be referred. On one occasion the Chair asks how many pirate radios there are in Jerusalem, and a Shas MK responds 'one, the state radio!' In March 1997

---

[3] It is widely believed that the radios interfere with air traffic control. On 2 September 2002 several flights had to be cancelled because the pilots could not communicate with the control tower, apparently because of the pirate radios, and there was talk of a protest strike by air traffic control staff. But the *Ha'aretz* report of August 2004 shows that this has been a real issue, not just a stick with which to taunt the radios and their friends.

the Shas Minister of Transport said that so long as the only pirate radios were those of the Peace Movement (Kol Hashalom) and the settlers (Channel 7) they were left alone, but as soon as religious groups started to broadcast they were persecuted. In May that year a Shas MK said the stations might not be 'very legal', but they do express the views of a 'hated and persecuted' section of the population. On another occasion a member complained that while the police leave undisturbed the Christian evangelical radios, 'which propagate a mistaken interpretation of the sources', leading astray gullible Jewish listeners, the Jewish religious radios, which broadcast 'love for Israel and the truth' are subjected to constant harassment. In 1997 an early 'Ben Izri Committee' had recommended the legalisation of the religious broadcasters, increased budgets for religious broadcasting by the state broadcasting authority, the establishment of a state-funded Jewish broadcasting service, the inclusion of religious programmes in the most popular state radio station (Station 2) and the installation of religious professionals in all state radio stations: a classic example of Shas playing its hand to the maximum. None of the proposed measures were adopted, nor were they when a second attempt was made at legislation in 1999.

Largely in response to complaints about air traffic interference, the increased eagerness on the part of the authorities to enforce the law (*Ha'aretz* 19 August 2004) brought the number of closures to 229 in 2003, compared with only thirteen ten years earlier in 1993. Ultra-Orthodox stations seem to have had dozens of transmitters confiscated, but quite often only their offices have been closed, while the stations continued transmitting. Even so, *Ha'aretz* continues: 'within three and a half months no less than nine transmitters were confiscated from Arutz 2000 located in the community of Har Bracha … On May 20, a transmitter was confiscated and the next day, on May 21, its replacement was confiscated'. This reflects levels of financial support, derived from donations, which belie the pleas of poverty we heard from station managers in 2001, and a dynamic 'rapid response' management style we have repeatedly found in Israel's social movements.

The views of the Shas MKs quoted above were, of course, echoed by the pirate station operators. The director of the Mikol Halev station also told us (in 2001) that although there are hundreds of pirate stations in the country, only the religious ones were troubled by the police. Asked whether there might be advantages to illegality, he responded guardedly: he did not see benefits from legalisation 'in all situations', especially because legal stations are watched by the authorities and he did not want any authority looking over his shoulder or, as he put it, 'telling him what to say'. (This may reflect anxiety over a law against incitement that was passed in the wake of the Rabin assassination in 1995, described by some, with customary hyperbole, as a device for muzzling right-wing voices.) A newspaper journalist explained to us also that becoming legal involves bidding for a wave band, which is very expensive, because of the heavy competition for the few legally available bands, and would probably be far beyond the means of any of these stations. Legality would also impose all sorts of time-consuming paperwork.

On the other hand, legal status would allow the stations to earn revenues from advertising. In short, while radio piracy was tolerated by the authorities, the attitude of the radios themselves was summed up in a broadcaster's comment that 'no revolution is ever made in legality'. But by 2004 the position seems to have shifted: a bill was in the Knesset and Ben Izri was trying to use legalisation of the stations as a bargaining chip in (notional) coalition negotiations. He was prepared to accept legal oversight of the stations and some stations seemed ready to disburse the very substantial sums required for a legal operation, including 'setting up studios for a cost of around $1 million and putting up millions of shekels for a deposit' (*ibid.*). The bill would allow for three new stations of which two would be religious—a proportion that would have been simply unviable a few years previously and which reflects the size and audience of the *t'shuva* movement even when Shas was out of government.

The radios' funds are raised from donors and collections for the radios are often made at public meetings in support of the *t'shuva* movement, held in basketball stadia and the like. At MiKol Halev the broadcasters and workers, even the website designer, are volunteers, yeshiva students or people who have adopted full time religion. The station receives many offers—or approaches—from people who want to broadcast, but the director only accepts those recommended by trusted individuals. For someone who wants to build a reputation as a Rabbi the radio is a good opportunity, as in the case of Rav Shalom Arush who heads a network of several yeshivas and broadcasts on Kol HaChesed (The Voice of Charity). There are also degrees of professionalisation, exemplified by Rav Gilles, an experienced broadcaster in several different idioms on several stations—sometimes answering phone-ins, sometimes delivering learned commentaries, sometimes interviewing a guest—and adept at switching his accent and style of speech between different audiences. Stations have now taken to recruiting media professionals who have made *t'shuva* or are at least sympathetic to their cause. Rav Gilles' ethnic/community identity is of no concern to the stations, who are eager to broadcast this well known and experienced voice.

The radios do not stand still. MiKol Halev, which looks and sounds like a shoestring operation, had a website which allowed listeners to hear native-speaking Rabbis expounding in Hebrew, Spanish, French and English. The size of their audience is of course impossible to know accurately, and many wavering listeners, responding to an audience survey, might not admit they listen until 'they have crossed a certain line' and are ready to say they have become more observant. Sometimes a public response reveals their audience, as when, in response to a call by Ovadia Yosef to remove television sets from the home, some 200 sets almost immediately appeared in a preannounced location. Rav Gilles estimates the size of an audience by the number of callers—on some stations he has long queues of callers while on others there are very few. All arrange for a few callers in advance to get the show going. On this basis he reckons that MiKol Halev is a small station, whereas its director says it is one of the biggest.

Some stations have achieved a degree of institutionalisation despite their ambiguous legal existence, and while on occasions of momentous importance they may join forces, many also carve out audience niches. Kol HaEmet has been on the air since 1995 and describes itself as the world's biggest *kollel* and yeshiva. Ovadia Yosef is its Chairman and various prominent Sephardi Rabbis are on its board. Radio 10, in which Reuven Elbaz, the leader of Or HaChayyim, is very active, directs its *t'shuva* message at academics and members of the élite. MiKol Halev, as we have seen, looks to the popular sectors for its audience, while Kol HaNeshama is the one most given to expressing hostile attitudes to the Ashkenazi élite. Finally—though there are many others—Kol HaMizrach (The Voice of the East) is devoted principally to transmitting North African and Middle Eastern Jewish music.

Pirate radios and the t'shuva movement

The pirate religious stations are linked with a range of grassroots and street-level activities. We have seen the links with evangelists, but the case of Kol HaChesed shows that these links can spread much further and that their multi-media capacity has the effect of shifting established social boundaries. Kol HaChesed is a nationwide broadcaster run out of Netania by a group who resemble a social rescue brigade, as described in Chapter 6. Asked about their mission the first word they say is 'family'—to broadcast a message of love, of reconciliation within families, and to do so in a language which is readily understandable to people unfamiliar with Judaism. They distribute didactic cassettes by giving a person 100 to sell as a good deed (*mitzvah*), they respond to requests for help and advice, especially on matters of family and education, and they provide a marriage guidance service whereby listeners can consult a Rabbi personally or by telephone, off the air. And, as so often, there are miracles: when a lady rang in saying she was having difficulty finding a husband, the Rabbi on the air told her she should sell 100 cassettes—three weeks later she was married!

Thus we can see how radios are linked with other activities and organisations, crossing boundaries which in the routine of everyday life would be much thicker. Kol HaChesed does not emphasise Sephardi or Ashkenazi traditions and uses Rabbis from different traditions and tendencies. However, their attitude to secular Jews remains uncompromising. They have been known to attack the Supreme Court judges and 'leftists' (described on Kol HaNeshama as having their 'days numbered') for their liberal or secular outlook, as well as the academic world, accused of infecting the whole of society. In contrast, the one Ashkenazi *haredi* station, Kol Simcha, was indifferent to reaching out to the Sephardi population or to potential returnees, each of which was dismissively equated with the other: '*T'shuva?*.. that is for Sephardim' was the revealing quip.

Partly perhaps because of its doubtful legal status, pirate broad-casting creates a complicity and an intimacy with its audience: callers are not all that numerous, so they have time to chat, they are invited to make their needs known, and the speakers follow up through their religious or political networks to satisfy urgent personal needs. Most programming consists of homilies or phone-ins, with musical interludes of varying length. MiKol Halev is hosted every morning by a former ice-cream seller known as Ovadia Mehaglida ('Ovadia Ice-Cream'), for whom nothing is too much trouble. While we were there, someone rang in with a request for thirty items of clothing for a group of students who want to begin adopting religious dress. They sounded like candidates for *t'shuva* and the radio's prompt call brought immediate offers of money or donations in kind. Once a week they run a programme to match buyers and sellers of anything from household goods to real estate. Many stations reserve airtime for requests from individuals for help in emergencies. They also broadcast on health issues and alternative medicine.[4] Whereas pre-viously the stations tended to shy away from explicit political state-ments, in the increasingly polarised context of the second Intifada some stations have become more vociferous on the subject of Jewish relations with Arabs and Palestinians.

The Sephardi element is not explicitly played up, but is an implicit presence through references to Shas or to Ovadia Yosef, through the accent of broadcasters, through music and through their chatty style, which stands in contrast to the formalism of the state channels, char-acteristic of the Ashkenazi (secular) élite. Boundaries are redrawn by bringing listeners into new networks, which at first may be only vir-tual, but, if the radios achieve their aims, their influence in reshaping the lives of individuals, families and even broader groups should not be underestimated, as their listeners put children into religious school, start attending synagogue, and become ever more involved in reli-gious life. The content of the broadcasts, like the videos and tapes directed to the popular, less educated sectors, could be described as 'folksy'. They also pander to popular stereotypes, for example where

---

[4] There is an affinity between movements of religious renewal and the 'New Age' culture, given their interest in healing, and in the case of Jewish ultra-Orthodoxy, an uneasy attitude to medical manipulation of the body, especially of women's bodies.

a negative figure—in this case a priest—is portrayed speaking with an Arabic accent. Their use of images, proverbs and examples from everyday life, edges listeners towards conclusions in the manner of folk wisdom. They can always invoke as a precedent the example of Ovadia Yosef's addresses—though not his writings—peppered as they are with popular language and anecdotes (Yadgar, 2003).

Women are an important section of the audience, and stations pay a great deal of attention to their needs and problems, especially family problems and their solutions. Some speakers allow women on the air (but only 'so long as they keep to the point'), while others only allow them to leave messages—questions which are read out and answered, and which listeners can then follow up with requests for further clarification. In response to frequent requests for advice in overcoming family conflicts, speakers tend to recommend patience, long-term commitment, love in the family. For these broadcasters, even major political problems have their solution in the rebuilding of the family, helped by a more observant lifestyle. A man wants more children but cannot convince his wife; a woman wants to convince her household to adopt more strict observance, but encounters re-sistance among her men-folk … Both men and women call to ask advice in resolving family conflicts. The responses tend to focus on 'peace-building' in the home, especially by advising women not to respond to their husbands' inconsiderate or offensive behaviour. As we have seen in other *t'shuva* contexts, and indeed in Pentecostal churches, callers worry about insubordinate children, drugs culture, family violence and the temptations of the media and the street.[5] Thus a woman calls to complain that her husband shouts at her con-stantly. In response the speaker tells a story about a Rabbi who gave a woman an amulet to put in her mouth and keep it there. As a result she could not speak of course, but each day her husband came with more and more generous presents—flowers, a diamond ring, and so on. Eventually the Rabbi tells her that the 'amulet' is nothing but an empty card… The reference to amulets, of course, is a discretely Sephardi allusion, and listeners might also see in it an allusion to the controversy which arose concerning their distribution by Shas in the 1999 election campaign.

---

[5] In the ultra-Orthodox Ramat Shlomo neighbourhood a social worker told us that when he organises, in conjunction with the religious authorities, adult education sessions, the theme of family problems is very frequently requested by the public.

Listeners identify quite readily with 'their' station, to the point that when asked to place themselves on a religious spectrum, they may use the name of their preferred station as a shorthand response. The format makes the station an extension of the home, helped in this by a sense of complicity with the speakers and their friendly, helpful, 'can-do' responses. Some daytime programmes are for children, often using cautionary tales to convey a message.

Thus we see a range of mechanisms whereby the activities of radios, when combined with other organisations and of course with politics, are redrawing some of the boundaries which separate the multiple ethnic, religious and cultural enclaves of Israeli society. Listeners can find a radio which uses a particular style of speech, uses a certain type of music, emphasises certain themes, and enables them to combine religious observance with an engagement with the media—something quite uncommon in the *haredi* world until the *t'shuva* movement took hold. They also feel at home among an audience with whom they have a strong religious and ethnic affinity, so the airwaves are used to form networks of solidarity. Politically, the organisations which the radios promote depend directly or indirectly on government funding, so it is not surprising that sometimes the stations 'overstep the mark': in the 2001 election campaign, the Chair of the Electoral Commission 'issued an injunction banning election propaganda from Shas' pirate radio stations' (*Haaretz*, 1 February, 2001). The newspaper had no hesitation in identifying all the stations mentioned here with Shas.

The cassette tape industry and the t'shuva movement

The radio stations draw their audiences from several symbolically bounded communities, and much of their broadcasting is designed to consolidate boundaries by persuading listeners to adopt a more stringent way of life. They also aim to shift individuals across boundaries, using popular Oriental music, transmitting hard rock late at night, and thus appealing, through their media-born intimacy, to new constituencies who might change their lifestyles and join the *t'shuva* movement. The thriving religious cassette industry is another facet of the same campaign (Amran, 2000): it contributes by using the private character of cassette listening to get a 'foot in the door' (Amran uses the English expression), and also more publicly, by locating distribution centres, complete with study rooms and attendant religious experts, in shopping malls or other unaccustomed locations such as the designated points where soldiers can safely hitch a lift to and from their units. Like the radio programmes, cassettes are designed for listening as a 'secondary activity', for example while people go about their housework or sit on a bus or in their cars. There are musical tapes with religious-cum-popular music, tapes directed at children and tapes produced for more and less learned or observant audiences. The audience is broadened by using the Sephardim who are not *haredi* but 'respect their traditions', as a bridge to the secular public.

Cassettes are cheap to produce and do not have large economies of scale, allowing producers to carve out ever more precise market niches. Their spoken output is broadly divided between moral uplift or lifestyle themes and exegetic content for a more learned audience. There is also material directed more specifically at an audience of potential candidates for *t'shuva*, emphasising the sharpness of the contrasts between the secular and the religious world. Yet the medium does affect the behaviour of listeners in unintended ways. For example, in principle *haredi* women are not supposed to listen to the exegetical discourses, but they do, as some Rabbis ruefully note even on the cassettes themselves, and to prevent them would be possible only by withdrawal of all these learned cassettes.

The market orientation and growing professionalisation of the religious cassette system is illustrated by the ability of preachers to shift their tone and content for different audiences, and also the appearance of fee-charging speakers side-by-side with others who regard their work as a service to the community. For the most part the market is dominated by three companies. One of these, the non-profit Kol Hadaf,[6] is closely identified with Agudat Yisrael, and has benefited from the support of a New York real estate developer, as well as from state funding through the good offices of the influential Agudat MK Menachem Porush, former Chairman of the Knesset Finance Committee. It focuses exclusively on exegetic material and is not identified with *t'shuva*. The other two producer/distributors

---

[6] 'Voice of the Sheet' because it belongs to an organisation which produces a daily page of text with commentary broadcast in New York and Israel, in English, Hebrew and Yiddish, and also on El Al flights to New York! ttp://www.shemayisrael.co.il/dafyomi2/index.htm.

concentrate on moral uplift and issues in everyday life, and do not produce exegetic tapes, focusing more on the potential *t'shuva* audience. Of these the more successful is Ner Lemea (A Candle for 100),[7] a for-profit concern which has produced 2,200 tapes on themes such as 'peace in the home' and children's education. Kol Hadaf tapes are sold only in ultra-Orthodox neighbourhoods where, tacitly avoiding untoward contact, men and women briskly make their purchases at different times, while Ner Lemea sells to a mixed, unsegregated, clientele. At the time of her research Amran found that a favourite subject was the 'reincarnation of autistic children', a theme to which we shall return in the latter part of this chapter.

Like the radios, the religious cassette business makes new connections between the public and private spheres, instrumentalising, in the propagation of *t'shuva*, the media and the inferential modes of popular culture. The distribution of these cassettes is not like the distribution of entertainment material, such as video films and games which are obtained from standard retail outlets. People who go to the religious cassette outlets are aware of their common religious affiliation, and the outlets themselves are designed and located to serve a community. It is in neighbourhood mutual aid libraries (*gemachim*), based in private homes, that the cassette companies find their core market. These libraries are an institution in an observant neighbourhood, providing a service to individuals but also adding to the observant community's social capital by extending co-operative activity.

T'SHUVA AND THE TENSION BETWEEN HIGH AND LOW CULTURE

For those whose knowledge or experience of Judaism is limited to the diaspora, it is hard to imagine the adoption of strict religious observance as a dissidence directed against high culture, or that the propagation of an observant lifestyle might be wrapped in symbols and motifs drawn from the sphere of popular culture. How can ultra-Orthodoxy, which seems so austere, so bound up with the written word and canonical texts, accessible only to the learned, be anything but high culture? In Israel the ultra-Orthodox communities seemed

---

[7] A Talmudic allusion to a passage in which it is said 'a candle for one is a candle for a hundred'.

for a long time to be erudite, austere and self-isolated, relating to the rest of society only through their leaders' indefatigable political pressure and occasional direct action against violations of their bodily inhibitions and Sabbath observance. Yet now their influence and example spread through society born on technologies, symbols and musical motifs which the 'core' members of these communities regard with contempt, if they are aware of them at all. So, from an analytical point of view, drawing the line between high and popular culture requires account to be taken of the diversity of the ultra-Orthodox world itself and of the difficulties of mapping the secular-religious contrast onto that between high culture and its popular counterpart.

The erudite-popular dualism can be used when contrasting worldly secular Jewish life to that of the ultra-Orthodox whose every minute seems drenched in the minor rituals of daily life and their supernatural allusions. But it could also be applied to the contrast between the activities of yeshivas and adult study centres (*kollelim*) where men sit bowed over multi-lingual Rabbinic texts and commentaries, and the ecstatic expressions of those same men (if they are Chassidim) on the great festivals and at celebrations of rites of passage. It could also be applied to the schism in eighteenth-century Eastern Europe between the austerity of the followers of the Great Rabbi of Vilna (the Vilna Gaon) and the ecstatic manifestations of the Chassidic movement—a schism which was marked by ferocious hostility for generations and only began to soften after the Holocaust, but is today expressed more in distinctive ritual practices, marriage choices, choices of school and yeshiva and dress codes (Jacobs, 1995).[8] Furthermore we have seen how the popular-erudite contrast has at least one, and most likely several, ethnic dimensions among Israeli Jews, one of which sets the country's Sephardi population apart from the secular Ashkenazim. The 'Ashkenaziness' of the latter is itself probably defined by other Israelis more by its affinity with the cultural and technological ways of life of modernity than with their previous European ancestry, including widespread participation in the popular musical cultures of the West (Segev, 2002). If the Sephardim

[8] Maybe the ideological element was already exaggerated in earlier accounts, and these ritual markers were the issue between the different schools and sects already in nineteenth-century Eastern Europe.

qua Sephardim are carriers of an Israeli popular culture, they are not thought to be in this camp of Western youth culture, yet both could be called 'popular'. *Qua* youth, of course, young Sephardim participate as much in Western-style youth culture as any other Israelis.

Further difficulties arise in the religious field. The Rabbinic erudition of the *haredi* communities stands in sharp contrast to the secular erudition of the university: while academics bring modern sciences such as archaeology and linguistics to bear on canonic texts, and place them in a historical context, in the yeshivas the Rabbis do not accept the treatment of those texts as historical documents. Although they cultivate an extraordinary command of the texts, as far as yeshiva scholarship is concerned, Rashi (1040–1105) in France, Maimonides (1135–1204) in Cordoba and Cairo and the authors and editors of the Talmud (500–200BCE) in Babylon and Jerusalem might as well all have lived at the same time and in the same place. Their dissidence *vis-à-vis* the philosophical claims of modern science and their evident hostility to innovation could therefore be said to place the Rabbis in the camp of popular culture.

As these remarks show, and as we have argued in other contexts (Lehmann, 1996), the popular-erudite opposition is suffused with reflexivity: each contains a certain conception of the other, and of the other's conception of itself. For present purposes, and remaining in the religious sphere, we shall understand popular culture as practices which refer explicitly to an inherited tradition and which to some extent express a dissidence *vis-à-vis* an élite culture considered to be hegemonic, respectable and cosmopolitan. In this conception, although élite culture is considered closed to popular culture, it is also perceived by the popular to be vulnerable to pressure from those who could explicitly or implicitly accuse it of betraying a heritage or building an illegitimate power base. The bearers of popular culture make claims on the élite, and for their part the bearers of élite culture develop and often co-opt a certain concept or model of the popular, as expressed in all sorts of contexts, from folk exhibitions to juridical disputes. Today's disputes (in Israel, in France, everywhere) about the extent to which the liberal state can permit illiberal practices in the name of respect for tradition presents another dimension of this dialectic, replete with multiple misapprehensions, misconstructions and inevitable mutual stereotyping.

To understand the popular dimension of the return to religion, it must first be recalled that the Israeli state constitutes a space in which the interaction of high and low culture is bound up not just with relations of power but with partisan politics. Although the Ashkenazi Rabbinical world may look down on the Sephardim, it has also imparted to its Sephardi followers its own hostility to the secular élite and thus brought them in as participants in the culture wars of Israel's Jews. The broader Sephardi population, for their part, especially those of North African origin, provide a stream of willing participants because they feel themselves marked out from the secular élite by a range of linguistic, educational and socio-economic markers, and those who speak for them repeatedly charge that élite with making them feel inferior in culture and social status. But even now, after two decades of Shas and its evangelisation, only a small minority of the Sephardim are brought up in the *haredi* world, so the vast majority have little experience of discrimination at the hands of the Ashkenazi ultra-Orthodox, and can without any ambiguity join in the chorus of class resentment and religious indignation.

This is the context in which the promoters of *t'shuva* have mobilised popular culture and strict religion against the secular élite and its cosmopolitan (European-Ashkenazi) practices. The streetwise tinge to the movement—evidenced in Ovadia Yosef's asides, the chatty style of some cassette tapes, the religious music on tape and the fabulous imagery of Amnon Yitzchak's apocalyptic discourses (see below)—provides a platform for its openness to the broader society and demarcates the *t'shuva* movement from the *haredi* association with closure, introspection and exclusion. The dissidence is further legitimated by the identification in Israel of the popular sectors with the Judaeo-Arab heritage, rather than with the Yiddish-speaking Eastern European culture, because the Sephardim are disadvantaged, because theirs is the language of the street, and even because the pronunciation of modern Hebrew itself derives from the Hebrew of the Northern and Southern Mediterranean shores and of Sephardi communities in historic Palestine. Similarly, much of Israeli popular music also derives from the North African and Middle Eastern musical modes, not from those of Eastern Europe or of the Judaeo-Spanish tradition, as do the staples of Israeli diet (falafel, houmous etc.).

Outside Israel *t'shuva* movements are scarcely associated with popular cultures. Chabad uses cassettes and co-opts popular music and

New Age themes and motifs into its activities, runs outreach programmes in the Jewish community and on many university campuses,
especially in the USA, and is well known for its missionary activities
worldwide. But these operate in a parochial Jewish cultural field in
the diaspora, not throughout a national cultural space as is possible in
Israel, and it is striking that Chabad, though it has extensive operations in Israel, including an entire settlement known as Kfar Chabad, does not have a high profile there, but rather a dispersed and
fragmented presence. In contrast, the Israeli *t'shuva* movement, with
Shas as its vanguard, has developed not just as a 'conversion' or 'return' movement but also as a politicised movement of cultural dissidence able to challenge the prevailing relationship between various
erudite and popular cultures. Furthermore the element of self-esteem,
and thus empowerment, on which Deri insisted, has to some extent
at least ensured that the message has spread rather than remaining
confined to a closed community feeding on its own animosities.

The mischievous millenarian: the use of parables
and myths to subvert official discourse

The confluence of popular culture, religious renewal and multi-media intervention is well represented in the figure of Amnon Yizt-
chak. Yitzchak is a one-man multi-media road-show: his video
cassettes are distributed for free at street intersections; he makes CDs
of his appearances in Israel, England and the United States (being
welcomed on a helipad by the Mayor of New York); and his personal appearances in Israel seem calculated to challenge and offend
the country's cultural élite. When he hired Tel-Aviv's *Hechal Hatar-
but* (Temple of Culture) auditorium legal moves were (unsuccess-
fully) taken right up to the High Court to stop his appearance there.
Consequently, the audience at his—by now unchallenged—appearance in the equally highbrow Jerusalem Theatre in November 2001
were gleefully treated to a video of those very protests. The shock
tactics go further. To support his campaign against television, Yitzchak promises that anyone who throws out their TV set will receive
a free copy of the Babylonian Talmud (Talmud Babli), and to demonstrate the success of his evangelising campaign, he exhibits a box
of earrings and ponytails discarded by women and men who have
publicly renounced their secular life at his meetings.

Yitzchak's Yemeni origin is central to his mediatic persona: his accent identifies him with that underprivileged and Oriental sector of society, even though the Yemenis are apart from the Sephardim in ritual and community, and he wears a *djellaba* (an Arab-style body-length tunic) with unique accoutrements, including a skull-cap which he jokingly refers to as his 'antenna'. In this slightly, but far from entirely, jokey vein, he litters his addresses with wordplay, talking of the 'tembelevisia' instead of the 'televisia'—an allusion to the mind-numbing effects of television[9]—and likening George W. Bush's name to the Hebrew word for embarrassment—*busha*. Yitzchak manages to soften stark choices and thick boundaries, presenting *t'shuva* as a gradual purification of social relations rather than a radical break, with an emphasis on joining a new community rather than on breaking bonds with the old, and as a solution to everyday problems of love, family and finding a spouse. By fashioning his 'act', to some extent, in the manner of a stand-up comic, he catches both the secular and the religious off balance: by joining the comic and the serious, the transcendent with the everyday, it has been said that he creates a mediation between the sacred and the profane which is novel at least in Judaism (Wasertzug-Rabid, 2002). He thus attracts young people who, he claimed, find his meetings 'better than cinema, theatre and TV all together'.

He also has many attributes of a Christian evangelist, including the theological, a domain in which he draws generously on Christian expressions or keywords. Thus in a meeting in 1997, when questioned about a two-year old child who had died in a terrorist attack, he gave his audience to understand that this death was a grace of God, for the child was a lost soul who would return to the higher world in an improved state. This was a price the parents had to pay so that God's grace could be carried out (Meler, 1998).

In another Christian fundamentalist variation, the road-show is also a business operation, benefiting from the cooperation of volunteers and from donations, and marketing itself with exaggerated claims. His Shofar organisation claims to have distributed a million videos for free in its first year, to have sold a further million a year after 1996, and to have brought 100,000 returnees per year back to

---

[9] *Tembel* is Hebrew for 'foolish'.

religion. The free distributions of video and cassette tapes are made in the expectation that a certain number of the recipients will then become buyers and sellers. At meetings he invites his audience to 'win' (i.e. buy) 1,000 cassettes by signing up to make ten monthly contributions of 100 shekels. If he persuades a mere twenty people, from 500 attending a neighbourhood meeting, to sign up, that makes 20,000 tapes in a small area. The 'winners' will then sell the tapes in their neighbourhood (and perhaps make a profit).

His Chayyim Keflayim (Living Twice) programme follows up people who provide their names at meetings and gives them cassettes. Thus the organisation builds up a database of people with whom it comes into contact, who might become more involved or donate funds. Like the radio stations, it encourages parents to put their children into religious schools and supports returnees on their road back to religious observance, but Yitzchak and his people have gone much further than the radio stations in creating a public of their own, in the application of business principles, and in adopting the content of American millenarian fundamentalism (Ammerman, 1987). His rhetoric also goes further than (almost) any Israeli politician would dare.

At the Jerusalem Theatre Yitzchak made constant reference to his cassettes: 'I am saying this now that we are on cassette 200, but I already predicted it in cassette 35'; in responses to the public he would say, 'but have you not listened to the last cassette?' Warm-up videos had already shown his supporters distributing cassettes for free at road junctions. The cassettes seem to be the emblem of his operation. To own and listen to them is to belong, and to distribute them among one's friends and relations is to draw even closer to his campaign.

Dressed in his distinctive attire, Yitzchak is his own trade mark. The format of his meetings includes him giving an address followed by questions from the floor. Many people want their personal problems resolved—one needs a husband, the other a wife, a young boy wants to attend religious school but his mother will not let him, and so on. Almost all the questioners—some of whom may be 'planted', like callers to the phone-in radio programmes, to get the process under way—speak with ease and eloquence, and Yitzchak responds in his own down-to-earth style. Those who have specific needs are asked to hand in a piece of paper and he blesses them all at the end of the meeting.

Yitzchak's mockery of the establishment is fuelled by wordplay and judicious use of accent and turns of phrase. In one video, filmed live, he defends the privileges enjoyed by *haredim* in Israel, using the analogy of a watermelon. This is a reference to a remark by Ezer Weizman, Israel's former Head of State (1993–2000) and, for the preacher's audience, an archetypal representative of the European, educated, secular élite. Weizman had picked out the development of the seedless watermelon as a source of great national pride, but for religious people, for whom Israel is above all not a state but a land, the notion that the country should take pride in such mundane achievements is itself laughable. Yitzchak uses the quote to weave a fable about Israel's religious and secular populations: the metaphor of 'black' as the colour of strict religious observance. For him, it is not surprising that Weizman, like all secular Israelis, wants an Israel without the black seeds—without the *haredim*.[10] For Yitzchak, in contrast, the *haredim* are not only black seeds, they are also the seeds of continuity of Judaism, while the juicy red flesh of the watermelon represents communism and dictatorship—i.e. the godless Zionist secular regime—and the green outer skin represents fertile pasture, an image of a fertile Israel. The kibbutz, secular and emblematically Zionist, took the juice of state subsidies first, so the *haredim* were forced to come and extort their due: if the *haredim* had staked their claim first, they would not have had to exercise so much pressure later on. He then attacks a towering icon of Zionism, namely the 'founding father' David Ben-Gurion. Ben-Gurion, he claims, had said that Israel had to make the Jews into a people with a culture—thus ignoring 5,300 years of Jewish culture—and introduced German high culture—that is, as he put it, anti-semitism. Israel's secular culture, he is saying, is anti-semitic. What, Yitzhak asks, of charity, of Sabbath observance, of respect for the sages—are these not also culture?

We had occasion to appreciate the effectiveness of Yitzchak's use of these devices in his address, entitled 'Before the End'—more or less word for word the same as a cassette he issued on 12 September 2001—the day after an event which offered a golden opportunity to merchants of apocalyptic millenarianism. He recalled his prediction

---

[10] The word 'black' is synonymous with *haredi*; thus a black neighbourhood is one dominated by the ultra-Orthodox.

at the time of the 1993 Oslo agreements that 'there is no peace with terrorists' (cassette no. 35). Two years before he had predicted that 'the great America would shrink ... no-one would have predicted it, not even in their worst nightmares.... A million Interpol agents ... millions of recorded telephone conversations ...', all these 'sources', he said, playing on the term 'intelligence sources', are of no use because those without *spiritual* sources' are unprotected. Only those who had the Jewish 'sources' knew it would happen.

The discourse then discusses the biblical origins of claims to the land of Israel, and quotes the Zohar, the thirteenth-century Kabbalistic text:[11]

there will come a time when their right to the Holy Land will expire. Then the sons of Ishmael[12] will wage war on the whole world, on sea, on land and near Jerusalem, and other peoples will participate in the struggle, but there will be no victor... there will be three months of war in a far-off place, and in the end only Israel will remain and the whole world will recognise the one God and his name is One ... No-one believed these or other prophecies, yet 'the sons of Ishmael' have made us—the sixth power in the world—and the Americans, look like circus performers, like dwarfs: they took away the King's crown and slapped him in the face.

Yitzchak ridicules the Americans—branded by implication as the global champions of the consumer society—and indeed the Israeli state itself, which places too much trust in military prowess. He predicts that two thirds of the world will perish in the war of Gog and Magog:[13]

in 9 months of catastrophe, there will be epidemics, and limbs will be cut from bodies. Two thirds of the world will die. It is all written down—there is nothing to be done. The American attempt to impose globalisation, democracy and liberalism, ignoring all religions, has come to this.

But there is a chance of salvation for Israel if the people make *t'shuva* and return to God. He reiterates the Prophetic theme of the life of the Jewish people as an endless alternation between abandonment of God and *t'shuva*, so 'maybe this is the last *t'shuva*, maybe we can be saved as in the Exodus from Egypt. Maybe now we have finally

[11] The legends and controversies are summarised by Louis Jacobs (1995: 628–30).
[12] i.e. the Arabs.
[13] A periodic theme in Jewish and Christian eschatology, derived originally from the Book of the Prophet Ezekiel, 38, 39.

understood and the Messiah will return in our times', a phrase which appears frequently in Jewish prayer.

Apart from the violence of the language and the message, there is a constant inversion of official language in the discourse, with the use of wordplay and caricature: the seedless watermelon, the Twin Towers and the tower of Babel; Bush juxtaposed with the Hebrew word '*busha*', the 'intelligence sources' juxtaposed with 'spiritual sources', and the ridiculing of a great power humiliated, an image of the 'world upside down'.

Written black on white, the speech seems extremely threatening, but in the auditorium, delivered in a low-key measured tone, sprinkled with jokes and ridicule of the great and powerful, including all Israeli political factions—save Shas—the audience did not respond with abnormal emotion or enthusiasm, as they might have done to fiery political rhetoric in a less genteel location.

The show should be interpreted in several different registers: a deft use of popular language to promote millenarian, anti-establishment religion; an allusive use of Yitzchak's persona to contribute to Sephardi religious empowerment but without openly espousing Shas; a straightforward invitation to *t'shuva*; or simply an occasion when people can come to receive advice, to engage in a ritual of conversion, or simply to receive a blessing from the sage.

Autistic and Alzheimer sufferers as oracles

There is a strain in the *t'shuva* movement and in Amnon Yitzchak's pronouncements which places returnees or converts on a higher or purer plane than the old-timers, and we have noted the Biblical idea that God takes greater pleasure in one sinner who repents than in a person who has been observant from birth.[14] But the superior status conferred on *ba'alei t'shuva* is not only a theological or rhetorical device: it draws on the fear of being unmasked and the fear of gossip, which are powerful motives in the dynamics of conversion, as will become clear below. One facet of this turns up in accounts of brain damage sufferers acting (or being used) as oracles, contained in pamphlets which circulate, rather discreetly, in Shas and *t'shuva* circles.

---

[14] Cf. Luke 15:7, 'there will be more rejoicing in heaven over one sinner who repents than over ninety-nine righteous persons who do not need to repent.'

One of these,[15] given to us by the lady who organises a worldwide chain of psalm-readers, is entitled 'A Faint Voice in the Void' and is sub-titled 'Messages from the Autistic and Brain-Damaged on the Situation of our Times: messages from the world of the souls'. The practice of such people acting—or being used—as oracles is not new, and the ideas attributed to them are classic revivalist themes. The autistic, and also Alzheimer sufferers, are quoted as denouncing the frivolities of the world and the danger of hypocrisy lurking where religious observance is not entirely authentic. They emphasise qualities of the heart and disinterested Torah study—Torah 'for its own sake' in the standard phrase—along similar lines to those preached by an Or HaChayyim tutor (Rav Eliezer) whom we have already quoted. Autistic children warn, in the delphic manner characteristic of oracles, that 'if they study Torah otherwise than for its own sake' the Torah 'will turn against them'; they denounce the current 'impudent and bare-faced generation' which 'will only understand when they encounter a heavy blow'; a 'plastic *yiddischkeit* [Jewish way of life] has been created'. All politics is described as polluted and tainted, and all those, including *haredim*, who are involved in politics are tainted. The Alzheimer sufferer addresses his son as if imprisoned in his body: 'I am shut in my own body ... I used to live only for my body but now it does not work, it is only soul, and you cannot run away from the truth ... do not wait till, God forbid, you are in the state I am in. You have to pray, but prayer is not enough, you have to keep the commandments ... it does not matter if your sister is divorced so long as she keeps the commandments ... you have to leave this world and go back to the life of my father and grandfather.' The old man says he is in touch with his dead father, who came to tell him 'the world does not have much time.' And when his son tells him he does not have an income, the father replies, 'God gave you a wife and a child and this is better than an income.'

On one hand these pamphlets emphasise innocence and purity: 'a Jew without heart or love of God is not a Jew'; 'although we do many righteous things and there are many expensive yeshivas, look closely inside the heart of the people and you will see there is no heart ... When we make *t'shuva* we will all find happiness and go up to Jerusalem and we will crown the Messiah and we will be at peace

[15] The publisher is identified by phone numbers in Israel and the United States.

with God and with ourselves.' But the warning that 'you cannot run away from the truth', that behind a façade of purity or observance there may be a different reality, opens the door to a darker side, to the power of those (in this case those behind the 'oracles') who claim to see through the façade.

Not only does this pamphlet, like Amnon Yitzchak's preaching, read as placing *hozrei bet'shuva* above the established *haredim*: the latter are denounced more or less explicitly as hypocrites and beneficiaries of political favours, which enable them to lead a luxurious lifestyle. 'The angel who receives our prayers never asks about the colour of a kippa, its size, or the material it is made of', says an autistic girl: 'religious people are the apex of the world but spend their time squabbling over government budgets; they say it is for God above but they hate each other in the name of God.' Those who return to religion will save the world, not those who engage in politics or worldly activity, and those who devote themselves to study have no guarantee if their heart is not in it.

The problem is: who can tell which heart is pure and who can be assured that the impurity of their own hearts, their own base thoughts, will not be detected? This anxiety, as we shall see, can open the way to a perverse power play.

THE RECOVERY OF FRAGMENTS FROM TRADITION

It is a commonplace that religious traditions, the movements which carry them forward and transform them, and the institutions which embody them and ensure their reproduction, survive by adapting to and also by fashioning immense change in their environments, while at the same time retaining an aura of deep resistance to change and faithfulness to tradition. But this commonplace is too general and vague to constitute the basis for coherent interpretations of social movements: who, after all, is to fix the boundaries which decide when change is change and when change is continuity? Who is to decide what counts as tradition and what does not? Instead of assessing from without what is tradition and what is change, it is worth asking how the power and authority to define and redefine tradition is itself subject to change.

The interest here is to make sense of how Shas and the *t'shuva* movement combine centuries–old ritual, scholarly and liturgical continuity, and continuity in the practical reflexes of daily life, with startling innovations such as the pirate radios we have been discussing and the vaudeville of Amnon Yitzchak. Rather than view this apparently incoherent and kaleidoscopic set of observations as a combination of the new and the old (the 'modern' and the 'traditional') we see it as a dialectic of co-optation and conflict which characterises the popular-erudite relationship in religious life. In this framework an intellectual or ideological élite has a certain conception of the content of religion and uses its bureaucratic and financial resources to codify and adjudicate through a deliberate, recorded process, trying to rationalise and domesticate the supernatural. For them the cult of the supernatural is largely an embarrassment. The mechanism of control is the establishment of bureaucracies, of which the Vatican and the Church of England are prime examples. When these institutions face the challenge of new circumstances, they respond by turning to doctrine and revising what their intellectual exponents regard as outdated or hard to sustain, in an effort to 'read the signs of the times'. Liberation Theology, for example, grew out of a massive theological effort leading up to the Second Vatican Council (Vatican II), and subsequently was propagated through a worldwide network of nuns, priests and activists in outreach activities, Catholic and secular educational institutions and Christian and secular developmental NGOs. This theology gained influence on popular movements especially in Latin America, but experience showed that its influence relied heavily on the support of religious institutions and professionals (Lehmann, 1990; Doimo, 1995; Vasquez, 1998). The modernising impetus (*aggiornamento*) of Vatican II and Liberation Theology, like Liberal Anglicanism, required downgrading 'superstition' and practical involvement with the supernatural, shifting the emphasis of religious practice away from ritual towards education, towards 'consciousness-raising' and awareness of the ways in which religious institutions and their followers could engage with the world, away from personal religiosity to the good of society. In Judaism the equivalent shift is seen in what is known in Britain as Reform Judaism and in the United States as Conservative Judaism, and to some extent in Modern Orthodoxy, followed by Liberal Judaism and innumerable unorthodox variants ('cool shuls', 'gay shuls', and so on). These are doctrinally aware, erudite departures which, if they have one thing in common, it is the downplaying of the supernatural.

But popular religion, with its affinity for a supernatural realm beyond bureaucratic control, is never quiescent, and finds adaptations to changing circumstances in less intellectualised, less centralised, and more inferential ways. It does not deliberate about the theological implications of this or that procedure, but relies on intuitive representations among its public about what fits and what does not, often with surprising results. Brazilian Pentecostals adapt the Catholic communion and call it the Holy Supper;[16] the Catholic Charismatic Renewal has borrowed wholesale from the Pentecostals, invoking fear of the diabolical, and practicing glossolalia and exorcism; Jewish evangelisers in Chabad must have learnt their method of organisation from the Pentecostals, and have also borrowed from New Age, as do some branches of the Bratslav Chassidim. Neo-Pentecostals (such as the Universal Church of the Kingdom of God) borrow directly from the Bible, anointing the foreheads of the faithful with oil and distributing purifying water from the River Jordan, and the *t'shuva* movement has no difficulty with ideas about divine intervention in political events, in wars and in people's personal lives. Innovation in popular religion is marked by a lack of authorisation, decorum or respect for established ceremonies and procedures, featuring offences against respectability and good taste, as in the spontaneity of Pentecostal 'gifts of the spirit' and glossolalia, or claims about the messianic qualities of their leaders (Chabad). Boundaries are forced back or violated in a process which resembles trial and error, or bricolage, in feints and prods from below rather than a concerted institutional strategy, so that in all probability the innovations which do become institutionalised are but a fraction of those which have been tried out. For example, in Israel one grassroots *haredi* development is the Zaka brigade of rescue workers who have now become a standard feature of post-bombing scenes, shown on television worldwide. As Nurit Stadler (2002) explains, they have taken upon themselves a service which involves the violation of many ultra-Orthodox norms, not least dealing with body parts, even on the Sabbath if necessary. From one point of view this can be seen as a

---

[16] The *Santa Ceia* is the taking of a beverage in small plastic cups distributed to those who are entitled.

way for *haredim* to gain legitimacy in the eyes of the Israeli public and state, but at the same time there is in their activity an element of satisfaction in this violation of ingrained ritual practices. Other examples of breaking down frontiers are the campaigns which take Jewish missionaries into hospitals and onto the street or into Metro stations in London and Paris.

Surprise and shock, then, are stock weapons in the armoury of popular religious revivals. They provocatively challenge authority: where official institutionalised religion undertakes elaborate procedures to authorise change, popular religion gains legitimacy for changes without such deliberation and with little concern for propriety. Authority is charismatic and embodied in persons, acquired only secondarily and sometimes *ex-post*, through rituals or procedures. Ritual innovation occurs through trial and error. Again, we only hear of the successful innovators and leaders: behind them are innumerable failures who remain forgotten and ridiculed as charlatans or pranksters.

Ideological modernists may depict such movements of regeneration as backward-looking or ridicule them as drenched in superstition, but the spokesmen for evangelical and charismatic movements retort that the modernists represent an entrenched power élite—a retort sometimes expressed in quasi-paranoid language, in which (for certain kinds of Christian) the Pope is the anti-Christ, the Catholic Church the 'great prostitute', and so on.

These are also the movements which have adopted most readily forms of organisation and communication appropriate to contemporary conditions, precisely because they are not burdened by the centuries-old procedures and bureaucracies of the Roman Catholic or Anglican Church. In contrast to the image of an inward-looking community studiously uninterested in the wider world, we find among evangelicals as well as in the *t'shuva* movement, a direct engagement with the practical and ideological problems of contemporary life (broken families, drug abuse, ill health, depression and of course poverty) and the co-optation or infiltration of whatever ideas and methods might find a reception among the target audience, irrespective of authoritative endorsement or compatibility with tradition. In short, there seems to be little contradiction between adaptation to modernity and resuscitation or continuation of practices and beliefs which deal unashamedly with the supernatural. Popular religion relates to supernatural forces which will cure illnesses, make people wealthy and give us insight into others' thoughts and purposes: through symbolic exchange relationships (such as pilgrimages and votive offerings), through acts of charity, through fasting, and through consultation with mediums, preachers, healers, priests and rabbis (Brandão, 1980; Lehmann, 2002).[17]

Even so, one must draw a line between the popular religion that is contained within the limits of toleration and even encouragement of institutional religion (pilgrimages, local cults etc.), and revivalist-cum-dissident movements that clearly challenge and confront institutional religion, especially by denouncing its hypocrisy, its finery, its political machinations, and claiming (as through oracles) additional, privileged insight into the minds of followers. One element which does seem to mark out revivalist-cum-dissident movements from the ways of day-to-day popular religion, is the call on people to change their lives. Movements of revival call for a change 'from within' a person, which often goes together with cutting off or at least attenuating existing ties of family and friendship and economic ties guaranteeing a livelihood. This sort of choice, once associated with hermits and other virtuosi, is now acquiring the characteristics of a mass phenomenon, made possible, among other things, by the prosperity of modern societies, which facilitates charitable giving, by subsidies from the state, and by the entrepreneurial character of contemporary revival movements. Subsidies from the state are evident in Israel, but elsewhere too we observe Pentecostal leaders, in Brazil for example, using the clientelistic channels to which their political involvement connects them to obtain state funds and subsidies in one form or another (Freston, 2001b). Furthermore, entrepreneurship for its part has at its disposal technologies which enable preachers and organisations to reach a wider audience than ever before and to communicate with unprecedented effectiveness.

These are external conditions, but the internal dynamics also need to be explained. The important role of exchange and interdepend-

---

[17] Carlos Rodriguez Brandão in his remarkable *Deuses do Povo* ('The People's Gods') (São Paulo, 1980), enumerates with a wealth of illustrative quotation and popular language from small-town Brazil the abundance of informal officiants who populate the world of unofficial worship.

ence in revival movements can link this inner change in people's lives, manifested in renunciation of worldly pleasures, to popular religion, despite the seeming incompatibility between the practical character of popular religion and this other-worldly agenda of personal transformation. As Boyer explains, people's 'inference systems for social interaction ...guide their intuitions about exchange and fairness' (Boyer, 2001: 229). The model of social exchange, which could be seen as a cognitive version of the classic formulation by Marcel Mauss (1950), is evidently applicable, for example, to pilgrimages and local cults: people go to ask for an intercession by a Saint or by a particular Virgin—viz. Guadalupe or Lourdes, and, in Israel, Baba Sali. Villagers all over Latin America and the Mediterranean ask favours from a local patron saint or Virgin—to pass an examination, to retain a boyfriend, to get a job—making a vow, *voto*, beforehand in hope, and after the fact bringing an *ex-voto* in recognition. At the shrine to Baba Sali in Beersheba pilgrims receive a blessing and make a contribution to the shrine's guardians (Weingrod, 1990). Thousands of Jews go to Uman in the Ukraine, the burial site of Rabbi Nachman of Bratslav, whether or not they are followers of the loosely bound movement which takes his name—the Bratslav Chassidim. In Israel we attended the annual festivities at Meron on Lag Be'Omer,[18] where Chassidim would emerge from their buses unloading fifty-four bottles of grape juice to offer to others in the hope of achieving a desire—not any kind of desire, of course: a desire which fits in to the cycle of Orthodox Jewish life, such as finding a wife or having a child.[19] A *voto*, in effect. When a child is born, or a wedding held, it is customary to mark the occasion by making a donation to the community—another *ex-voto*. Boyer's 'inference system', or Mauss's social exchange, come into play because to ignore one's obligation to repay the favour is to invite disapproval and eventually sanction: stated another way, such practices reinforce the guilt felt by those who do not meet their reciprocal obligations.

---

[18] The 33rd day of the Omer, which is the period running from Passover to the Feast of Weeks (Shevuot). While 'counting the Omer' observant Jews cannot get married or cut their hair—except on this day—a sort of Shrove Tuesday. Practices vary, inevitably, between Sephardim and Ashkenazim, and within the two communities as well.

[19] Fifty-four is three times eighteen, the number which in Hebrew letters means 'life' and which is often used in religious contexts. For example, people may make charitable donations in multiples of eighteen.

Modern revival movements reproduce this mechanism of exchange and guilt in innumerable contexts. Pentecostal converts may find protection in multiple social obligations and frequent church attendance, but at a price: conversion involves 'burning bridges', or 'cutting the lines' as the Rabbi quoted in Chapter 3 so graphically put it, and their newly adopted web of exchanges carries sharp sanctions. The new convert is heavily dependent on a single set of connections, having cut links with pre-existing, more diverse networks. Not infrequently, converts cut themselves off not just from old drinking mates or party circuits, but also from their immediate family. Our Shas-related informants in Israel said they discouraged this, but they may well have been expressing the desirability of a smooth transition while leaving the final destination of separation unchanged. In fact, several young men told us that they had broken off marriage commitments as a result of their *t'shuva*. As a result of this dependence on a new group, the sanction of guilt is very effective indeed in disciplining converts, and the group leadership can impose very great sacrifices on its membership in exchange, implicitly, for protection and support (Iannacone, 1997; Berman, 2000). These mechanisms are managed by an abstract organisational power and a distant leadership who fulfil the function of inspiring fear normally ascribed to the local, accessible deities of popular religion, and construct the personality cult which so often surrounds the leaders of revival movements. This we have seen in the person of Ovadia Yosef, and it is well known in the case of Chabad, an unknown number of whose followers believed and still believe that their Rebbe (d. 1994) was and is the Messiah[20] (Berger, 2001), while outside Judaism the phenomenon of personalistic charismatic leadership is pervasive in Pentecostalism. In very rare extreme cases, which count as cults rather than sects or movements, members hand over all their possessions, even their lives, to the leadership (Berman, 2003).

Popular religion in the t'shuva movement

Shas, and the *t'shuva* movement in which it is a leading force, ease themselves into the interstices of the social fabric with no need for a centralised 'brain', and have recaptured, or simply retained, the

---

[20] Recall the dual commemoration of his death noted in Chapter 1.

supernatural element of religion. By setting themselves up in local synagogues and disused building site caravans, their activists institute inter-personal circuits of exchange and advertise the solution of daily problems of love, money and family. This interstitial and entrepreneurial aspect dynamises revival movements in competition—and in contrast—with other religious institutions whose legitimacy derives from ancient existence. Unencumbered by doctrinal concerns, mobilisation moves rapidly in response to very local issues such as the lack of kindergartens or teenage crime, and in the process deploys, visually and orally, all sorts of imaginative baggage in the form of associations, allusions and affinities with people who are moved by the accent, garb, even the physiognomy of the protagonists, and by their antagonisms against the Ashkenazi élite. Activists may not even preach: they simply embody a stance by their presence and their manner of making themselves present. In this context inherited beliefs about evil spirits, as about the dangers which can befall those who violate the Sabbath or the rules governing sexual relations, are gathered up and proclaimed as self-evident truths validated by the *mise en scène*. The example of Zeev in the previous chapter shows the mechanism at work, for the young men he sends into those farming co-operatives simply get on with restoring the synagogue and bringing it back into use, conducting services and studying Torah—just being present: their start-up agenda does not seem to involve any preaching at all.[21]

Successful conversion campaigns seem to adopt a certain style of story-telling, in which the listeners' standard set of beliefs, about health or about history for example, are unsettled. Religious narrative comes in innumerable styles, formats and genres, from heroic myths to esoteric disquisitions, and it would be impossible to specify the suspension of disbelief which makes them 'religious'. One tactic which we observe among both Christian and Jewish evangelists is the confrontation between religion and science. Preachers see in this confrontation a major battlefield, and they deal with it in two ways: on the one hand they quote inexplicable recoveries by people whose cases have been given up as hopeless by 'the doctors', with much

---

[21] Revivalist roadshow evangelists in the tradition of Billy Graham do preach, but the real work of conversion is done on the ground by local pastors for whom the roadshows serve as a type of advertising to attract newcomers.

emphasis on how the doctors could not explain the recovery, while on the other there is a specifically Jewish claim, with reference to modern science, that 'it is all in the Torah' or 'it is all in the Gemara'. We saw earlier how an institution has been established to try and place such claims on a modern academic footing, and we know that evangelicals and fundamentalists want to show that the claims of religion can be demonstrated—or at least that the doubts of the anti-religious can be rebutted—scientifically. A pamphlet entitled 'Replies and one question',[22] describes, for example, near-death experiences and the apparition of the dead.[23] It is presented in the format of a scientific paper, with footnotes, while its back page advertises evangelising radio stations and organisations such as Arachim and Amnon Yitzchak's Shofar. The text takes up accounts of near-death experiences in which, for example, 'the dead see a great and strong life which is the reality of someone who gives boundless love', or where a person sees their whole life passing in front of them in strict chronological order in a few seconds, or where all their friends and relatives come to see them. These descriptions are then said to echo the words of the Mishnah—'when a person detaches himself from the world all his actions pass before him'. The pamphlet also goes into the question of séances, where the dead return to address the living, and which are not explained by science. The cases or stories contained in it are characterised, in the manner of popular legends, by sudden unexpected twists of fortune, and often, though not always, conclude with a person's return to religion.

If these pamphlets are in the form of fables, listeners' beliefs can also be shifted by allusions to their own self-image, especially to assumptions they may have about their origins. The claim that 'it is all in the Torah' is related to the character of *t'shuva* as a return to a heritage as well as a life-changing experience: preachers pay much attention to linking the *ba'al t'shuva* back to the stories of the Rabbis

---

[22] Written and edited by Zamir Cohen and published by the Or VeArachim (Light and Values) Institute in Beitar Elit (a newly built town in the Occupied Territories with a predominantly *haredi* population), with the support of the Ministries of Education and of Religious Affairs.

[23] It says that research on people who revive after 'clinical death' is mostly on non-Jews, and so cannot be applied to Jews, for Jews observe all 613 commandments whereas non-Jews only observe seven, and also Jews have access to 'higher spheres'.

and the history of his or her people. Such evocation requires only the smallest of hints in the recounting to evoke a Jewish heritage: even the mere formula 'there was once…' or 'it is said…' is enough. The discourse is peppered with stories about events and personages in a past which, though undefined, is assumed to be a Jewish past: for example, a Rabbanit, addressing her class of newly religious women, begins her cautionary tales by evoking the Sephardi past with the phrase 'Once, in Baghdad…'. Stories of miraculous cures, often with much symptomatic detail, also fit onto this template of Jewish heritage. The hope must be that feelings of guilt and betrayal will be stimulated among those who have drifted away, whether they have consciously abandoned observance or whether they are, in the standard phrase heard in the *t'shuva* movement, 'kidnapped babies', innocent victims of an irreligious upbringing.

All these hints, props and inferential allusions in the language and even the setting of these story-tellings create an aura, a suspension of disbelief, in which people who in different circumstances would laugh off the claims of miraculous cures and exorcisms, sit and listen dutifully. Of course, they have usually agreed to attend, as in the Arachim seminars or a mass meeting at the Yad Eliahu stadium, so they come with a predisposition, and the setting is not as a rule imposed upon them, unless they are prison inmates (favourites for the propagation of *t'shuva*). For example, at a meeting organised at the Yad Eliahu stadium in Tel Aviv by Arachim in mid-2001 and attended by the Or HaChayyim leader Reuven Elbaz among other dignitaries, attractively packaged bottles of water blessed by Yitzchak Kedourie were being sold at $500 each (payable in instalments and by credit card). Stories were told of the water's miraculous qualities—for example how it helped somebody escape the bailiffs who had come to take away their last possessions—while people kissed the bottles and held them aloft, and the names of the purchasers were announced over the public address system to much applause.

T'shuva may start out as a project of indoctrination or may be just education, but when we take all these events, performances and spectacles together with the intensity of involvement, the dedication of campaigners, the enthusiasm with which they engage potential converts and returnees, we are perhaps most impressed by the diversity of the instruments used and by the movement's ability to marshal resources across so many spheres and boundaries, avoiding, ignoring or breaking down the frontiers established by institutionalised religion. To be sure, religion in Judaism is not hierarchically organised as it is in the Catholic or Anglican churches, but it is rich in institutions and it is also extremely diverse: the *t'shuva* movements bring together that which institutions separate and separate some of that which they bring together, and within the religious world that produces major change.

From giving to gossip

In the Jewish ultra-Orthodox community giving is of enormous importance. In fact, just like Pentecostals have to give 10 per cent to their churches, so, *haredim* are expected to give a tenth of their income to charity. But giving is also surrounded by a degree of superstition. On several occasions we were told that 'one does not count', that recording exact numbers as in a Census was something Jews should avoid. One reason was that King David once took a census and all sorts of disasters followed—and indeed, in two places in the Old Testament the story is told, in almost exactly the same words, of how God punished Israel as a result of the Census David had taken (Chronicles 21:1; Samuel 24:1).[24] Eventually, however, one underlying version was told to us by a Moroccan whom we met in a *kollel*: you should give charity secretly, in case someone sees you giving and becomes jealous, asking 'why not me?', consequently attracting the evil eye to the donor. And then he continued, as if by association of ideas, to say that 'not counting' also means that one should never settle accounts, because it always ends badly: for example, with your wife it is best not to try to 'get to the bottom' of an issue, or to 'settle it once and for all'. It is better to let things calm down, to leave well alone.

So charity is not a simple matter of giving—in fact it can be risky. This is not unusual, as we can see in a Ghanaian example where urban migrants, finding themselves under pressure from their village kin to share in their prosperity, join Pentecostal churches apparently in order to protect themselves from those pressures (Meyer, 1998).

---

[24] The major difference between the two accounts is that Chronicles says 'Satan incited David to count the people of Israel' and Samuel says 'the Lord incited David against them and gave orders that Israel and Judah should be counted'.

Their relatives expect them to share their good fortune, for example by taking them into their houses while they obtain an education, and the ungenerous can expect retribution in the form of curses and spells. The upwardly mobile find a way out of the trap by switching to another exchange system, namely a Pentecostal church, which is perhaps no less demanding, but may offer them a preferable bargain in terms of social status and networks, and also enables them to exorcise once and for all the demons to which they are vulnerable. Giving to a church also has the advantage that one is giving to an abstract entity, an institution, or at least to a pastor as the organiser of that entity, in effect funding him for the function he performs, or just paying him a wage—rather than giving to a private person in a gesture which risks arousing jealousy and invites retaliation.[25]

Likewise, among *haredi* Jews, giving to an institution such as a rotating credit society, or *gemach*, which is also seen as a charity, or simply putting money in a charity box on the street, may free them from importuning by fellow *haredim*, many of whom are poor because they spend so much time learning and because they do not have the skills necessary for pursuing a career in the secular world. Wealthy people seem quite happy to have their names inscribed on the entrance to a yeshiva or a synagogue, so they do not exactly want to be anonymous, but they may well wish to avoid arousing rivalry among individual beneficiaries of their generosity. Also, by donating to institutions they gain political influence, for they enhance the status and power of the leading figures in those institutions, who in turn will pay due deference to their donors.

Beyond the issue of giving and the jealousy it may arouse, there is a more general question of concealment, linked to the obsession with the drive to evil (*yetzer ha-ra*), and its twin the evil tongue (*lashon ha-ra*)—in other words with gossip. It is a constant subject of concern among our interviewees, reflecting life in a community where so much depends on keeping up appearances, and where curiosity about people's origins—and thus about sexual matters—and about their personal habits is pervasive and invasive. This constant exposure to criticism and prying eyes helps to explain the extreme uniformity

---

[25] Unfortunately there is no guarantee that pastors will not mishandle church funds, and there are innumerable accounts of financial disputes in Pentecostal churches.

of modes of dress and deportment in the *haredi* world, since conformity is the best way to avoid being 'picked out'. As mentioned, students at the Or Hachayyim yeshiva listen to detailed lists of prohibited clothes and perfumes and so on; likewise at the women's *chugim* or consciousness-raising classes, run by a Shas-related outreach operation, the address given by the *Rabbanit* who was leading the group focused with great detail on, for example, how to keep one's hair covered, how to prepare meals on different occasions and other similar details of private life. She also dwelt on the dangers of gossip—both to the object of the gossip and also to the gossip-monger, who can suffer a curse which brings failure through all her life.

If the fear of gossip is easy to understand, it is unusual to read or hear of the source of that fear—namely, the manipulation of the dark side of gossip. An undergraduate thesis from the Hebrew University illustrates this with a description of events in the impoverished Jerusalem neighbourhood of Shmuel HaNavi, located on the edge of the Boukharim neighbourhood (Berger, 1999). Here we are removed from the world of carefully staged seminars and public meetings, and taken to one in which the narrative of *t'shuva* is borne on stories with much harsher, more lurid, even threatening imagery and content than those we have mentioned. In Berger's interpretation, this is classic gang behaviour repackaged as religious enforcement. A Modesty Committee, presumably self-appointed, watches over morals. Kiosks are forced to stop selling secular and provocative publications. A street bench is burnt in case men and women sit on it together. Arab students are forced out of the neighbourhood and their house set alight. The less observant are subjected to malicious gossip, so that if they are unwell they are said to be involved with witchcraft, to have committed immoral acts, or even to have had immoral thoughts—and they are pressed to go and see a Rabbi instead of a doctor; while autistic children are manipulated to point accusing fingers at individuals.

Berger also refers to publications distributed only to trusted *t'shuva* activists, which present a range of dark images and warnings. *Yom LeYom* ('From one day to the next') (October 1999) contains a quotation from Ovadia Yosef about the impurities which the Land of Israel must expel (literally 'vomit'): 'If you do not expel the causes of pollution, it may become contagious, like in hospitals where infections stick to the walls and the only solution is eventually the total destruction of the building ... Do not listen to the secular radio because its message sticks to the walls and then corrupts the souls of your children.' *Zeman HaBira* ('Capital Times') (25 November 1999) warns that those who have relations with menstruating women may go mad.

The ultimate solution to the problems of a person plagued by gossip may be exorcism: the newspaper *Sodot HaNeshama* ('Secrets of the soul') describes the effect of an exorcism performed by Rav Batzri—a 'warm-up' speaker at Ovadia Yosef's regular Saturday night address at the Persian Synagogue (located near the same Shmuel HaNavi neighbourhood). When Batzri diagnoses a *dibbuk*—a possessing demon—in a woman, it speaks from the victim's stomach (Geschiere, 1995),[26] its voice is recognised as that of a familiar person, and it knows all the details of her husband's life.

If a community does fall under the influence of such moral guardians, they may indeed acquire invasive powers, because people will be fearful of their reprisals and diagnoses, and also because they may acquire the authority to distinguish between bursts of madness and mental illness and moments of divine inspiration. The account shows that the activists, or moral guardians, in the community, have to be on their guard with respect to everyone including observant people. Exaggerated behaviour—as when someone claims to be a Prophet or to speak with the voice of God—has to be controlled, especially in a neighbourhood like this one where drug abuse is present.

The nature of religious norms

Whether the norms of *haredi* life are more numerous than those in any other social space is impossible to say: indeed the question of the number of norms can quickly be seen to be meaningless and unanswerable since what appears as one norm can readily be subdivided into many others, and vice versa. Are *haredi* norms more rigorous? Even that question has to be unpacked: by more rigorous we must surely mean that violations are punished with unusual severity, that

[26] Geschiere describes possessing demons located in people's stomachs in West African folklore.

observance seems to be highly uniform, and that changes tend to stiffen rather than soften resistance to outside influences and pressures.

Among *haredim* there is a widely reported anxiety about exposure, or shame: people go to extraordinary lengths to cover up a source of dishonour from fellow *haredim* and from the secular world. It is said that if a child abandons the *haredi* life for one in secular society, the family may possibly never mention the child's name again, though the very nature of such reports makes them unverifiable if the field researcher is not to turn into a detective. The co-operation of *haredim* with the police in matters such as family violence is apparently difficult if not impossible to obtain, and even in medical matters one hears that there is a degree of reluctance to consult doctors who do not have the trust of a Rabbi.

This anxiety is related to an underlying feature of the norms of *haredi* behaviour, which is not their number but their uncertainty, which in turn is related to the idiosyncratic, personalistic ways in which rules are developed: although some big, usually political or quasi-political, issues—like the observance of the Jubilee year[27]— may go to a Rabbinic Council, most day-to-day issues arising in individuals' daily lives are decided by individual Rabbis, case by case, on their own. Uncertainty arises because both precedents and the Rabbinic texts are innumerable and therefore open to innumerable interpretations. Also, there are all sorts of Rabbis, recognised by different communities and differing in their status. So, in practice, norms evolve under pressure, often 'from below' towards creating and thickening boundaries, as a result of the fear of gossip and dishonour, and of Rabbinic disapproval. So the loop is looped: in addition the power of that disapproval arises partly because certain Rabbis, as beneficiaries of charitable giving, and as intermediaries in the distribution of state resources to yeshivas, to yeshiva students and to adult *kollel* learners, are in a position of power.

---

[27] In 2001 a change was imposed by certain Rabbis on the Israeli Chief Rabbinate to casuistic arrangements which had enabled Jewish farmers to remain within the halakhic rules while still cultivating in the Jubilee (seventh) year during which, according to Leviticus 25:2–7, the land should be left fallow. The practical implication is that food grown on such land, or at least sales from that food, is not kosher and will not be so certified by the Rabbinic authorities in Israel.

Memorability: converts learn fast

Religious dress has the qualities of a uniform, yet it is readily recognisable as religious: finding people who might mistake the uniform of even the Salvation Army for, say, a military uniform would be hard. Religious dress also has qualities that largely transcend the boundaries of the great religious traditions: its modesty, and its asexuality, especially when applied to women: traditional nuns' habits cover their entire bodies save the face and hands; ultra-Orthodox Jewish women, who are not religious professionals or even 'virtuosi', dress and carry themselves in such a way as to downplay their sexuality. Male officiants and professionals—priests, men in holy orders, choir boys, in Anglican and Catholic churches—dress in non-male attire. In this way they exhibit their non-availability for sexual relations, and also advertise the cost they are paying for membership in an élite—in the case of the clergy—or in a very tightly knit and mutually supportive community—in the case of the *haredim* (Iannacone, 1997).

A uniform also provides an opportunity for controlled variation: it is based on an archetype designed out of a limited number of elements, so that slight variations stand out. This is obvious among the police, the military and other armed corporations, where slight variations denote rank. Parish priests are distinguished from Bishops by the different colour of their shirts; choristers at Ely Cathedral in England all wear cassocks, but seniors and juniors wear different colours and their cassocks have a slightly different design.

Among ultra-Orthodox Jews the basic uniform—the core archetype—for men is a black suit, a white shirt and a tall hat, a white tassel or fringe and of course a beard for married men. The various sects and sectors of the ultra-Orthodox are distinguished by variations in beard, type of suit, and hat, by how they exhibit the white tassel (*tzitzit*), and a few other details.[28] The point is that the uniform is made up of a more or less set number of 'variables': thus some wear their tassels outside their jackets, while others do not; some wear long, curled sidelocks, others do not; hats range from the 'Lithuanian' perpendicular homburg to a tall imitation of the Shakers (worn by Chabad) and the Borsalino worn by Shasniks.

---

[28] On the Sabbath the regalia worn by men of different Chassidic sects is more radically distinguished, since in some cases they do not wear suits at all, but tunics and fur-rimmed hats.

Over time we can observe how the range of variation is incre-
mentally extended: one hears stories of an extreme and secretive sect
in the Old City of Jerusalem who wear blue tassels, and one observes
the 'hippy' branch of Chassidism, the 'Bratslav' followers, who have
almost abandoned the archetype, with their large white crocheted
skullcaps. The most ideologically driven West Bank settlers[29] increasingly appear as outlier variations on the theme: the men among them
almost invariably sport beards, and exhibit their white tassels with
ever less discretion over self-consciously ragged dress, while the women
have come to cover themselves more and more completely in long
sleeves and long skirts, even when carrying rifles on their shoulders.
They also have adopted the *haredi* pursuit of very high fertility.

Modifications in the ultra-Orthodox archetype introduced by
Sephardi *haredim* in Israel and by their *t'shuva* movement are minor,
but sufficient to mark its wearers out as unmistakably Sephardi to the
local population. Their innovation lies partly in the mere fact of
being Sephardi *haredim*, and visibly so, a category unknown before
the 1980s outside the yeshivas: an oxymoron, so to speak, or at least
an ill-assorted pairing.

Sephardi identity (independently of a carrier's religious life) is dis-
played in Israel by, for example, individuals' accents, by their sur-
names, perhaps by their use of Arabic slang and doubtless by physical
appearance. Sephardi liturgical customs are also distinctive in many
ways, but are not visible on the street. Together, these elements make
an archetype, though they do not build a thick or multi-layered
frontier: setting aside their subordination to the Ashkenazi *haredim*
and the effects of their undoubted economic disadvantage *vis-à-vis*
other Jews, Sephardim live everywhere, occupy all sorts of positions,
and encounter no barrier (in the secular world) to marriage with
non-Sephardim. But Shas has begun to tweak the archetype, as a
nascent ultra-Orthodox ethnic and religious revival movement, and
in accordance with the pattern of incremental modification described above, has retained the *haredi* stereotype with small but crucial
modifications: the black suit has become very dark navy blue with
wide lapels Armani-style, the hat has become a Borsalino, the beard

---

[29] The vast majority of inhabitants of the West Bank settlements are motivated by
cheap housing and other subsidies more than by ideology.

is groomed and the women wear hair nets instead of wigs. That, though, is enough to make the combination recognisable in public spaces.

For Sephardim and Ashkenazim the religious texts—the Torah, the Talmud and its many offshoots, the prayers—are word for word the same. In ritual Sephardi-Ashkenazi differences concern the prayers themselves hardly at all, but, for example, sequencing, repetition and details about the date or time of certain observances.[30] To some these may be details, but Israelis, and observant Jews in particular, are usually acutely aware of them. Because each sect has small deviations from a 'core' model or archetype, the deviations become easier to remember, especially since they only exist within quite limited spheres. One's clothing and beard have to conform to a particular community or sect—they cannot be chosen freely. Once a person is in one or another community, he or she will very quickly sense what is proper and what is different. Deviations across community lines within the ultra-Orthodox world are not regarded as offences against divine law, for which one pays in the world to come, but they do induce the more immediate sanctions of unspoken disapproval, embarrassment and shame. A novice, once his or her bridges are burnt, will be eager to please now that the retreat is cut off, and will have powerful incentives to learn.

Boyer provides amusing examples of potentially religious beliefs which we intuitively know would never catch on: 'We worship this woman because she gave birth to thirty-seven children... We pray to this statue because it is the largest artefact ever made...' (Boyer, 2001: 93). These counter-examples in turn lead us to understand that beliefs which successfully claim to be counted as religious have certain common features. Boyer and, with slightly different reasoning and evidence, Atran develop a complex cognitive argument about 'violated ontologies'. These are described by Atran (2003b: 101ff.) as the way in which memorability is enhanced by counterintuitive elements in an otherwise straightforward narrative. A 'belief set that is mostly intuitive combined with a few counterintuitive

---

[30] This refers to the prayers of repentance said daily before the New Year (Rosh Hashanah), which Sephardim say at midnight and Ashkenazim in the early morning; or the celebration of Lag Be'Omer, which varies somewhat.

elements' (*ibid.*: 106) has better chances of survival than one which is counterintuitive throughout. In a similar line of reasoning, the taboos which permeate *haredi* (or for that matter Pentecostal) life and which *ba'alei t'shuva* (or converts) adopt with little intellectual effort, also seem to have a memorability feature which allows individuals of little or no Talmudic knowledge and no religious upbringing to assimilate them very quickly.

Newly religious people seem to adopt the way of life without learning formally or didactically a long list of prohibitions and obligations: in a short time they have assimilated dietary laws, dress codes, prayer routines, Sabbath laws, the subtle differences between festival observances and of course the music and the responses to the most frequently repeated elements of the liturgy. Like innumerable illiterate converts to Pentecostalism (who will rapidly memorise the hymns and sing them with gusto), people who have set out on the road to *t'shuva* learn with remarkable speed practices which would seem mind-numbingly complicated if listed 'cold' on a page and presented, for example, to a group of uncommitted secular individuals. Learning to read and understand Rabbinic Hebrew, let alone Aramaic, takes longer, even for speakers of Modern Hebrew who can find the Talmudic and liturgical versions unfamiliar if they are not part of their upbringing, but the *t'shuva* movement is less concerned with such erudition than with the accomplishment of a strictly observant lifestyle.

In Israel, admittedly, *haredim* are an established part of the social landscape, so joining them is not a leap into the unknown on the part of secularised people, but still one may wonder at the adoption of a package of mostly unscripted practices and routines: we have observed among Chabad recruits in London, not only the rapid adoption of prayer timetables and modes of dress, but also of a certain gait, of turns of phrase, of diet ruled not just by dietary laws but also by a highly standardised menu, for example, of roast chicken on the Sabbath eve, and by the adoption of a hundred other little humdrum rituals, such as kissing a *mezuzah* on entry to a room, washing hands with a blessing before taking any food, and saying a blessing before eating any food or drinking any drink. Linguistic nuances and 'niches' which may appear fiendishly complicated to the secular outsider, such as the different Hebrew pronunciation used for prayer as opposed to daily speech and the mixing of Yiddish expressions with the vernacular, seem to be adopted with ease.

Cascading demarcations and the increasingly central role of the t'shuva movement in the haredi world

The movement of Sephardi renewal is an epidemic proliferation of points of demarcation: the institutional manifestations of the process are there in the development of a party and its innumerable religious and educational offshoots, but that does not account adequately for the rapid evolution of a diffuse combination of ethnic and religious renewal into a sub-culture featuring, among other things, Rabbinical control of personal habits, the standardisation of modes of dress, the synchronisation of people's daily, weekly and annual chronologies and a constant inflow of new recruits. These habits could not have been imposed through a centralised strategy of political propaganda and mobilisation, if only because the leadership were inexperienced in modern forms of political mobilisation and in the ways of bureaucracy. With only a few symbolic starting hints—ten minutes of electoral air time in their first campaign showing a Rabbi performing the simple family ceremony ushering in the Sabbath—the system installed itself as if ready-made. Evidently they 'touched a nerve', but that is too vague as an explanation.

An alternative way of thinking about this proliferation of demarcations and prohibitions—some directed by Rabbis, but many arising 'from below', from the anxieties of potential non-compliance or non-conformity—might be in terms of a lateral channelling of the contagion behaviour characteristic of ritual systems. This would not apply only to this case but also to the combination of rituals both delineating ethnic demarcations and taboos of cleanliness, which of course are also found in many other cultures. Boyer (2001: 136–7) quotes various sources about how the slightly compulsive character of pollution avoidance rituals can have evolved: once a relationship was noticed, but not of course understood, for example once a connection was noticed between contact with corpses and illness, practices to avoid such contact were elaborated in an extremely prudential, risk-averse fashion, accentuated by ignorance of the causal mechanism involved. This contagion system is in turn linked to obsessive-compulsive disorder, which 'the discoveries of neuro-imagery and physiology suggest... may amount to a small tweaking of a normal function' (*ibid.*: 274). '[S]ome elements of rituals trigger activation of those particular mental systems that work on overdrive, as it were, in obsessive disorders...' (*ibid.: 275*). Rituals activate the contagion system, and this makes them 'highly salient cognitive gadgets' (*ibid.*: 276). The argument is not that rituals and taboos are functional, because obviously they can become highly dysfunctional, as when they prevent a woman from going to the doctor because she is shy about her body; rather the argument is that ancestral functionality, as explained above, has given rise to self-per-petuating patterns of behaviour.

We observe in fundamentalist forms of religion how this conta-gion system goes somehow out of control and the overdrive becomes a collective phenomenon. Ultra-Orthodox Judaism has several dif-ferent sorts of frontier: that which divides Jews from non-Jews; those which divide the ultra-Orthodox from secularised Jews as well as from the less stringent modern Orthodox; and those which divide the various ultra-Orthodox communities and sects from one another. Why this proliferation of dividing lines has arisen, and whether it makes Judaism 'different', are matters for another discussion, but new-comers, fearful of disapproval, are liable to multiply sources of pol-lution and to make conservative rather then generous interpretations of prohibitions. To this must be added the particular system of autho-rity of ultra-Orthodox Jews in which the personal judgment of indi-vidual Rabbis is unpredictable, engendering pre-emptively conservative behaviour among their followers.

A more conventionally sociological interpretation for cascading demarcations, arising from the power relations in which the newly observant become entangled, is not hard to adduce: if they are to join fully then they must give up old jobs, old ties and eventually old family: we have mentioned the opposition of Shas spokesmen to breaking up families, but the dynamic of commitment leads indi-viduals to develop a new quasi-family, and also, probably, to acquire a spouse who will meet with the approval of the religious authority such as the head of a *kollel* or the tutor at a yeshiva—an approval more important than that of parents who have been 'left behind'. Having cut their pre-existing ties of employment, family and friendship, eventually burning their bridges, they are highly dependent on the new source of authority, so the motivation to abide by rules and the anxiety associated with non-compliance must be very strong. When a prestigious figure like Ovadia Yosef or Reuven Elbaz appears at a synagogue or yeshiva, the young men surge forward to kiss his hand in an elaborate gesture of respect and obedience. Proliferating gestures of blessing—for example every time one takes food or drink—and kissing are expressions of the same anxiety: they mark a moment, even a split second, of hesitation and precaution before the next act, as if guaranteeing that it will not be polluted or infringe any unknown norm. For the norms can and do proliferate, so one must worry not only about those one knows but also about those one does not know.

Thus in this secular society the injection of new blood into religious sects may be an important element in their preservation in ways that are not immediately obvious. Whereas secular observers assume that the preservation of ultra-Orthodoxy and fundamentalist religion is the work of introspective and backward-looking traditionalists, it is possible that the new entrants are not only important in a quantitative sense for the skills they bring into the community, and in a demographic sense for the additional numbers who add to those existing and replace those who leave, but also because, on account of the mechanisms explained here, new entrants may be as important a force in the continuous drive to ever more stringent observance as are the traditionalist Rabbis.

Among Pentecostals, for whom proselytising is almost a *raison d'être* and who are all converts, to a greater or lesser degree, this is not surprising. But in ultra-Orthodox Judaism it is more so, yet *t'shuva* is already the *raison d'être* of one highly influential and large international sect—Chabad—and of a major Israeli movement—Shas. Furthermore, other sectors of the *haredi* world, which have tended in the past to view the *t'shuva* movement with some disdain or even distrust—especially on account of the prominence of Chabad with its highly controversial views and methods—are gradually shifting their attitude. Indeed, our interviews have shown that beyond the 'specialised' *t'shuva* movements, among Chassidic sects and the Lithuanians the *ba'al t'shuva* is now a readily recognised figure, so that they speak for example of special Torah classes for returnees, and express less disdain for them than they might have done in the past. So *t'shuva* has gradually acquired institutional recognition, and thus we observe the reshaping of religion in Judaism as in the other great traditions.

7

CONCLUSIONS

FRAGMENTATION AND COALESCENCE: ENCLAVES AND THEIR BOUNDARIES

Neither of us imagined, when we set out on the project of studying Shas, that it would prove so rich in itself, as a prism through which to study Israel, and as a springboard for deepening our understanding of social movements. We thought this would be a case study of religious revival and of the counterintuitive use of religious rituals, markers and traditions. The initial puzzle was simply 'why do these Sephardim adopt Lithuanian habits and practices?'

In exploring the issue, we came to realise that the link between ethnic markers and their content is not what might be assumed in everyday life. Shasniks seemed utterly indifferent to what appeared, in their dress, as a fragmentation or dispersal of the packaged markers of Lithuanian identity and a denial of the markers of Sephardi identity. The wearing of a formal hat or a dark suit in Eastern European *haredi* style did not mean they had 'become' anything different from what they or their North Africans or Middle Eastern forebears had been, and in no way contradicted the Shas motto of 'recovering the glory of old'. If markers can be changed without necessarily a change in substance, then ancient boundaries and conflicts too can be invented overnight as much as they can be forgotten, depending on political conditions—on pressures and power relations. We see this in the imperceptible shaping of a Sephardi identity in Israel encompassing and admitted by people whose background lies in far-flung and historically disconnected places from Morocco to Afghanistan, which in the past shared neither language nor musical traditions (in contrast to the Ashkenazim of Western and Eastern Europe). The intuitive reaction of a Western reader is 'why not the Yemenis too? Are they not also from the Middle East?', to which the answer is 'why should one have expected any particular group to adopt the Sephardi identity?' Because they are black? Because they are poor? These are labels, even stigmata, external impositions which may be quite irrelevant to the motivations involved.

Identity, for obvious reasons, looms large in Israeli cultural life, in politics, in religious institutions and in the street. But the loyalties and affiliations, as elsewhere, are shaped by innumerable factors other than a person's ancestral line. To start with, intermarriage is rife across ethnic lines, and education and employment drive deep spatial and occupational wedges between people of otherwise similar backgrounds. There is also some active recruitment, notably by the *t'shuva* movement, which brings people into one of the quasi-ethnic *haredi* communities. Israelis thought they had a melting pot, but today the word among the educated who use such language is that they don't. In fact, from a sociological point of view, there is much in Israel, especially intermarriage, which resembles a melting pot. But the rise of Shas forces us to ask questions about the production of ethnicity which go well beyond intermarriage.

The enclave system is an indispensable political aspect of the production of ethnicity. The system, and underlying it the proportional representation system, rewards those who nurse their clientele carefully: even a few seats in the Knesset can provide significant clout in coalition and budgetary negotiations. So political leaders have every incentive to consolidate a following, to delineate it from others, and to construct material and symbolic walls around it. These include, for example, special allocations for large families, special schools for Shas, exemptions and credits for settlers, subsidised credits for building and house purchase for *haredi* communities, and so on. Political competition in this system may encourage an accentuation of differences and points of tension, even if, however acute and shrill, they sometimes prove short-lived. Yet at the same time the frontiers may criss-cross, and may vary in their thickness, and individuals can hold apparently inconsistent loyalties, as well as change their sentiments of identification and hostility. To say that frontiers may be both conflictive and fluid does not invalidate our thesis about enclaves. The enclaves are rooted in politics and institutional design: they become self-perpetuating because they generate interest groups and mobilisation. Since there are incentives to create new enclaves, the pattern is in constant flux.

The concept as we use it is quite different from that of Sivan, who applies it to a particular sort of fundamentalist movement or sect (Sivan, 1995), and from others' usage of this and similar terms in the Israeli context. We wanted to detach the idea of an enclave from the assumption that loyalties are permanently ascribed, inscribed and entrenched, and also from similar assumptions of permanence and indelibility of ethnic markers. In Shas we see how, through mobilisation from below and hard political bargaining at the top, an enclave was fashioned. It is very important to repeat that, in emphasising the changeability of these markers, we are not trying to denigrate, belittle or dilute the resulting loyalties and affiliations. Every collective identity can be shown to draw, in its self-justifying rhetoric and narrative, on flawed, distorted and even utterly fictive historiography. But that does not mean, and must not be taken to mean, that it is illegitimate. On the other hand it might lead one to ask why those claiming rights as impersonal members of an interest group or a market-based interest, like 'workers' or members of a professional group, are any less entitled to a hearing or to certain rights than those who choose to base claims in the nomenclature of religion, ancestry or cultural distinctiveness.

The element of flux is possible because identifications and oppositions are distributed through different fields: religious, linguistic, ethnic, political and social class (Barth, 1969). Only in the case of the exclusion of the Arab population are several fields superimposed. The multiplicity of fields obliges us to be careful when making statements about the depth or sharpness of social divisions among Israel's Jewish population because while common usage among them may make exclusions appear extremely sharp, there are also fluidities that cannot be overlooked: we have seen how the settler movement has borrowed habits and dress from the ultra-Orthodox repertoire, thus bridging a very deep-rooted chasm between the conquest of the land, historically associated with the secularism of the kibbutz, and strict religious observance. The spectacle of Rabbis in black suits and white shirts with their flowing beards calling for civil disobedience, and occasionally more, has become a standard feature of the settler movement's more militant factions, as are prayers and psalms and religious songs at their demonstrations.

We have described in detail the bridging of another gap, as Shas leaders and activists knitted together a social movement across the religious-secular divide, bringing traditionally minded and secularised Sephardim into their institutions and their electoral constituency. Sometimes conflicts are ephemeral: we observe the periodic appearance and disappearance of conflicts over religious observance, of conflicts and disputes involving Yemenis, or Russians, or whoever, and we see that whatever the rhetoric, total rupture is avoided, as illustrated by the Likud-Labour coalition briefly reinvented in 2005. There is no government coalition that does not include representatives of groups who disagree ideologically and even pursue mutually exclusive lifestyles.[1] Boundaries can be managed, and the hurly-burly of politics can thicken them or, in contrast, dilute them.

These remarks should serve as a warning that when we write of one or another cleavage or division and especially the sharpness of the language used to describe them, readers should constantly keep in mind the multiplicity of fronts and fields which define the points of friction, sometimes confrontation, among Israeli Jews. An issue which today appears overwhelming and determinate may tomorrow seem like a distant memory. The enclave system should therefore be understood analytically as a battery of boundary-creating and preserving mechanisms, but not as a fixed constellation of individuals, lineages or organisations whose relationships are unchanging over the long term.

The discussion of enclaves obviously raises the question of what makes Israeli democracy produce the outcomes it does. And here we found that its undoubted exclusionary features, notably *vis-à-vis* the Arab population, have another face, because the enclave system does offer a way for new groups to 'elbow' their way in. Whether, as we repeatedly ask, Shas's success in thus raising the profile of a certain idea of being Sephardi and carrying 'Sephardiness', has been or will be translated into an improvement of measurable well-being for those on whose behalf the movement claims to speak, is another matter.

Shas is also a social movement. Although some—mostly hostile—Israelis dismiss it as little more than a vehicle for the political and

---

[1] The criss-crossing of affiliations and loyalties and style and substance is illustrated by the tactic of the Russian party—Yisrael Ba'Aliya—which sent two Orthodox and two traditionalists out of its seven members to the Knesset in 1996, even though it represented a highly secularised constituency (Elazar, 1998).

economic ambitions of its leadership, we think the evidence is that it has many of the attributes needed to qualify as a movement, as do the West Bank and Gaza settlers, but not any of the established political parties. In being a movement it draws on Israeli Jewish habits not just of mobilisation, but also of turning mobilisation into institutions. Shas qualifies as a movement because of, among other features, its ability to knit together different publics, people of varying family and religious background, and to fit them into a number of institutional niches—educational, recreational, ritual and religious. It could, perhaps should, have gone further, and engaged with a wider variety of opinion-forming élites, if it was to make quite as much of a revolution as the leaders have sometimes proclaimed. It is clear from our account that the force of the movement owed much to the *t'shuva* element: this tempered the potential divisiveness of the 'purely' ethnic discourse, which has had little legitimacy among Israeli Jews. The *t'shuva* element also afforded Shas the institutional mechanisms of building a cadre of activists in yeshivas, which would not have been provided by a mobilisation based only on party affiliation. The word *t'shuva* had resonance even among the mildly religious because it is the keynote of New Year and Day of Atonement services—the two days when even the minimally observant attend synagogue. Return to observance—or to a Jewish way of life—has also become a global phenomenon, transcending ancestral, cultural, ethnic and national frontiers. As we explain, Shas did not start out with precisely this dual ethnic-religious agenda, but the pioneers quickly realised its potential. From then on the formula spread epidemiologically, making links, connections and affinities in a variety of institutional, territorial, ethnic and religious contexts.

Our analysis did not only link macro and micro—or institutional politics and social mobilisation. It also encompassed the imaginary, the mediatic and the symbolic dimensions of religion, and showed how, through unenunciated and allusive markers, these contribute to the political and religious movements, occasionally by mechanisms which may offend the mainstream liberal sensibility. A range of radio stations and other media come to fuel the machine of *t'shuva*, not because of a centrally agreed strategy, but by competition and imitation. Habits of language, of radio listening, of deference to leaders whose names are endlessly and admiringly repeated, begin to spread.

Stories of miracle cures and exemplary punishments become fixed in the mind. These media are not indoctrination, but they are habit-forming, and the campaigns benefit from the memorability of such stories. The media may also knit real sociability by encouraging listeners to support certain schools or to attend meetings, or by making cassettes available at dedicated outlets.

The penetration of Shas in society and its strategy of building a public profile is also undertaken through occupation of public space: the political management of housing projects and the energetic building of synagogues and ritual baths. If those efforts are of a symbolic kind in their reference to Shas, indoctrination may be more overt in the movement's schools and kindergartens. This is where the movement hopes to educate future generations of leaders, and it is certainly privileged to have such a well endowed, state-funded, instrument at its disposal for the purpose. Yet the indoctrination and recruitment may not work in the way the leadership hopes. The pupils have other opportunities, and the best may be 'poached' by Ashkenazi institutions. It is impossible to predict what will be the socio-political fruits of Shas's educational venture. In addition, it is in these educational and consciousness-raising institutions that patron-clientelism may find its main expression. This is the feature most noticed by secularist Israelis, and although we hope to have shown that it is not the 'whole story', Shas would clearly not have grown as it did without access to substantial resources and without distributing them in the discretionary and lumpy fashion characteristic of systems of patronage. This factor may in the end rebound: it may undermine trust and act as an obstacle to the movement's graduation from social movement to a full institutional partner in Israel's educational and welfare system.

Our analyses have also had a persistent underlying comparative theme. Much of this chapter explores these comparisons further; one summary of our discussion is that if Shas differs substantially from the evangelical and Pentecostal churches to which we have frequently compared it, it is more likely to be because of the influence of the Israeli political setting than because of differences between religious traditions in the broad sense. Indeed, we hope to have shown that differences within traditions are no less important, sociologically, than differences between them, and that contemporary con-

version-based movements are a phenomenon whose common characteristics straddle conventionally defined religious divisions.

SHAS AND POLITICS: A TROUBLESOME GUEST

The rise of Shas has been accompanied by a redrawing of the secular-
religious divide in Israel. The other religious parties, originating in
Agudat Yisrael, which had monopolised the voice of ultra-Orthodoxy in politics until the arrival of Shas, were an inward-looking
minority, concerned with the preservation of their own way of life,
whose worldview did not accommodate the idea of a Jewish state
governed on democratic and secular principles. They adapted, to be
sure, and at least from 1977 they played the political game, but they
kept away from the major polemics and devoted themselves to ensuring a flow of funds to their institutions and to protecting their core
of institutional prerogatives—control of the nationality qualification,
of marriage among Jews and of Sabbath observance in the public
space. Even their decisions about political manoeuvring in the public
sphere derived from internal disputes and alliances within the *haredi*
world: there was no reaching out, politically or even religiously. Religious outreach was the affair of Chabad, and when Chabad became
too influential Rav Schach instigated a split in Agudat Yisrael.

But Shas took a very different approach. For one thing, the party,
or at least Ovadia Yosef, does not take a doctrinaire view of the state
of Israel: Yosef's non-Zionism is definitely not anti-Zionism. It re-
sides in 'detaching the legitimacy of the state from the legitimacy of
Zionism' (Fischer, 2004b). The state is not some sort of culmination
or destiny of the Jewish people, but neither does it represent a violation of the Torah or an illegitimate foreshadowing of a messianic
future, or—as messianic nationalists would have it—a concrete task
for those who would bring forward the coming of the Messiah. It is
simply a legitimate Jewish institution by whose laws its citizens should
live, and also without doubt a great moment in the history of the
Jewish people (Chen and Pepper, 2004). This leads to Fischer's conclusion that Shas can contribute 'to the basic tenor and pattern of
Israeli society' by a 'lessening of ideological charge and mobilisation.'

On the whole, though, Shas leaders avoid these issues. Surprised
by their initial success in 1983 among lower-class Sephardim in

Jerusalem, its leaders dared to proclaim religion and ethnicity in the political-ideological sphere. This placed political and intellectual élites on the defensive, denouncing the gulf separating the Jewish identity of the state with the population's irreligious way of life and embarrassing them by giving voice to subterranean, but omnipresent, racial divisions. As Deri said to us, at a certain point he and his colleagues came to understand the rules of the game and threw themselves into the political process. This brought them much success but also contributed to his personal downfall. Maybe he did not realise how serious his offences were, or how seriously the courts would take them. Maybe he failed to understand that newcomers should 'know their place'. Maybe he thought he was the eternal golden boy who could get away with anything, even with his habit of rebelling against the father, first against Rav Schach, later against the Labour Party establishment which had taken him into their bosom. He has yet to rebel openly against Ovadia Yosef, but clearly their paths have diverged.

No wonder the political establishment found Shas a troubling guest at their feast: on religion and on race, they broke taboos or at least raised issues of exclusion and ethnic bias in a new way. But their success at the grassroots made them a danger as well as a potentially useful ally. Deri's vociferous recourse to the court of public opinion while the Supreme Court was considering his numerous appeals, especially during the 1999 election campaign, may well have made politicians wary of the party even after his imprisonment. Barak and Sharon needed Shas, but Sharon was quick to replace Shas with its diametrical opposite—the heavily Ashkenazi and fiercely anti-*haredi* Shinui—when the opportunity arose after the 2003 elections. Later, when the withdrawal from Gaza split his party in 2004 and 2005, Sharon was not prepared to pay for the participation of Shas with concessions in welfare expenditure: if Sharon and his Finance Minister Netanyahu had offered enough carrots, surely Shas would have supported the withdrawal. Deri had gone too far, by both exploiting the 'rules of the game' and at the same time, in adopting his shrill rhetoric, denouncing them. Despite these fluctuating political fortunes, though, Shas has institutionalised the seeds of an Israeli Judaism. Deri and Ovadia Yosef had the foresight to create institutions and enshrine them in law, thus ensuring their continuing survival, so the *t'shuva* movement and the related Sephardi awakening continues, underpinned by the Shas school network and the party's strong presence in local government. They have already created their own enclave, and, by tingeing the secular-religious divide with the theme of ethnicity, have created, or brought to the surface, a sharp guilt-ridden boundary, as well as contributing to the widespread Israeli opinion that the once-standard melting-pot metaphor cannot be applied to their society's diversity.

GLOBALISATION

Beyond Israel and Judaism, the case of Shas can also be seen in the context of a global style of cultural politics, for many of our themes can be found to underlie the most diverse movements, from Mexico's Zapatistas and Bolivia's coca producers to far right parties in Western Europe and patriotic reaffirmation in Russia, all of which can be called 'ethnic' in one sense or another: they are described as movements of ethnic renewal, even 'ethnorenaissance', and, whether their language is identified with the 'right' or with the 'left', they invoke a hostility to globalisation.

In the 1996 Israeli elections something similar seemed to manifest itself: a substantial number of the Jewish electorate had somehow expressed their suspicion not just of the peace process as conducted by Shimon Peres and other, younger, left-secular figures, but also of what they saw as an emerging agenda of an 'Israel linked to the global village while rejecting the Jewish foundations of the State' (Elazar, 1998). The margin of Netanyahu over Peres in that election had been less than 1 per cent, but in the Jewish vote his margin was very wide—11 per cent—and the size of the margin could be said to represent a mélange of largely ill-articulated fears aroused by the pressures on Israel not only from the Arab world but also from the liberal West. Both parts of this observation can be connected to the Shas phenomenon.

Shas expresses its distrust of that 'global village' in its strong distaste for, even fear of, the perceived corrosive effects of globalisation on cultural heritage and family structures: television is regarded as a source of much evil and drugs are a perpetual cancer. As we have seen, one of Shas's earliest and most enduring appeals was to parents who, as first generation immigrants from North Africa, were utterly disconcerted by what they saw as the waywardness and disobedience of their children, which they blamed on the media and the tolerance of liberal élites.

In addition, Shas may also reflect—though it does not precisely express—the disintegrative effects of globalised markets on employment opportunities, on job security and on social welfare nets (Peled, 1998). After 1967 Israel experienced a spurt of economic growth and later, after 1977, a gradual opening to the world economy. During the 1990s this trend became an explosion, with the penetration of globalised mass media, the emergence of a 'yuppy' culture, of a successful hi-tech industry and a world class knowledge élite. At the same time, social forces changed fundamentally: the once all-powerful Histadrut, or Trade Union Congress, lost its industrial empire to privatisation, the kibbutz ethos lost its influence, and the kibbutzim themselves became much more like private concerns. Social welfare entitlements have been subject to steady erosion ever since the Netanyahu government of 1996–9, and the collapse of the dot-com boom and the second *intifada* led to deep recession, pushing unemployment over the 10 per cent mark.

SOCIALISATION AND CONVERSION

Family

Curiously, sociologists of religion in general seem to have little grasp of what is surely self-evident: that in all known societies, however modern, religion has been inculcated in children by their parents and their extended kin, and that this fact must have a strong influence on the way in which, once they have grown into adulthood, they come to think of their own religion and that of others. Of course the family is not the only agent of religious socialisation and family structures vary enormously, but it is regrettable that the moulding of religious behaviour by family relationships has not had its place in general theories of religious sociology. It is in the course of childhood that individuals learn, as intimate reflexes, the 'second nature' rhythms of the day and the week: church, mosque and synagogue attendance, the music of religion, the small domestic rituals, the incantations uttered in sometimes incomprehensible but rote-learnt formulae in an archaic version of their own language or in a completely foreign tongue, before meals, on going to sleep, on learning good news or bad. Even more intimate details are assimilated: Jews and Muslims learn about circumcision, Christians, Jews and Muslims assimilate codes of modesty which are imperceptibly linked to religious affiliation and the resulting obligations, relating for example to marriage and the upbringing of the next generation. But now conversion-based religion is changing this model radically: parents and grandparents lose some, and sometimes all, of their predominance in religious socialisation, and so the childhood resonances of religious behaviour throughout an individual's life are replaced.

The case should not be exaggerated, to be sure. It would be mistaken to assume that 'traditionally' (a much-abused word) the family has been the only agent or space of religious socialisation: we have but to recall catechism classes, and the influence of the village priest in Catholicism, or the importance of the Talmud Torah attended by Jewish children in pre-Holocaust Eastern Europe, to place the family's role in perspective. But if we are witnessing a change of emphasis it is possible that it has reached a 'tipping point': as conversion and 'reversion' grow, extra-family mechanisms and institutions acquire increasing authority and power to shape the religious socialisation of young people, of converts especially and even of the intra-family socialisation processes themselves. Although this research does not focus on religious socialisation as such, the involvement of the institutions we describe in education and in the inculcation of religious rituals and procedures, is self-evident, and not only in the case of converts and returnees themselves and their children. In addition, religion appears to become more demanding, and its stipulations more meticulous and invasive, even as individuals in religious communities find in them networks of relationships which, having been built up in institutions of education and learning, or in their process of returning to the faith of their forebears, are quite separate from their kinship networks.

From one point of view, it can be said that these trends show that religion is being modernised and adapting to secularisation. Secularisation, understood as the detachment of religion from the state and from the compulsory control of marriage, of education, and of much else, is part of a generalised process of differentiation, which—over the long run—also detaches many functions, for example the organisation of production, from kinship relations. So, in itself, the shift of functions from home to institutions might be no more than a detail in the march of modernity. But they are not just a detail: these changes in religious socialisation are taking place in parallel with severe conflicts within the great religious traditions over the scope of religious authority, over authoritative interpretations of sacred texts and what legitimises such authority, over the extent to which religious authorities should dictate people's sexual behaviour, over the extent to which the state should submit to religious tutelage. Above all, the change in mechanisms of socialisation is occurring at a time when mass conversion movements are setting the agenda, and setting the pace, in the religious sphere. Whatever the causes of these multifarious changes, they cannot be subsumed under an overarching schema of modernity. We need to take account of discontinuities.

Rationalisation and the miraculous

When one tries to explain discontinuities, one looks to social movements. In trying to interpret the break in continuity in the religious sphere that we are witnessing, we see that social movements, in interaction with the broad features of modernity, namely differentiation and secularisation, have challenged institutions that try to monopolise the administration of the supernatural. As a result innovative institutions of religion increase their power over popular religiosity, changing its content. This changing content is the belief in textual inerrancy and in the veracity of the miraculous, which enjoy widespread acceptance even in a public imbued with modern popular culture and a standard awareness of the rationality of science. The uniquely powerful pressures to which individuals are exposed in the confluence of conversion-based religion and modernity would thus find an explanation not in 'modernity in general' but in a vulnerability arising from the family's loss of its role in religious socialisation, combined with the pressures arising from their involvement in movements of religious revival and conversion.

The argument is that in the sphere of religion pressures for rationalisation and pressures for popular self-affirmation converge—the latter being a penetration or transcendence of the opacity of modern science and bureaucracy by the untutored pursuit of directly apprehended truth.[2] Modernity and secularisation theories assume that religion is identified not with feeling but with doctrine: preachers and theologians and academics emerge into the public sphere to talk about religion in terms of a theodicy rationally reached by the individual's own reflection, rather than followed out of a sense of duty or habit. The same conception also assumes that religion is a private affair and a matter of individual choice, and indeed the modern state in its ideal type treats religion as a choice rather than as an identity— though this is changing under the impact of identity politics and multiculturalism. If it is widely accepted that religion is a matter of individual choice, then the idea that it is chosen because it is true, and demonstrably true, and that an individual's choice should be defendable in those terms, acquires an appeal. Experience tells us that for some people this sequence (not a 'logic') becomes quite compelling, as in the examples of creationism, 'proofs' of miracles, faith healing, alternative medicine, Fatima secrets and so on.

The same environment creates opposite pressures for élite, or historic, institutions of religion to become more learned and more rational and specialised: theology becomes an academic profession on a par with philosophy in general, or with sociology, under the guise of 'religious studies', drawing its legitimacy from the domain of ethics, sociology, philosophy or history, rather than the supernatural. Clergymen come increasingly to resemble social workers and counsellors. Religious institutions identified with the establishment, with a time-honoured way of doing things, become more detached from the daily practice of the supernatural, accentuating their classic role of subordinating the supernatural to rational administration. This is the story of the Church of England, and is also the trend detected by John Paul II in post-Conciliar Catholicism, which he then tried to reverse by encouraging the movements of evangelisation and by turning the hierarchy's attitude to canonisation on its head.

The question of popular religion

We thus observe two divergent patterns of rationalisation: the previously hegemonic institutions of religion fall victim to classic *entzau-*

[2] A challenge which goes back to Jean-Jacques Rousseau, as interpreted in Jean Starobinski, 1971, *Jean-Jacques Rousseau: la transparence et l'obstacle*, Paris: Gallimard, (English translation, Chicago University Press, 1988).

berung (stripping the magic out of religion), while the new ones appropriate the rhetoric of science in support of the esoteric, which can be grasped without prolonged scientific training: the opacity of a mysterious language can be penetrated through the adoption of a rival esoteric which requires little training but much concentrated suspension of disbelief, as in the jargon developed by evangelicals, Jewish sects and so on. This tension helps to explain the fierce anti-intellectualism of conversion-led religious movements: their hostility to the use of modern science, archaeology, linguistics etc. to interpret holy texts, and also to the culture of academia generally. In the eyes of the tribunes of this revivalist popular religion, it is the language of the experts and the scholars which is opaque and esoteric, while their own beliefs are founded in the immediate evidence of experience.

Max Weber prefigured some of this in more direct language than we might use now, especially on the subject of class differences in religious dispositions. 'Once a salvation doctrine and an ethic of intellectualist origin has become a mass religion, an esotericism or aristocratic status ethic arises that is adjusted to the needs of the intellectually trained groups. Meanwhile, however, the religion has been transformed into a doctrine of a popular magical saviour, thereby meeting the needs of the non-intellectual masses' (Weber, 1978: 505–6). The intellectual class, in Weber's schema, bifurcate, resolving their quest for meaning through either contemplative withdrawal or romantic populism, like the Russian *narodnichestvo*, more popularly known as the *narodniks*.[3] In Weber's scheme the intelligentsia and the popular classes are mutually alienated either by intellectualism and contemplation, or by the inauthenticity of sponsored popular culture. But he also enumerates examples of 'quasi-proletarian', 'petty-bourgeois' or 'pariah' intellectualism among, for example the Russian peasantry and the German proletariat of his time, whose religious needs 'tended to assume either an ethically rigorous or an occult term' (*ibid.*: 507–8), as well as in early Christianity, where it was exempli-

---

[3] Bitterly and sarcastically derided by Lenin (but appreciated by Marx in his later years, as in his *Letter to Vera Zasulich*), the *narodniks* (literally populists) were a movement of intellectuals who put their faith in the people and in the institution of the peasant commune as a way for Russia to become a modern, developed country. See Franco Venturi, 1960, *Roots of Revolution: a history of the populist and socialist movements in nineteenth century Russia*, New York: Knopf.

fied by Paul. Weber describes how Saint Paul's 'conception of the relationship between the spirit and the community' and of 'the manner in which spirit is accommodated to the facts of the everyday world' is taken up by successors but 'eventually dispersed with the slow growth of the bishops' and presbyters' monopoly of spiritual leadership of the community' (*ibid.*: 511). For Weber, anti-intellectualism is a 'hallmark' of Christianity, but the tension between anti-intellectualism and the institutionalisation of religious knowledge and power is present throughout his discussion, albeit more as the leading *leitmotif* than as the object of a definitive pronouncement. It re-emerges in the seventeenth-century Anglo-Saxon 'popular religious intellectualism' created by the 'unparalleled diffusion of knowledge about the Bible and interest in extremely abstruse and ethereal dogmatic controversy' (*ibid.*: 514). Weber also undertakes extended discussions of the relationship between dogma, priests and congregational forms on the one hand, and faith, preachers and the masses on the other, with allusions to the role of texts, of magic, of virtuosi, and to numerous examples ancient and modern, Eastern and Western.

Today's popular religious intellectualism, in Christianity, is that of evangelical preachers. Their hold over their followers is much more powerful than that of their more erudite, more educated opposite numbers in the Roman Catholic or Anglican churches. Religious entrepreneurs and propagandists combine a degree of organisational and political sophistication drawn from the resources of modern communication with a sensitivity to popular culture which does not fit straightforwardly into the polar opposition taken for granted by Weber and many since. To be an intellectual can also mean to master the 'science of the popular', namely communications and mass media. They are communicators and, unlike the classic stereotype of an intellectual, they are skilled in conveying the message of the doctrine or the text in the idiom of popular culture. This means somehow conciliating the message with modernity's faith in science. The upshot is something like a cult of the scientific—or of a jargon of science. The translation of Biblical or supernatural stories into the jargon of the *vraisemblable* demythologises the religious narrative, making it a source for very concrete prescriptions for everyday life. After all, if science can convince the layman of the truth of what is incomprehensible, and therefore miraculous, such as black holes, even evolution itself, why can religion not prove that the miraculous is scientifically demonstrable (but only explicable in supernatural terms)? Thus the cures recounted by Pentecostals, and also by the more evangelical Jewish sects, are invariably accompanied by statements such as 'the doctors had no explanation, but it is true and they confirmed it', while Ovadia Yosef tells of the rewards of religious observance and his followers recount how a present from a venerated and elderly Rabbi has, for example, brought an end to infertility. Grand narratives become fables: the miracles of Jesus, once cautionary tales with a moral attached, become straightforward incidents of healing which we can all imitate, mimic and reproduce.

In matters religious the supernatural is never kept under control, and the popular is never fully subjected to official management, least of all by the religious institutions of high culture associated with political and intellectual élites. Consequently, movements of religious renewal take charge of these elements that have been sidelined in the 'establishment',[4] but they bring to their mission now what might be called a pseudo-rational modernist rhetoric, or a simulacrum of rationalised religion: miracles are not depicted by evangelical preachers as legitimising myths embodying ethical or identitarian truths, with a core of mystery impenetrable to the lay person, rather they are advertised as scientifically and demonstrably true instances of the supernatural, and become part of everyday routine.

Any visitor to a Pentecostal church will observe how the Gospel miracles are evoked and marvelled at, but closer inspection will reveal that they are retold with a quite different message from that in the Gospel: where so often they involve Jesus challenging the established order by healing people who are regarded as unworthy—prostitutes, beggars or just poor people—the retelling emphasises only the miraculous quality of the cure and the moral is politically unchallenging: faith heals and Jesus cures. Pentecostal Christianity, and to some extent its Jewish counterpart in the conversion movements

---

[4] It is unfortunate that in English the word 'established' has a technical, legal meaning as well as an everyday connotation. Legally, it refers to the special status of the Church of England as the 'established' Church—the official state Church headed by the monarch. In common parlance, however, it has come to refer to opinion-forming élites who have acquired a status ('social capital' in Bourdieu's sense) which confers authority on their pronouncements and tastes, especially in matters cultural and political. It is used here in the latter sense, obviously.

(Shas and Chabad), have detached the miraculous from the unique: the once-hegemonic narratives of Christianity described miracles as the work of exceptional individuals, namely Christ and the saints, rendered not only exceptional but mythical by the fact that their very material existence was not always beyond doubt. Contemporary religious movements, especially the neo-Pentecostal churches like the Brazil-based Universal Church of the Kingdom of God, empower quite ordinary office-holders to administer *cura divina*.

This literal quality, the dis-enchantment or *banalization* of the miraculous, goes together with the fetishism of textual inerrancy. The doctrine of textual inerrancy according to which everything in the sacred text is literally true, is inseparable from the fetishisation and the authoritarianism with which its interpretation is proclaimed by preachers. The divine is portrayed as the human writ large: God, it is implied, is just like us but omnipotent and omniscient. His morality is ours not only in the general sense of, for example, the Ten Commandments, but in the detailed punishments and rewards that govern our daily lives. The expression 'fetishisation of the text' is used in part to denote its detachment from context, but it is also intended to denote the great power which is placed in the hands of those who claim a monopoly over its interpretation—the guardians of the fetish. For one paradox of the idea of inerrancy is that although it proclaims the democratisation of the text by saying 'everyone' can have access because the true message is self-evident in its words, in practice all followers of charismatic and fundamentalist movements share the same interpretation, which is proclaimed by the movement's leadership (Boone, 1989). In parallel, there is an esoteric dimension to this culture which fetishises the text by reading meaning 'into' its secret correspondences, on the basis of numerology and the like. This can be a harmless pastime, or a harmless erudition, but it can also be abused, as in the current celebrity-cult of the Kabbalah led by a former insurance salesman who has restyled himself 'Rabbi Berg'.

In revivalist religion the miraculous is talked of as an almost routine everyday occurrence. We see this in the most varied of circumstances: in the pilgrimage centre at Lourdes, with its copious records of cures and an official apparatus to decide when a cure is proven, and when it is not (Harris, 1999); in the attempts to make creationism (rebranded as 'intelligent design') a science 'like any other'; in the displays of discarded crutches in evangelical churches; and in the case cited in this book of an institution created to demonstrate the popular ultra-Orthodox Jewish claim that all modern science can be found in Maimonides, or in the Talmud. Followers of text-based fundamentalists are told that Biblical personages were flesh and blood like they are, so the followers too are capable of great feats and miraculous deeds.

While revivalist religion is in some ways, then, more literal, more concerned with demonstrating the truth of its claims, in a parody of empirical science, the secularised intelligentsia can appear more comfortable with, perhaps less threatened by, 'old-style' religion. To judge by opinion pieces in liberal newspapers such as *Ha'aretz* in Israel (Lefkowitz, 2001) or the *Folha de São Paulo* in Brazil, they seem to approve of traditional religion embedded in the rituals and rhythms of everyday life and the family, or in the safe controlling structures of a hegemonic church, while reserving their doubts, even hostility, for evangelical and fundamentalist varieties. The *Folha*, for example, has described neo-Pentecostal churches as purveyors of the 'fast food of religion' (Birman and Lehmann, 1999).[5] To modernist intellectuals the evangelical attempt to justify religious observance on the grounds that supernatural beliefs are true, and can be proven to be true, poses a severe challenge, much more so than a defence based on a certain reverence for tradition or on a concept of the supernatural. They find the passionate conviction that infuses the discourse of the converted either offensive or simply incomprehensibly irrational. Recalling Max Weber's remarks about those intellectuals who edge towards romantic populism, they can more easily tolerate the ritual life of the supernatural, which requires less conviction than conformity and fits with the preconception that religion is a matter of tradition, of the past. Thus in Brazil among the educated classes, possession cults, sometimes known as Afro-Brazilian (though they are nowadays more Brazilian than African), command much more respect, as heritage, than the evangelical churches, and in Ghana the state has sought to promote indigenous possession cults, as heritage, even though, maybe because, Pentecostalism has long overtaken them both quantitatively and in terms of political legitimacy (Meyer, 2004).

[5] Using the English phrase 'fast food' in the Portuguese.

Bryan Turner, implicitly admitting that he is taking a strong position, says he would go 'further' than those who state merely that fundamentalist movements are not opposed to modernity, to argue that 'by embracing modern technology and rational organisational forms, fundamentalist movements are, often as an unintended consequence, ushering in radical modernity', a view reminiscent of Weber's interpretation of the Protestant sects as, in Turner's words, 'the reluctant midwives of modernisation' (Turner, 2004). S. N. Eisenstadt is a little more hesitant: in the Chicago Fundamentalism Project's concluding volume, he describes the basic ideology of fundamentalism as 'anti-modern: the negation of some of the basic tenets of modernity—of the autonomy of the individual, of the hegemony of reason, of the ideology of progress', but Eisenstadt enumerates various 'distinct modern characteristics' of fundamentalism, such as a predisposition to a 'totalistic worldview', in addition to an affinity for modern technology and methods of organisation (Eisenstadt, 1995: 264). Gabriel Almond and others who write the concluding chapters are also cautious, noting only fundamentalist movements' exploitation of the techniques and technology that secularisation affords them (Almond, Sivan *et al.*, 1995: 405).

The difficulty of finding a coherent view is partly rooted in the quasi-legalistic artificiality of the question 'are they modern?', for the more relevant question is 'what are their implications and effects in the contemporary (modern) world?' Depending on our conception of modernity, we can take the view that fundamentalist movements are backward looking and anti-modern, and for that reason a threat to the modern way of life, or that they are a threat to that way of life precisely because they are modern. Even if these movements are part and parcel of modernity, that may not be much of a consolation, for they may still threaten the well-being or peace of mind of many 'equally modern' individuals and collectivities. Some theories speak of the 'disembedding' of habits, institutions and customs (Giddens, 1990), or the 'remooring of tradition' (Thompson, 1995) as central features of modernity, opening the way for incorporating revivified traditions, and above all traditions transposed to diasporas or via mechanisms of cultural appropriation. In this framework, however 'traditional' the content of a practice might be, it nevertheless can, on account of these reflexive factors, become very modern. Certainly, whatever such movements may lack or exhibit in modernity of outlook, they are capable of competing in contemporary political and mediatic arenas.

The purpose of this discussion, which began by considering the decline of family control of religious socialisation and shifted from there to the questions of popular religion and modernity, has been to show that although conversion-led religion does represent an important break, it is still religion and, modern or not, it still does for its followers many of the things religions invariably do. So when we compare the text-based fundamentalists and the more spirit-based charismatics, we should not conclude that a focus on the text implies an absence of the supernatural from daily life. Nor does the institutionalisation of the shaping of religious souls, which we have described as to some extent replacing the family in religious socialisation, dispel belief in omens or negotiation with supernatural forces through modern genies and fortune-tellers, as we saw in Chapter 5.

RELIGION, FAMILY AND SOCIAL CAPITAL

Religious movements in the contemporary world can, in simple language, make a lot of noise, but it is not easy to interpret that noise and its effects. The number of people practicing their religion in one way or another seems to be on the increase, but even if this is not the case, the numbers visibly practicing and proclaiming their religion in the public sphere are increasing, religious voices are making ever more confident interventions in politics, and the conversion-based movements to which we have paid so much attention are transforming the meaning of religion in public and private spheres. Finally, religious organisations—especially those campaigning for conversion—seem able to mobilise the undivided and all-consuming energies of their followers and are making themselves felt in elections, in the media and very occasionally by violence.

Which of their aims are fundamentalist movements most likely to achieve and under what conditions? The case analysed in this book has a particular contribution to make to answering this question because, although in some ways Shas has much in common with Christian and Muslim conversion-based movements, it has developed in a very particular institutional context, and in these remaining pages we ask to what extent that context has shaped the movement's ability to achieve its aims, returning to some of the major themes proclaimed by conversion-based movements in different parts of the world. The themes of particular interest can be divided into the private sphere (family, children's upbringing, education) and the public (social capital and politics).

Shas activists share with Pentecostals and Islamists a deep anxiety about the difficulty parents experience in keeping the respect of their children and in keeping them away from the temptations of the street, notably drugs. They also share with many, but not all, Pentecostal churches and with Islamists, a desire to control their children's sexual activity by keeping them away from the temptations of the television, videos and the like. The prohibition of contraception which is standard (save on medical grounds) among *haredi* Jews is also found among the Brazilian Assemblies of God and similar traditional Pentecostal churches, with none of the theological reasoning marshalled by the Catholic hierarchy. The neo-Pentecostal Universal Church of the Kingdom of God is silent on this matter and, instead of prohibiting television, has opened its own network which transmits morally acceptable entertainment by day and religious programming by night. In order to gain or regain control over wayward and potentially wayward children Shas has provided kindergartens and schools with extended hours and a strong culture of obedience to teachers, and a timetable of activity which aspires to govern almost all a child's waking hours at home and at school. In principle, in the schools for children from the most observant families, when the children are not learning they are praying. Evangelicals have nothing like this: in Brazil, in the absence of documented information, we can only say that their education activities are limited to Sunday school and occasional kindergartens where municipal subsidy can be obtained. But the expanding presence of evangelical politicians in local government will probably make more resources available to them for educational activities especially at the pre-school and primary level.

This is no universalistic, secular social-democratic improvement programme. The analysis would be impoverished if it excluded the role of the supernatural, especially in family matters. Pastors and Rabbis try to convince their followers that the problems they experience in their families—indiscipline, violence, infidelity—are rooted in their irreligious way of life and in the work of diabolical forces. The

invocation of past sins, even going back to earlier generations, explains children's poor behaviour: among Jews it may be said that the
mother conceived when she was in the menstrual period of abstin-
ence, and among evangelicals that some ancestor had become involved with a possession cult in order to overcome infertility or to obtain
the love of a particular man or woman. Either way, present misfortune is tied to a corrupt contract, to the pursuit of a desired outcome
at low cost. To combat the misfortune a sacrifice must be made, by
joining a church or by making *t'shuva* and studying Torah, and developing a different set of reciprocities.

The evident fact that people living in poverty are the principal—
though by no means the only—constituency from which movements
draw their converts, has a place in this account, because joining a
church or becoming an activist in a movement like Shas costs above
all time, whereas the alternative responses to poverty and marginality,
such as medical attention, or joining a club, cost money. If one joins
this type of religious movement one can achieve recognition and a
type of citizenship by adopting an austere and observant way of life
and giving of one's time, even just by sweeping the church floor, and
it is in the leadership's interest to reward such behaviour rather than
to discriminate against the poor or the dark-skinned. Experience
suggests that once movements succeed and become wealthy and institutionalised—as in the case of Methodism—these patterns change
and privilege sets in.

Leaders want to succeed, and they want their movements to expand, but to pursue this over a long period exclusively on the basis of
the sacrifices of their followers is not only wearing, it can also become dangerous at the extreme. It can lead to the involution we
witness in cults and catastrophes like the 1978 Jonestown massacre of
US citizens in Guyana, to armies of volunteers exposing themselves
unprotected to modern weaponry, or to the epidemic of suicide
bombing we witness in the Middle East (Atran, 2003a; Berman,
2003). So, to avoid imposing excessive sacrifices, organisations look
to politics and the state as sources of funds, offering in return the
votes of their disciplined followers. Shas has gone further because its
access to state funds has alleviated the impositions on its core followers and activists, and because it has even been able to build itself
up as an independent political force. All over Latin America—in

Brazil, Guatemala, Peru—evangelical church leaders have gone into politics with a corporate, not an ideological agenda: they hope to be rewarded with contracts to run charitable activities, schools and the like. But doubts remain concerning the extent to which these movements bring about structural or even significant cultural change in their societies. In politics and in the media they have presented a challenge and embarrassment to established political élites (Birman and Lehmann, 1999), but the political establishment in Brazil, at least, overcame its initial distaste and by now has co-opted the evangelical politicians quite successfully in time-honoured fashion. Evangelicals do not take part in debates on the major issues in society, preferring to keep a low profile and reserve their electoral firepower for issues of concern to themselves. They may also have reached a plateau in their grassroots expansion: except for the inflated case of Guatemala, and despite very high rates of growth which would, if maintained, have taken them beyond the 20 per cent mark, in no Latin American country have the Protestants passed that proportion.

Shas has used the funds at its disposal to go further and intervene systematically in the family life of its activists and followers. The state funds, directly or indirectly, yeshivas for *ba'alei t'shuva*, who then live on the yeshiva premises, or find a wife through the good offices of the yeshiva tutors, or if they are married, and if they show they have truly changed their way of life, may even find housing through Shas channels. Thereafter, if they are living in a Sephardi religious neighbourhood, they are under pressure to have large numbers of children, and also to send them to Shas schools. The numbers involved are doubtless below the total of those who might potentially qualify on account of their ethnicity and having made *t'shuva*, but the mechanism is quite unique for a conversion movement, and shows how with state support the movement responds to the crisis of the family.

Many of the themes we have discussed can thus be brought together under the heading of social capital, and the question with respect to Shas is whether the movement's dependence on the state has affected its ability to create social capital. For that, translated into sociological jargon, is what underlies the Shas leadership's calls for a return to religion and a recovery of Sephardi self-esteem.

If we base ourselves on a simplified version of Putnam's account of Italy (Putnam, Leonardi *et al.*, 1993) social capital is the confluence of trust in institutions and a rich associative culture. Ashkenazi Jewish society in the diaspora exhibits what must surely be a remarkably high level of social capital: there is hardly a single cause for which that society does not provide an organisation of some kind, as a cursory perusal, for example, of the London *Jewish Chronicle* demonstrates.[6] We saw early signs of this propensity in the establishment of yeshivas in Eastern Europe in the nineteenth century: independent self-financed institutions detached from the personal dependencies and family ties of village and small town. But our account of North Africa showed that only in the exceptional case of the island of Jerba—where Africa's first printing press was established—was the magic formula found. Indeed, the resistance to the attempt to establish yeshivas in Morocco shortly after the establishment of the French protectorate in 1912 was symptomatic of the difficulties of securing long term institutional autonomy among North African Jews, since it ran into opposition from local élites accustomed to running institutions as if they were their personal fiefdoms. We remarked on the consequences for North African Jews when they arrived in Israel, for even though they had survived the physical destruction of the Holocaust, they did not match the achievement of the Ashkenazim in preserving their institutions. To be sure, the Israeli power structure and cultural bias was not on their side, and the North African élites, presented with more options than the Holocaust survivor generation, and little touched by the ideological Zionist movement, had tended to migrate elsewhere. But that is not an adequate explanation. Even if they had encountered the most caringly politically correct and multicultural reception—in other words a welcome way ahead of its time—the shock would still have been severe. They were coming from a society in which religion, family and tribe were determinants of social position to one which was, on the one hand, ferociously individualist and competitive and, on the other, guided by a socialist ideology utterly foreign to them. Their skills as artisans were poorly rewarded or not in demand at all. The Hebrew they

---

[6] Recently the London Institute for Jewish Policy Research, as part of its 'Planning for Jewish Communities' programme, published a report reflecting the awareness of this in Jewish organisations: Ernest Schlesinger, 2003, *Creating Community and Accumulating Social Capital: Jews associating with other Jews in Manchester*, Report no. 2, 2003.

knew was not an everyday spoken language and their Arabic was quite different from that of the local Arab-speaking population. In short, even without violence, the trauma of the migration must have been great, greater probably even than the shock experienced by those going through the great migrations between Europe and the Americas, or between countryside and city in poor countries. Migrants usually join a long term trend, and encounter networks of earlier migrants in place ready to receive, support and socialise them. The waves of North African migration, in contrast, were sudden and massive.

The children and grandchildren of the North Africans have already dispersed throughout Israeli society, not least through intermarriage with people of Middle Eastern and Ashkenazi origin, but their distribution in the socio-economic hierarchy is uneven and their above-average exposure to social problems is widely recognised. The Shas leaders seized on their malaise and constructed the ideal of returning 'to the source' (*El HaMa'ayan*), of recreating a world free of the travails of modernity. In practice, this means making *t'shuva*, and preserving or restoring Sephardi versions of ritual and music—it does not mean patronising secular Israeli popular music, despite its strongly Sephardi-Arab elements.

Recreating a lost way of life is a dream, even a fantasy, for Shas as it is for many other movements of cultural rebirth. Where Shas was successful was in mobilising at the grassroots for *t'shuva* and for political purposes. To build on what they have already achieved, Shas and its followers have to face modernity not only in their methods of mobilisation but also in the content of their message. This means building social capital, and recognising the dream for what it is: a dream.

The theory of social capital in Putnam's book on Italy tells us that what Shas lacks is still a basis for high levels of trust and transparency to match their grassroots mobilising skills. His later, and now more famous, *Bowling Alone*, which is about the United States, places more emphasis on social capital as a product of the associative life: it is an idea of personal community involvement in a manner which reaches out to others and binds them together. The research on religion finds that in the United States, although participation in voluntary activity is particularly prevalent in churches, it tends to be the preserve of the most committed, the true believers, who then drive their churches and the political ginger groups allied to them towards uncompromising positions, and away from consensus: evangelical churches, which resist the trend toward disengagement from institutionalised religion, do not encourage 'civic engagement with the wider community' and focus on their own needs and the needs of their own faithful (Putnam, 2000). The social capital thus built does not strengthen the ties that bind society together. The upshot, we might add, is forceful organisation based on tightly knit groups bound by personal as much, or more than, institutional ties, to the detriment of trust and transparency.

In the case of Shas the disjunction between personal involvement and institutional construction may be quite glaring. People may love Shas and vote for it, but just as innumerable Americans attend church without participating, or claim to be part of a church without attending (Putnam, 2000), they may not be faithful to the party when it comes to actions which affect their own or their families' welfare, such as their children's schooling: this is because clientelism makes individuals feel vulnerable and dependent on unpredictable decisions by political intermediaries or party leadership, so if they can, and depending on circumstances, they may prefer a more anonymous, although less emotionally appealing, alternative. Israel offers such alternatives—in other places they may not exist.

Unfortunately, a major obstacle to the consolidation of Shas is precisely one of the causes of the movement's success, namely its reliance on the state and the political habits of the enclave system. This reliance encourages clientelism and focuses efforts on the search for state or state-supported employment at the expense of building a secure base in a supportive constituency. The problem is far from unique: popular movements in Latin America—indigenous and other—have tended to look for their reproduction to international and governmental funding rather than to a contributory base (material or nonmaterial) among their own rank and file. As a result they have suffered from a dependence on external contacts and financing (Assies, 1999).[7]

---

[7] Although the Brazilian Landless Workers' Movement (Movimento dos Sem-Terra—MST) has a vast following, it obtains support by contributions from members working in the land reform cooperatives established on land expropriated as a result of the movement's campaigns, and managed under the auspices of the MST itself. In other words, it is indirectly funded by the state.

On the other hand, it is striking that Pentecostal churches are able to fund themselves from their own followers. It is notorious that in Africa, even amid the total institutional collapse which afflicts certain regions, the one institution which exists is the, usually evangelical, church. In Latin America, churches, from tiny local one-man operations to vast apparatuses like the Universal Church of the Kingdom of God, seem able to raise funds even from the poorest followers.

The demands of Shas on its followers are more religious and social than financial, while the leadership has not renounced its rhetoric claiming discrimination and disadvantage among the country's Sephardim. The question is: is this cause best served by continuing dependence on the state? The evolution of Shas has been determined not just by the grassroots mobilisation talents of its activists but also by the strategy of turning the fruits of that activism into state support. Economic theorists of religion (Iannacone, 1997) would argue that this success has been bought at the expense of their autonomy—an autonomy which would in its turn require greater sacrifice on the part of the users of institutions. Already parents of children in Shas schools are pressed, even required, to make sacrifices by leading a religiously observant life, but is that enough? They do not have to pay much in fees, if anything, and they are not expected to contribute their labour to constructing school buildings.

Arieh Deri complained that the brightest young Sephardi students gravitate towards Ashkenazi institutions, depriving the movement of its future cadres. Is this a case of 'false consciousness' or a degree of lack of trust? The one highly distinguished and over-subscribed Shas-related yeshiva we know of is the Tunisian Al Kisei Rachamim in Bnei Brak, but significantly it does not receive subsidies from the state, rather campaigning for donations and charging fees and receiving a proportion of students from outside Israel. Also its founders and Director come from Jerba, the island with a unique history of creating Jewish institutions in North Africa. Its political links seemed to us limited to a respect for Ovadia Yosef rather than active involvement. The one Sephardi yeshiva we visited which was unconnected with Shas (Yekiri Yerushalayim) was a thriving institution, much larger than any Shas yeshiva, even Al Kisei Rachamim: the tutor (*mashgiach*) who talked to us claimed that the yeshiva prospered with no government support at all, was well over-subscribed and suffered no leakage of its brightest students. He was ferociously hostile to political Rabbis—among which he counted Shas *en bloc*. Maybe this was just political point-scoring. But maybe there is also a lesson here: reliance on the state may have helped Shas build up numbers, but that dependence may have sown doubts in the minds of its constituency about the quality of its institutions and the transparency of their procedures, and about the extent to which teachers may be appointed more for their political loyalty than their professional merits. Of course they would never raise the matter in public, but when issues of schooling are at stake word of mouth is a powerful influence on opinion, and hierarchies of prestige are subject to fine-grained evaluation. If Shas has to hold down its material and religious demands on the parents in order to maintain school rolls, then the project of forming a Sephardi élite is in trouble. Somehow, if it is to consolidate its roots in society and raise Sephardi self-esteem, the movement may have to choose whether or not it should try to reduce its reliance on the state and increase the demands made on its followers.

BIBLIOGRAPHY

Adler, Ch. and M. Inbar, 1977, *Ethnic Integration in Israel: a comparative case study of Moroccan brothers who settled in France and Israel*, New Brunswick: Transaction Books.

Almog, O., 2000, *Sabra: the creation of the New Jew*, Berkeley, CA: University of California Press.

Almond, G. A., E. Sivan *et al.*, 1995, 'Fundamentalism, phenomenology and comparative dimensions' in M. Marty and R. S. Appleby (eds), *Fundamentalisms Comprehended*, Chicago University Press.

Ammerman, N. T., 1987, *Bible Believers: fundamentalists in the modern world*, New Brunswick: Rutgers University Press.

Amran, M., 2000, 'Cassette culture in the Haredi community' (Hebrew), MA thesis, Dept. of Communication, Hebrew University, Jerusalem.

Aronoff, M. J., 1974, *Frontiertown: the politics of community building in Israel*, Manchester University Press.

Assies, W., 1999, 'Theory, practice and "external actors" in the making of new social movements in Brazil, *Bulletin of Latin American Research*, 18, 2, 1211–26.

Atran, S., 2003a, 'Genesis and future of suicide terrorism', www.interdisciplines.org

———, 2003b, *In Gods We Trust: the evolutionary landscape of religion*, New York: Oxford University Press.

Barrett, J., 2001, 'Do children experience God as adults do?' in J. Andresen (ed.), *Religion in Mind: cognitive perspectives on religious belief, ritual and experience*, Cambridge University Press.

Barth, F., 1998 (1969), 'Introduction' in F. Barth (ed.), *Ethnic Groups and Boundaries: the social organization of culture difference*, Prospect Heights, IL: Waveland.

Bar-Yosef, R., 1968, 'Re-socialization and de-socialization: the process of immigrants' (*olim*) adaptation', *International Migration Review*, 2, 3, 27–45.

Barzilai, G., 2003, *Communities and Law: politics and cultures of legal identities*, Ann Arbour, MI: University of Michigan Press.

Bayart, J.-F., 2005, *The Illusion of Cultural Identity*, London: Hurst.

Beinin, J. and J. Stork (eds), 1997, *Political Islam: essays from the Middle East Report*, Berkeley, CA: University of California Press.

279

Beit-Hallahmi, B., 1991, 'Back to the fold: the return to Judaism' in B. Beit-Hallami and Z. Sobel (eds), *Jewishness and Judaism in Contemporary Israel*, Albany, NY: SUNY Press.

Ben-Ami, I., 1998, *Saint Veneration among the Jews in Morocco*, Detroit, MI: Wayne Sate University Press.

Ben-Ari, E. and Y. Bilu, 1994, 'Saints in the crossroads of meaning: on the metaphysics of Baba Sali' in D. Ochana (ed.), *The Presence of Myths in Judaism, Zionism and Israelism* (Hebrew), Tel Aviv: Hakibbutz Hameuchad.

Berenstein, D., 1979, 'The Black Panthers: conflict and protest in Israeli society', *Megamot* (Hebrew), 15, 1, 65–80.

Berger, D., 2001, *The Rebbe, the Messiah and the Scandal of Orthodox Indifference*, London: The Littman Library of Jewish Civilization.

Berger, M., 1999, 'Social deviance: the case of Hazara Bet'shuva in a deprived area' (Hebrew), Research paper submitted for BA Degree, Dept. of Education, Hebrew University, Jerusalem.

Berman, E., 2000, 'Sect, subsidy, and sacrifice: an economist's view of Ultra-Orthodox Jews', *Quarterly Journal of Economics*, 115, 3, 905–53.

———, 2003, *Hamas, Taliban and the Jewish Underground: an economist's view of radical religious militias*, Washington, DC: NBER Working Paper no. 10004.

Bick, E., 2001, 'The Shas phenomenon and religious parties in the 1999 elections', *Israel Affairs*, 7, 4, 55–100.

———, 2004, 'A party in decline: Shas in Israel's 2003 elections', *Israel Affairs*, 10, 4, 101–29.

Bilu, Y. and E. Ben-Ari, 1992, 'The making of modern saints: manufactured charisma and the Abu-Hatseiras of Israel', *American Ethnologist*, 19, 4, 672–87.

Bin Nun, Y., 2003, 'La quête d'un compromis pour l'evacuation des Juifs du Maroc' in S. Trigano (ed.), *L'exclusion des Juifs des pays arabes. Aux sources du conflit israëlo-arabe*, Paris: Editions In Press.

Birman, P., 1998, 'Feminine mediation and Pentecostal identities', *Cambridge Anthropology*, 20, 3, 66–83.

———, 2006, 'A mirror to the future: the media, evangelicals and politics in Brazil', in Birgit Meyer (ed.), *Media, evangelicals and the Public Sphere*, Bloomington, IN: Indiana University Press.

——— and D. Lehmann, 1999, 'Religion and the media in a battle for ideological hegemony', *Bulletin of Latin American Research*, 18, 2, 145–64.

Boone, K., 1989, *The Bible Tells Them So: the discourse of Protestant fundamentalism*, Albany, NY: SUNY Press.

Boyer, P., 2001, *Religion Explained: the human instincts that fashion gods, spirits and ancestors*, London, Heinemann.

Brandão, C. R., 1980, *Os Deuses do Povo. Um estudo sobre a religião popular*, São Paulo: Brasiliense.

Burdick, J., 1994, *Looking for God in Brazil*, Berkeley, CA: University of California Press.

Campbell, J. T., 1995, *Songs of Zion: the African Methodist Episcopal Church in the United States and South Africa*, New York: Oxford University Press.

Campos, L. S., 1997, *Teatro, templo e Mercado. Organização e marketing de um empreendimento neopentecostal*, Petrópolis, RJ: Vozes, São Paolo: Simpósio e UMESP.

Caplan, K., 1997, 'God's voice: audiotaped sermons in Israeli *haredi* society', *Modern Judaism*, 17, 253–79.

————, 2003, 'The internal popular discourse of Israeli haredi women', *Archives des Sciences Sociales des Religions*, 123, 77–101.

Caspi, D. and Y. Limor, 1999, *The In/Outsiders: the media in Israel*, Cresskill, NJ: Hampton Press.

Castells, M., 1998, *The Power of Identity* (vol. 2 of *The Information Age: Economy, Society and Culture*), Oxford: Blackwell.

Chen, N. and A. Pepper, 2004, *Ovadia Yosef: the biography* (Hebrew), Jerusalem: Keter.

Chesnut, A., 2003, *Competitive Spirits: Latin America's new religious economy*, New York: Oxford University Press.

Chouraqui, A., 1985, *Histoire des Juifs en Afrique du Nord*, Paris: Hachette.

Cohen, E., 1972, 'Black Panthers in Israel', *Jewish Journal of Sociology*, 14, 1, 93–109.

Comaroff, J., 1985, *Body of Power, Spirit of Resistance: the culture and history of a South African people*, University of Chicago Press.

Corten, A., 1999, *Pentecostalism in Brazil*, Basingstoke: Macmillan.

Crewe, E. and E. Harrison, 1998, *Whose Development? An ethnography of aid*, London: Zed Books.

Csordas, T., 1997, *Language, Charisma and Creativity*, Berkeley, CA: University of California Press.

Davie, G., 2000, *Religion in Modern Europe: a memory mutates*, Oxford University Press.

————, 2002, *Europe: the exceptional case: parameters of faith in the modern world*, London: Darton, Longman and Todd.

Dayan, A., 1999, *The story of Shas*, (Hebrew) Jerusalem, Keter.

Dein, S. and R. Littlewood, 1995, 'The effectiveness of words: religion and healing among the Lubavitch of Stamford Hill', *Culture, Medicine and Psychiatry*, 19, 339–83.

Deshen, S., 1982, 'The social structure of southern Tunisian Jewry in the early twentieth century' in S. Deshen and W. Zenner (eds), *Jewish Societies in the Middle East: community, culture and authority*, Washington, DC: University Press of America.

————, 1989, *The Mellah Society: Jewish community life in Sherifian Morocco*, Chicago University Press.

———— and M. Shokeid, 1974, *The Predicament of Homecoming: cultural and social life of North African immigrants in Israel*, Ithaca, NY: Cornell University Press.

Dieckhoff, A., 2003, *The Invention of a Nation: Zionist thought and the making of modern Israel*, London: Hurst.

Don-Yehiya, E., 1997, 'Religion, ethnicity and electoral reform: the religious parties and the 1996 elections', *Israel Affairs*, 4, 1, 73–102.

Doimo, A. M., 1995, *A vez e a voz do Popular. Movimentos sociais e participação política no Brasil pós-70*, Rio de Janeiro: ANPOCS, Relume Dumar.

Doron, G. and R. Kook, 1999, 'Religion and the politics of inclusion: the success of the ultra-Orthodox parties' in A. Arian and M. Shamir (eds), *Elections in Israel, 1996*, Albany, NY: SUNY Press.

Eisenman, R., 1978, *Islamic Law in Palestine and Israel*, Leiden: E. J. Brill.

Eisenstadt, S. N., 1985, *The Transformation of Israeli Society: an essay in interpretation*, Boulder, CO: Westview Press.

————, 1995, 'Fundamentalism, phenomenology and comparative dimensions' in M. Marty and R. S. Appleby (eds), *Fundamentalisms Comprehended*, Chicago University Press.

Elazar, D., 1998, 'Introduction: the battle over Jewishness and Zionism in the post-modern era' in D. Elazar (ed.), *Israel at the polls, 1996*, London: Frank Cass.

El-Or, T., 1994, *Educated but Ignorant: ultra-orthodox Jewish women and their world*, Boulder, CO: Lynne Reiner.

———— and E. Neria, 2004, 'The unorthodox flâneur: toward the pleasure principle: consuming time and space in the contemporary haredi population of Jerusalem' in Y. Carmeli and K. Applebaum (eds.) *Consumption and Market Society in Israel*, Oxford, Berg.

Evans-Pritchard, E. E., 1937, *Witchcraft, Oracles and Magic among the Azande*, Oxford: Clarendon Press.

Feldman, A., 2001, 'The Shas Party: a review of factors contributing to its development' (Hebrew), PhD thesis, Bar-Ilan University, Ramat-Gan.

Fischer, S., 2004a, 'Amulets and political liberalism: the conceptual organization of social reality and the legitimation of the state according to the Shas movement' in Y. Yonah (ed.), *A Maelstrom of Identites: a critical look at religion and secularity in Israel*, (Hebrew) Jerusalem: Van Leer Institute/Hakibbutz Hameuchad.

————, 2004b, 'The program and themes of the Shas movement', Jerusalem, unpublished manuscript.

———— and Z. Beckerman, 2001, 'Church or sect?' in Y. Peled (ed.), *Shas: the challenge of Israeliness* (Hebrew), Tel Aviv: Yediot Aharonot.

Fishkoff, S., 2003, *The Rebbe's Army: inside the world of Chabad-Lubavitch*, New York: Schocken.

Flint, G. and B. Sorj, 2000, *Israel: terra em transe. Democracia ou teocracia?*, Rio de Janeiro: Civilização Brasileira.

Fox, J. and L. D. Brown (eds), 1998, *The Struggle for Accountability: the World Bank, NGOs, and grassroots movements*, Cambridge, MA: MIT Press.

Freston, P., 2001a, *Evangelicals and Politics in Africa, Asia, and Latin America*, Cambridge University Press.

——, 2001b, 'The transnationalization of Brazilian Pentecostalism: the Universal Church of the Kingdom of God' in A. Corten and R. Marshall-Fratani (eds), *Between Babel and Pentecost: transnational Pentecostalism in Africa and Latin America*, London: Hurst.

Friedland, R. and R. D. Hecht, 1996, *To Rule Jerusalem*, Cambridge University Press.

Friedman, M., 1986, 'Life tradition and book tradition in the development of Ultra-Orthodox Judaism' in H. Goldberg, *Judaism Viewed from Within and from Without: anthropological studies*, Albany, NY: SUNY Press, 235–55.

——, 1994, 'Habad as messianic fundamentalism: from local particularism to universal Jewish mission' in M. Marty and R. S. Appleby (eds), *Accounting for Fundamentalisms: the dynamic character of movements*, Chicago University Press.

——, 1995, 'The structural foundation for the religio-political accomodation in Israel: fallacy and reality' in S. I. Troen and N. Lucas (eds), *Israel: the first decade of independence*, Albany, NY: SUNY Press.

——, n.d., 'Rabbi Eliezer Menachem Schach', unpublished manuscript.

Gellner, E., 1981, *Muslim Society*, Cambridge University Press.

Geschiere, P., 1995, *Sorcellerie et Politique en Afrique. La viande des autres*, Paris: Karthala.

Giddens, A., 1990, *The Consequences of Modernity*, Stanford University Press.

Gladwell, M., 2001, *The Tipping Point: how little things can make a big difference*, London: Abacus.

Goldberg, H. (ed.), 1996, *Sephardi and Middle Eastern Jewries: history and culture in the modern era*, Bloomington, IN: Indiana University Press.

Greenberg, D. and E. Witztum, 2001, *Sanity and Sanctity: mental health work among the ultra-orthodox in Jerusalem*, London and New Haven, CT: Yale University Press.

Grinberg, L. I., 1991, 'The Israeli labor movement in crisis: the political economy of the relations between Mapai, Histadrut and the state' (Hebrew) Ph.D. thesis, Tel Aviv University.

Gros, C., 1999, 'Evangelical protestantism and indigenous populations', *Bulletin of Latin American Research*, 18, 2, 175–98.

Haar, G. ten, 1998, *Halfway to Paradise: African Christians in Europe*, Cardiff Academic Press.

Harris, R., 1999, *Lourdes: body and spirit in the secular age*, London: Penguin.

Heilman, S., 1990, 'The Orthodox, the Ultra-Orthodox and the elections for the Twelfth Knesset' in A. Arian and M. Shamir (eds), *The Elections in Israel, 1988*, Boulder, CO: Westview Press.

———, 1992, *Defenders of the Faith: inside ultra-Orthodox Jewry*, New York: Schocken.

Helman, S. and A. Levy, 2001, 'Shas in the Israeli press' in Y. Peled (ed.), *Shas: the challenge of Israeliness* (Hebrew), Tel-Aviv: Yediot Aharonot.

Herrman, T. and E. Yar, 2001, 'Shas's doveishness: image and reality' in Y. Peled (ed.), *Shas: the challenge of Israeliness* (Hebrew), Tel-Aviv: Yediot Aharonot.

Herzog, H., 1995, 'Penetrating the system: the politics of collective identities' in A. Arian and M. Shamir (eds), *The Elections in Israel, 1992*, Albany, NY: SUNY Press.

Horowitz, D. and M. Lissak, 1987, *Trouble in Utopia: the overburdened polity in Israel*, Albany, NY: SUNY Press.

Horowitz, N., 2000, 'Shas and Zionism: historical analysis' (Hebrew), *Kivunim Chadashim*, 2, 30–60.

Hulme, D. and M. Edwards (eds), 1997, *Too Close for Comfort? The impact of official aid on non-governmental organizations*, Basingstoke: Macmillan.

Hunt, S. and N. Lightly, 2001, 'The British black Pentecostal 'revival': identity and belief in the 'new' Nigerian churches', *Ethnic and Racial Studies*, 24, 1.

Iannacone, L., 1997, 'Introduction to the economics of religion', *Journal of Economic Literature*, 36, 3, 1465–95.

Jacobs, L., 1995, *The Jewish Religion: a companion*, Oxford University Press.

Katz, J., 1973, *Out of the Ghetto: the social background of Jewish emancipation, 1770–1870*, Cambridge University Press.

Kedourie, E., 1989, 'The break between Muslims and Jews in Iraq' in A. Udovich (ed.), *Jews among Arabs: contacts and boundaries*, Princeton, NJ: Darwin Press.

Kepel, G., 1987, *Les banlieues de l'Islam: naissance d'une religion en France*, Paris: Seuil.

———, 2002, *Jihad: the death of Political Islam*, London: I. B. Tauris.

Lefkowitz, D., 2001, 'Negotiated and mediated meaning: ethnicity and politics in Israeli newspapers', *Anthropological Quarterly*, 74, 4, 179–90.

Lehmann, D., 1990, *Democracy and Development in Latin America: economics, politics and religion in the post-war period*, Oxford: Polity Press.

———, 1996, *Struggle for the Spirit: religious transformation and popular culture in Brazil and Latin America*, Oxford: Polity Press.

———, 1998, 'Fundamentalism and globalism', *Third World Quarterly* 19, 4, 607–34.

———, 2001, 'Charisma and possession in Africa and Brazil', *Theory, Culture and Society*, 18, 5, 45–74.

———, 2002, 'Religion in contemporary Latin American social science', *Bulletin of Latin American Research*, 21, 2, 290–307.

———, 2003, 'Dissidence and conformism in religious movements: what difference—if any—separates the Catholic Charismatic Renewal and Pentecostal churches?', *Concilium*, 2003, 3, 122–38.

Leon, N., 1999, 'Sephardim and haredim: an ethnographic inquiry into the meaning of the influence of the Shas movement on the perception of Oriental Haredi identity and discourse thereon' (Hebrew) Master's thesis, Department of Sociology, University of Tel-Aviv.

———, 2001, 'The glory of a generation, the persecuted and the "television dupes"' (Hebrew) in R. Rosenthal, *The Dividing Line*, Tel Aviv: Hemed, 285–98.

Lijphardt, A., 1969, 'Consociational democracy', *World Politics*, 21, 207–25.

Louer, L., 2003, *Les citoyens arabes d'Israël*, Paris, Balland.

Lupo, Y., 1999, 'The rescue of Moroccan Jewry for Torah: the transfer of Moroccan students to Lithuanian *Yeshivoth* after the Shoah' (Hebrew), *Pe'amim*, 80, 112–28.

———, 2003, 'La métamorphose ultra-Orthodoxe des jeunes juifs du Maroc', PhD thesis, Université de Paris-X. (The author's name appears in the thesis as Lupu, but in other publications as Lupo.)

———, 2004, *Shas de Lita: the Lithuanian takeover of Moroccan Torah scholars* (Hebrew) Tel Aviv, Hakibbutz Hameuchad.

Martin, D., 1990, *Tongues of Fire: the Pentecostal revolution in Latin America*, Oxford: Blackwell.

———, 2001, *Pentecostalism: the world their parish*, Oxford: Blackwell.

Mauss, M., 1950, 'Essai sur le don' in M. Mauss, *Sociologie et Anthropologie*, Paris: Presses Universitaires de France.

Mazlish, S., 1984, *Hazara Bet'shuva: movement and people* (Hebrew), Jerusalem: Masada.

Mazower, M., 2004, *Salonika: city of ghosts*, London: HarperCollins.

McAdam, D., J. D. McCarthy *et al.*, 1996, *Comparative Perspectives on Social Movements: political opportunities, mobilizing structures, and cultural framings*, Cambridge University Press.

Meler, Z. D., 1998, *Soul's Hunters: an answer to t'shuva* (Hebrew), Tel Aviv: Zamora Bitan.

Melucci, A., 1989, *Nomads of the Present: social movements and individual needs in contemporary society*, London: Hutchinson Radius.

Menocal, M. R., 2002, *Ornament of the World: how Muslims, Jews and Christians created a culture of tolerance in medieval Spain*, Boston, MA: Little, Brown

Metcalf, B. D., 2002, '"Traditionalist" Islamic activism: Deoband, Tablighis and Talibs', *ISIM Working Papers*, 4.

Meyer, B., 1998, '"Make a complete break with the past": memory and post-colonial modernity in Ghanaian Pentecostalist discourse', *Journal of Religion in Africa*, 28, 3, 316–49.

———, 2004, '"Praise the Lord...": popular cinema and pentecostalite style in Ghana', *American Ethnologist*, 31, 1, 92–110.

Miller, S. G., 1996, 'Kippur in the Amazon: Jewish emigration from Northern Morocco in the late nineteenth century' in H. Goldberg (ed.), *Sephardi and Middle Eastern Jewries: history and culture in the modern era*, Bloomington, IN: Indiana University Press.

Molina, O. and M. Rhodes, 2002, 'Corporatism: the past, present, and future of a concept', *Annual Review of Political Science*, 5, 305–31.

Morin, E., 1989, *Vidal et les siens*, Paris: Seuil.

Morris, B., 1999, *Righteous Victims: a history of the Zionist-Arab conflict, 1881–1999*, New York: Knopf.

Muratorio, B., 1980, 'Protestantism and capitalism revisited; in the rural highlands of Ecuador', *Journal of Peasant Studies*, 11, 1, 37–61.

Nussbaum, M. C., 2000, *Women and Human Development: the capabilities approach*, Cambridge University Press.

O'Donnell, G., 1977, 'Corporatism and the question of the state' in J. Malloy, *Authoritarianism and Corporatism in Latin America*, Pittsburgh University Press.

Peled, Y., 1998, 'Towards a redefinition of Jewish nationalism in Israel? The enigma of Shas', *Ethnic and Racial Studies*, 21, 4, 703–27.

Peres, I., 1977, *Ethnic Relations in Israel* (Hebrew), Tel Aviv: Sifriat Hapoalim.

Podselver, L., 2002, 'La *techouva*: nouvelle orthodoxie juive et conversion interne', *Annales EHC*, 2, 275–96.

Putnam, R., 2000, *Bowling Alone: the collapse and revival of American community*, New York: Simon and Schuster.

———, R. Leonardi *et al.*, 1993, *Making Democracy Work: civic traditions in modern Italy*, Princeton University Press.

Rajagopal, A., 2000, *Politics after Television: Hindu nationalism and the reshaping of the public in India*, Cambridge University Press.

Rostas, S., 1999, 'A grass roots view of religious change amongst women in an indigenous community in Chiapas, Mexico', *Bulletin of Latin American Research*, 18, 3, 327–41.

Sartori, G., 1976, *Parties and Party Systems: a framework of analysis*, Cambridge University Press.

Sasson, S., 1993, *Urban Social Movements in Jerusalem: the protest of the second generation*, Albany, NY: SUNY Press.

Schmitter, P., 1974, 'Still the century of corporatism?', *Review of Politics*, 36, 1, 85–131.

Schroeter, D. and J. Chetrit, 1996, 'The transformation of the Jewish community of Essaouira (Mogador)' in H. Goldberg (ed.), *Sephardi and Middle Eastern Jewries: history and culture in the modern era*, Bloomington, IN: Indiana University Press.

Segev, T., 2002, *Elvis in Jerusalem: post-Zionism and the Americanization of Israel*, New York: Metropolitan Books.

Shafir, G. and Y. Peled, 2002, *Being Israeli: the dynamics of multiple citizenship*, Cambridge University Press.

Shalev, M. and S. Kis, 1999, 'Social cleavages among non-Arab voters' in M. Shamir (ed.), *The Elections in Israel, 1999*, Albany, NY: SUNY Press.

Shalev, M. and G. Levy, 2003, 'The winners and losers of 2003: ideology, social structure and political change', unpublished manuscript.

Shenhav, Y., 1999, 'The Jews of Iraq, Zionist ideology, and the property of the Palestinian refugees of 1948: an anomaly of national accounting', *International Journal of Middle East Studies*, 31, 605–30.

———, 2000, 'What do Palestinians and Arab-Jews have in common? Nationalism and ethnicity examined through the compensation question', *Hagar: An International Social Science Review*, 1, 71–110.

———, 2004, *The Arab-Jews: nationalism, religion and ethnicity* (Hebrew), Tel-Aviv: Am Oved.

Shine, C., 2003, *The Jewish State: the final summary. Rabbi Ovadia Yosef and Chief Justice Aharon Barak* (Hebrew), Tel-Aviv: Peri.

Shitrit, S., 2001, 'Catch 17: beween harediut and mizrachiut' in Y. Peled, *Shas: the challenge of Israeliness* (Hebrew), Tel Aviv: Yediot Aharonot.

Shokeid, M., 1971, *The Dual Heritage: immigrants from the Atlas mountains in an Israeli village*, Manchester University Press.

———, 1998, 'My poly-ethnic park: some reflections on Israeli-Jewish ethnicity', *Diaspora*, 7, 2, 225–46.

Sivan, E., 1995, 'The enclave culture' in M. Mary and R. S. Appleby (eds.), *Fundamentalisms Comprehended*, Chicago University Press.

Soloveitchik, H., 1994, 'Rupture and reconstruction: the transformation of contemporary orthodoxy', *Tradition*, 28, 4, 64–130.

Sperber, D., 1996, *Explaining Culture: a naturalistic approach*, Oxford: Blackwell.

Sprinzak, E., 1991, *The Ascendance of Israel's Radical Right*, Oxford University Press.

Stadler, N., 2002, 'Is profane work an obstacle to salvation? The case of ultra Orthodox (Haredi) Jews in contemporary Israel', *Sociology of Religion*, 63, 4, 455–74.

Stillman, N., 1991, *The Jews of Arab Lands in Modern Times*, Philadelphia, PA: Jewish Publication Society.

Stolow, J., 2004, 'Transnationalism and the new religio-politics: reflections on a Jewish Orthodox case,' *Theory, Culture and Society*, 21, 2, 109–37.

Sundkler, B., 1948, *Bantu Prophets in South Africa*, London: Lutterworth Press.

Swirski, S., 1998, *Government Budgets for the Jewish Haredi Sector*, Tel-Aviv: Adva Centre.

————, 1999, *Politics and Education in Israel: comparisons with the United States*, London: Falmer.

Tapper, A. J., 2002, 'The "cult" of Aish Hatorah: *ba'alei t'shuva* and the new religious movement phenomenon', *Jewish Journal of Sociology*, 44, 1, 2, 5–29.

Tessler, R., 2001, 'The price of the revolution' in Y. Peled (ed.), *Shas: the challenge of Israeliness* (Hebrew), Tel-Aviv: Yediot Aharonot.

————, 2003, *In the Name of God: Shas and the religious revolution* (Hebrew), Jerusalem: Keter.

Thompson, J. B., 1995, *The Media and Modernity: a social theory of the media*, Cambridge: Polity Press.

Touraine, A., 1973, *Production de la société*, Paris: Seuil.

Trigano, S. (ed.), 2003, *L'exclusion des Juifs des pays arabe. Aux sources du conflit israëlo-arabe*, Paris: Editions In Press.

Turner, B., 2004, 'Fundamentalism, spiritual markets and modernity', *Sociology*, 38, 1, 195–202.

Van Cott, D. L. (ed.), 1994, *Indigenous Peoples and Democracy in Latin America*, Basingstoke: Macmillan.

Vasquez, M. A., 1998, *The Brazilian Popular Church and the Crisis of Modernity*, Cambridge University Press.

Vilaça, A., 2002, 'Missions et conversion chez les Wari: entre protestantisme et catholicisme', *L'Homme*, 164, 57–80.

Wasertzug-Rabid, O., 2002, 'Rhetoric of performance art in a meeting of hazara bet'shuva' in *Israel at the Beginning of the 21st Century: society, law, economy and communication* (Hebrew), Tel Aviv: Gumah—Books on Science and Research, 123–58.

Weber, M., 1978, *Economy and Society: an outline of interpretive sociology*, edited by Guenther Roth and Claus Wittich, Berkeley, CA: University of California Press.

Weingrod, A., 1990, *The Saint of Beersheba*, Albany, NY: SUNY Press.

Weissbrod, L., 2003, 'Shas: an ethnic-religious party', *Israel Affairs*, 9, 4, 79–104.

Willis, A., 1995, 'The Sephardic Torah guardians: religious "movement" and political power' in A. Arian and M. Shamir (eds), *The Elections in Israel, 1992*, Albany, NY: SUNY Press.

Yadgar, Y., 2003, 'Shas as a struggle to create a new field: a Bourdieuan perspective of an Israeli phenomenon', *Sociology of Religion*, 64, 2, 223–46.

Yashar, D. J., 1998, 'Contesting citizenship: indigenous movements and democracy in Latin America', *Comparative Politics*, 31, 1, 23–42.

Yiftachel, O., 1998, 'Democracy or ethnocracy? Territory and settler politics in Israel/Palestine', *Middle East Report*, 207, 8–13.

Young, L., 1997, *Rational Choice Theory and Religion: summary and assessment*, London: Routledge.

Zohar, Z., 1996, 'Traditional flexibility and modern strictness: two halakhic positions on women's suffrage' in H. Goldberg (ed.), *Sephardi and Middle Eastern Jewries: history and culture in the modern era*, Bloomington, IN: Indiana University Press.

———, 2001, *Restoring the Crown to its Ancient Glory: Rabbi Ovadia Yossef's vision of a Unified Israeli Judaism*, Ramat-Gan and Jerusalem: Bar-Ilan University and Shalom Hartman Institute.

INDEX

292 *Index*

ethnic boundaries and markers: their porousness 18–20; and radio 206; and
religion 2; meaning of terms 20–12; *see
also* enclaves, social boundaries
enclaves: 5–10, 252; cross-cutting 101; and
education 10–13; and ethnicity 20; and
Israel's NGO system 187; legal aspects
8–10; in Ottoman empire 8–9; and proportional representation 252; Shas's use
of 7–8. 105, 252–4; and social life 18–21;
and territory 13–18; and voting 16
education: a 'cover' for obtaining budget
allocations 186; as a religious profession
89–90; as an instrument of t'shuva 81–2;
Shas school curriculum 176–8; David
Yosef on need to modernize it 149; distribution of pupils across school systems
11; funding issues in Shas schools 139,
175; Israel's system 10–13; monitoring of
child and parental behaviour 177–8;
racial discrimination and quotas in haredi
schools 100; school admissions policy
176; school replaces family in religious
socialization 144; Shas pedagogical centre
109, 140–1; Shas schools with 'outward
looking' and 'strictly religious' policies
178–80; Shas's education network 168;
Shas's education statistics 171; Shas's
teachers training and pay 176; Shas's
ventures in modern style of education
140–1; and social class 10–11; *see also*
enclaves, family, Shas
ethnicity: 'ethno-classes' 17–18; and religion
21–3; and ritual 22; and the Shas vote
164–5; ethnic demands as demands for
citizenship 96; its absence from Shas's
programme 167; quasi-ethnicity 23;
redrawing boundaries 2, 23; *see also* social
boundaries, enclaves
Evangelical Christians: 3, 28, 29, 37, 71, 113,
144, 241, 230; and boundaries 23; and
charitable giving 241–2; Chabad and
110n.; conversion as moral change 110;
against modernist elites 231; in prisons
51; and sex 36; social consequences of 35,
37, 125; their promises compared with
t'shuva 83; *see also* Pentecostalism

family: loss of parental authority as Shas
leitmotif 92, 93, 144, 214, 260–2; loses
role in religious socialization, 144, 260–2

fundamentalist movements: 71; and contagious spread of ritual practices 247–50;
and modernity 269–70; reasons for their
failure 124–5

gossip: in haredi society, 239–42

Halakhah 52
healing 266–7
Hindus 25

intellectuals: their lack of role in fundamentalist movements 38–9, 120–2; and popular religion 263–4, 268–9; their role in
religious institutions 122–3; their role in
social movements 120–1
Islam: political Islam 38, 126

Jerba 62, 64, 181, 274, 277

Kabbalah: abuse of 106n; study of 106;
Yitzchak Kedourie as Kabbalist 106
Kedourie, Yitzchak 72, 106, 156, 191

'Lithuanians': main features 43; mitnagdim
44; and Sephardi 'superstititons' 73
Labour Party: and Shas 135, 136
Latin America: 273; Liberation Theology
229; popular and indigenous movements
96,276; *see also* corporatism, evangelical
Christianity, Pentecostalism, social
boundaries

marriage: among haredim 97–8; between
Sephardim and Ashkenazim 98–9
Methodism 122
miracles: in contemporary religion 265–8
modernity: 261–2; and conversion 262; and
fundamentalism 269–70; elements in
Shas which reject it 145; modernizing
education in Shas schools 139–41, 180;
modernizing Shas management 144–5;
modernizing trends in Shas 133–45; and
secularization 263; and the t'shuva
movement. 231–2
Moshavim 67, 196–79

North Africa: early haredi missions 63–4; *see*
Sephardi Jews